To Morgan Patterson

THE
FORGOTTEN HERITAGE

THE FORGOTTEN HERITAGE
A Lineage of Great Baptist Preaching

by
Thomas R. McKibbens, Jr.

MERCER

ISBN 0-86554-179-5 (cloth)
ISBN 0-86554-186-8 (paper)

The Forgotten Heritage
Copyright © 1986
Mercer University Press, Macon, Georgia 31207
All rights reserved
Printed in the United States of America

The paper used in this publication meets
the minimum requirements of American National Standard
for Information Sciences—Permanence of Paper
for Printed Library Materials, ANSI Z39.48-1984.

Library of Congress Cataloging-in-Publication Data
McKibbens, Thomas R.
   The forgotten heritage.

   Includes index.
   1. Preaching—Great Britain—History. 2. Preaching—United States—History. 3. Preaching. 4. Baptists—Clergy. I. Title.
BV4207.M38   1986   251'.0088261   86-705
ISBN 0-86554-179-5
ISBN 0-86554-186-8 (pbk.)

CONTENTS

Preface ix

PART I
BAPTIST PREACHING IN GREAT BRITAIN

Chapter 1
PREACHERS OF LEARNING AND PIETY 3

Chapter 2
FREEDOM TO PREACH
Baptist Preaching in the Eighteenth Century 21

Chapter 3
LIFTING THE LIMITS
The Emergence of the New Evangelical Calvinism 41

Chapter 4
JOHN CLIFFORD
A Rigorous Gospel 67

Chapter 5
ALEXANDER MACLAREN
This One Thing I Do 79

Chapter 6
HENRY WHEELER ROBINSON
In Debt to Life 91

PART II
BAPTIST PREACHING IN AMERICA

Chapter 7
A "HAZARD TO THE COMMONWEALTH"
Colonial Baptist Preaching 105

Chapter 8
THE REVOLUTIONARY PULPIT
Baptist Preaching in The Eighteenth Century 125

Chapter 9
TOGETHER WE PREACH
Baptist Preaching from 1800 to 1845 157

Chapter 10
JOHN A. BROADUS
The Preparation and Delivery of John A. Broadus 187

PART III
LIVING THE HERITAGE

Chapter 11
GIVING SHAPE TO THE HERITAGE 201

Chapter 12
MAKING CLEAR THE GOSPEL 213

Chapter 13
BACK TO THE OLD GRIND 225

Chapter 14
A WAY WITH WORDS 237

Epilogue
THE CHALLENGE OF WORLD PREACHING 245

Index 253

*This book is dedicated
to my father*
THOMAS R. McKIBBENS
*whose pulpit ministry
constantly lived the tradition*

PREFACE

A spirited conversation took place within a small group of Baptists, animated by one layman who was disgusted by a sermon he had recently heard delivered by a Baptist minister. "He yelled and screamed; he pounded the pulpit and told emotional stories that made people cry, *but he didn't really say anything.*" "What do you mean?" asked another in the group. "What I mean is that the sermon had no content—it was all emotionalism," the first went on to explain.

We all know what he meant; and as their pastor, I knew from firsthand experience how easy it is simply to play on the emotions of a congregation, especially when sermon preparation is inadequate. When I was in college, an older minister once told me in all seriousness, "Tom, when I don't have time to prepare for a sermon, I just yell louder—they never know the difference!"

But they do know the difference, as any preacher knows who respects as well as loves his congregation; therefore, I could sympathize with the frustration of that layman as he shifted his weight from one foot to the other. He was genuinely frustrated and angry, and he had every right to be. He had given an hour of his time, hoping to be inspired and strengthened with content as well as emotion, and all he got was mindless ranting and raving. This man was not a theological liberal prone to conceiving of religion only in terms of cold intellectual discussion. On the contrary, he had recently experienced a rather emotional conversion to the Christian faith. He knew what it was to *feel* as well as *understand* the gospel, and he desperately wanted to grow in the faith he had so recently professed.

Many Baptists have mistakenly concluded that the only alternative to boring intellectualism in the pulpit is a mixture of program promotion and mindless emotionalism, which grows in part from the old frontier camp meetings. Honest lay people hear this kind of preaching week after week, and although many of them sense deep down that they are not being fed the most wholesome gospel food, at least its table setting is attractive and the pulpit-pounder is entertaining. Not a few thoughtful laymen, however, are very much like my friend who was complaining about the sermon he had endured. While they would readily confess that the frontier-revivalistic tradition has much to offer in the name of Christ, they have become tired of the appetizers and want to dig in to the main course of the gospel.

We stood there for a while listening to our friend describe the sermon he had heard, but then other subjects intruded and we eventually began to disperse for other responsibilities. As we were leaving, however, one rather thoughtful layperson, who had obviously been pondering the preaching issue raised earlier, said something to our disgruntled friend—something that startled me. "About that emotional sermon you heard," she said, "why should you be so bothered? Isn't that kind of preaching representative of our heritage as Baptists?"

What she did not know is that although such emotional ranting is indeed part of the Baptist heritage in preaching, it is not the primary tradition in which the Baptist denomination was organized; neither has it been the moving force behind the phenomenal growth of Baptists in the past three centuries. There is a great tradition of Baptist preaching that combines both intellectual rigor and evangelistic warmth in a happy homiletical marriage that has never been put asunder. The greatest Baptist preaching has done more than produce large churches; rather, it has nourished strong Christians who have experienced both the passion and the depth of the gospel. When the Apostle Paul prayed that "Christ may dwell in your hearts through faith; that you, being rooted and grounded in love, may have power to comprehend with all the saints what is the breadth and the length and height and depth . . . and that you may be filled with all the fullness of God" (Ephesians 3:17-19), he was referring to the results of that kind of preaching.

Although the pages that follow give an account of the development of that tradition among Baptists, this book is *not* a history of Baptist preaching. If it were, the territory covered would be much more immense. It would include, for example, a far greater treatment of Separate Baptist preaching than will be found within these pages. It would treat the tremendous influence of black Baptist preaching, as well as preaching among Baptists of nations other than England and America. A general history of

Baptist preaching could easily expand into a multivolume work that would likely collect dust on the shelves of a few specialized libraries.

Such is not the purpose of this book. I have attempted to trace the lineage of a *particular kind* of Baptist preaching. Unfortunately it has become a forgotten heritage among many Baptists. It is a heritage characterized equally by intellectual rigor and evangelistic warmth, the union of head and heart in the pulpit. It is an openness to the knowledge of the times, yet an insistence upon the truth of the gospel. It is conservative in theology, but liberal in spirit. Above all, it is gracious, born of the grace of God. By the term *gracious,* I do not mean mere tolerance of others. Rather, I mean a genuine love of others even when they differ from us.

Many Baptists today, both in the pulpit and the pew, may be surprised to find that such a legacy of preaching has been fundamental to the development of the Baptist denomination from the beginning. The common assumption is that Baptist preaching has grown from what Charles H. Spurgeon quaintly called "elongated nonsense, paraphrastic platitude, wire-drawn commonplace, or sacred rhodomontade."[1] For many, to think of Baptist preaching is to think of flailing arms and labored breathing, of wild allegory and irresponsible prooftexts—in short, of ignorance made bliss. For those who have lived and labored under such an assumption, this book may very well be good news. You need no longer be embarrassed about your preaching heritage.

For that vast body of Baptist laity who have felt intuitively that there is something in their tradition that appeals to more than emotions, this book will confirm their suspicions. Some, I hope, may be challenged to remain within the denomination they have considered leaving in search of more substantive fare from the pulpit.

There is also a message here for those who are or aspire to be preachers within this tradition. This message is *not* that preachers should imitate the great preachers of the past who are presented here. Good preaching is not that simple. "The forgotten heritage" is not a static entity that can be appropriated unreflectively. True learning and piety do indeed stand on the shoulders of giants in generations that have preceded us, but those who would employ them rightly must also seek to interpret that heritage to meet the needs of the age they address.

---

[1]Charles H. Spurgeon, *Lectures to My Students,* first series (New York: Sheldon and Company, 1875) 248.

But there is a lesson to be learned from this account of Baptist preaching. Like other denominations Baptists have experienced both a revival and decline of preaching in a constant rhythm through the years. The early settlers of America, for example, first modeled their sermons on the preaching they had known in the Old World. Soon the fervor began to decline until the gospel broke out of the old forms and the Great Awakening was born.

Preaching has always followed such a rhythm—from revival through decline to revival—as though we never can find the key to sustained renewal of preaching. Is there a common factor when preaching begins to decline? Yes, sermons in a period of decline are always locked into the form and style of a past era of preaching. The revival of preaching happens when through the newness of God's Spirit sermons take the shape of the age in which they are preached.

The Apostle Paul could not preach in Athens the same way he preached in Jerusalem. Neither can we preach the same way as Thomas Helwys or John Bunyan, Robert Hall or Alexander Maclaren, Samuel Stillman or even John A. Broadus. Their preaching spoke clearly in their day and in their locations. In the great spiritual "There is a Balm in Gilead," a verse begins, "If you can't preach like Peter, if you can't pray like Paul." Let it be said clearly, preachers of today should *not* preach like Peter (or pray like Paul); they should preach the same gospel but in a form suited to the waning years of the twentieth century.

A word about organization may be helpful. This book is divided into three parts. Part one treats Baptist preaching in England where the Baptist family tree first sprouted. I have traced British Baptist preaching from its beginning in the seventeenth century up into the twentieth century. Whatever Baptist preaching in America has become, it will always owe a great debt to its English heritage.

Part two crosses the Atlantic both in space and time and takes up the exciting story of Baptist preaching in America from its beginnings in New England. The lineage is traced from the colonial era through the Revolutionary War century and on to the continuing influence of John A. Broadus.

Part three takes a different turn. No longer is the story purely historical. In five chapters under the rubric "Living the Heritage," I have attempted to assess the legacy of Baptist preaching that I described in the first two sections of the book and suggest ways to prepare sermons that honor that heritage. Some may call the third section "practical." I prefer to call it "contemporary," for to my mind there is nothing impractical about the two historical sections.

One question will occur to many as they glance at the table of contents: what happened to Spurgeon? The answer, in short, is that nothing has happened to Spurgeon. He still holds his place as one of the most naturally gifted and influential preachers ever to live among the Baptists or any other denomination. His greatness is not diminished by his exclusion from the main body of this book. I would readily agree that his exclusion says more about this book than it does about Spurgeon. It simply says that this book traces a different branch of Baptist preaching. Charles H. Spurgeon represents a tradition of Baptist preaching that is just as influential and important to the Baptist heritage as the tradition I have described. Spurgeon's is a grand heritage of preaching, and I can easily sympathize with the statement of Helmut Thielicke that one should "sell all that you have (not least of all some of your stock of current sermonic literature) and buy Spurgeon (even if you have to grub through the second-hand bookstores.")[2] Spurgeon's evangelistic fervor, his devotion to the Scriptures, his extraordinary speaking ability, and his keen wit place him in the forefront of a branch of Baptist preaching that has done great service in the Kingdom of God.

Like all others who presume to write a book, I am deeply in debt to a host of good people. No sooner had the trustees of Southeastern Baptist Theological Seminary elected me to the faculty than they also voted, at my request, to allow me a year's study leave to do the research for this book. Constant support from seminary President W. Randall Lolley, as well as Dean of the Faculty Morris Ashcraft and my colleagues on the faculty, has made this year possible. I am grateful to them all.

While I did research in many places both in England and America, my home base for the year has been Andover-Newton Theological School, Newton Centre, Massachusetts. The theological and historical libraries in the Boston area have proven to be an ideal setting for my work. President George W. Peck and librarian Ellis E. O'Neal, Jr., of Andover-Newton have proven to be gracious hosts.

---

[2]Helmut Thielicke, *Encounter With Spurgeon,* trans. John W. Doberstein (Philadelphia: Fortress Press, 1963) 45.

Adequate funding both for living expenses and research and travel costs has been crucial. Without such financial help I could never have begun the work. My special thanks is due to John H. and Carla Baker of Houston, Texas, without whose early and continued support this work could never have been attempted. Other individuals I especially want to thank for either contributing or raising funds are Peter Rhea Jones, Chevis F. Horne, James R. Boswell, Jeff L. Norris, William E. Hull, W. Levon Moore, Henry Fields, Mamie B. Mahaffey, Bill Mahaffey, William C. Burriss, Alton H. McEachern, Larry W. Kennedy, Julian W. Fagan III, Paul J. Craven, and Thomas and Janice Greene.

Churches have supported this work through special offerings or funds. To list all who contributed from such churches would be impossible, but I want to mention the fact that the First Baptist Church of Bristol, Virginia, where I was serving as pastor until this project began, has been a source of continual support and encouragement. In addition, members of the First Baptist Church of Martinsville, Virginia, the First Baptist Church of Laurel, Mississippi, and the First Baptist Church of Pontotoc, Mississippi, have added much needed support. There have also been anonymous contributions through the First Baptist Church, Shreveport, Louisiana, and the First Baptist Church, Waycross, Georgia.

Three foundations have added significant support. The First Baptist Church Foundation, Decatur, Georgia; Calvary Baptist Foundation, Roanoke, Virginia; and First Baptist Church Foundation of Laurel, Mississippi are due my sincere thanks.

Family members have also joined in the support of this project. T. R. and Betty McKibbens, Ben M. and Loren O. McKibbens, and Pearl Callahan have all been enthusiastic supporters of the work.

My mentors and colleagues—all valued friends—have read parts or all of the manuscript and have made valuable suggestions. Among those who have been especially helpful are Ellis O'Neal, Jr., S. Mark Heim, John W. Carlton, Chevis F. Horne, and John E. Steely. There are others with whom I have discussed the manuscript at length and who have made pertinent and very helpful suggestions. Among those are Gene F. Bartlett, Robert G. Torbet, W. Morgan Patterson, Barrington R. White, W. M. S. West, Norman H. Maring, William G. McLoughlin, Tina T. Saxon, Browning Ware, and William H. Brackney. They cannot be held responsible for the contents, but the dialogue with them has always been stimulating, and I am grateful to them all.

More than by any other institution, I have been encouraged by the Southern Baptist Historical Commission. My files are thick with letters of encouragement from Lynn E. May, Jr., executive director-treasurer. He, and especially his administrative assistant Carolyn Patton, have always seemed to have just the right word at just the right time. My thanks goes to them and the entire staff of the Historical Commission. Two of the chapters of this book have been published by *The Quarterly Review,* January–March 1985, and appear here with permission. Portions of chapters 3, 8, 9 were used in an article entitled "Disseminating Biblical Doctrine Through Preaching," published in *Baptist History and Heritage* 19 (July 1984): 42-52, and also appear here with permission.

The typing for this book was done by Evelyn B. Carter and Diane S. Stewart. They each justly deserve my deepest thanks I am also grateful to Peggy Haymes and Michael Langston for their assistance in preparing the index.

Through it all, my wife Donna and our children Katherine and George have made this year of research and writing one of the best years of our lives. They have willingly lived in a two-room apartment and have often found me preoccupied with some aspect of this book. But they have never failed to get my mind back where it should be while at home. This has been a united project, and I am in their debt.

Newton Centre, Massachusetts *Thomas R. McKibbens*
Summer, 1984

PART I

BAPTIST PREACHING IN GREAT BRITAIN

Chapter 1

PREACHERS OF LEARNING AND PIETY

I shall now give a brief account of some of the Baptist *ministers who lived in the times to which preceding history refers, whereby it will appear, that men of the greatest* learning *and* piety, *have neither been ashamed nor afraid in the worst of times to stand up in vindication of a principle truly* apostolical, *though ever so much despised and hated.*

Thomas Crosby, 1738

Baptist preaching emerged on the heels of the turbulent sixteenth century, when the Christian world was shaken by a movement sparked by an Augustinian monk named Martin Luther. The Reformation was not just built on a renewed interest in the Scripture and the doctrine of justification by faith. It was built on the *preaching* of the Scripture and the *preaching* of justification by faith. Joining Luther were Zwingli, Calvin, Latimer, Knox—all of them preachers. All the Reformation leaders emphasized preaching as the key to reform. Hugh Latimer even went so far as to say, "Take away preaching, and take away salvation."[1] It was in the context of that great revival of preaching that the Baptist movement took shape.

The particular context of seventeenth-century England presented peculiar concerns. King James I (1603-1625) had inherited a troublesome religious situation from his Tudor predecessors. The Anglican Church was a cauldron of controversy, and religious Separatists on the one hand and loyal Catholics on the other hand made life difficult for the ruler of the realm, who assumed that he was responsible for the religious as well as the civil life of his subjects. While he authorized the venerable translation of the Bible that bears his name, he also authorized the harassment and persecution of anyone who dared to differ with the Church of England.

---

[1] Quoted in T.H.L. Parker, *The Oracles of God* (London: Lutterworth Press, 1947) 115.

The earliest Baptist preachers shaped their sermons to fit this context and to reflect the reformed religious mind-set of the early seventeenth century. Theologically radical, politically dangerous, ecclesiastically Nonconformist, they preached sermons that spoke so clearly to their age that they often found themselves in prison.

THE CAMBRIDGE CONNECTION

John Smyth and Thomas Helwys

Prominent among this group of Dissenters was John Smyth, who bore a common name but was no common man. His dis-ease with the Church of England was nourished by the intense Puritan atmosphere of Christ's College at Cambridge University, where he earned a Master of Arts degree in 1593 and was elected to a Fellowship in 1594.[2] He had left his university post at the end of the century to become City Preacher at Lincoln, but when his hopes for true reform in the Church of England were snuffed out by the accession of James I, he left his post to minister to a little Separatist congregation in Gainsborough. By 1608 Smyth and his entire congregation were forced to move to Amsterdam to escape persecution, and while there, Smyth came to the conclusion that only believers should be members of the church. By rejecting infant baptism and forming a voluntary association of Christians into a church based on believer's baptism, Smyth became the first pastor of an English Baptist church.

What was Smyth like? Surely he was a rigorous thinker. Twelve years at Cambridge and the turbulent religious controversies that engaged his short life forced him to think clearly and deeply. Yet his devotion to Christ and his sincere desire to win others to the Christian faith fitted him to be an able forerunner of the kind of preaching that shaped the denomination of which he was a pioneer. In later years a professor of Ecclesiastical History at Cambridge, not a Baptist himself and therefore not prone to be sympathetic toward Smyth, said that "none of the English Separatists had a finer mind or a more beautiful soul than John Smyth."[3]

---

[2]Walter H. Burgess, *John Smith the Se-Baptist* (London: James Clarke and Company, 1911) 42.

[3]Quoted in W. T. Whitley, ed., *The Works of John Smyth* (Cambridge: Cambridge University Press, 1915) cxviii.

Smyth never returned to his English homeland, but the influence of his evangelistic preaching and his religious writings was felt not only in England but also in America. The religious covenant adopted by the Puritans in Salem, Massachusetts, in 1629 reflected the stance of Smyth's church "to walk in all His ways revealed or as they should be made known unto them."[4] From Smyth's church in Amsterdam a group led by Thomas Helwys returned to London to form the first Baptist church on English soil. Some, who had remembered Smyth's preaching in Lincoln, obtained copies of his sermons and other writings, and soon a Baptist church was formed in Lincoln. Others who met Smyth in Holland returned to England to form Baptist churches in Coventry, Salisbury, Tiverton, and other places. Whenever a Baptist resolves to preach and publish the gospel in clear and understandable language, whenever a Baptist resolves to struggle with the intellectual currents of the day and address current issues with the claims of Christ, whenever a Baptist resolves that duty calls for the spreading of the gospel to all the world, that Baptist is reaping a harvest planted by John Smyth.

Thomas Helwys led part of Smyth's church to settle at Spitalfields, located just outside the London city walls. Convinced that he must bear witness to the gospel in spite of danger, Helwys brashly wrote a strong defense of freedom of conscience and planned to present a copy of it personally to James I. In his case, such an idea was not impossible, for Helwys was no ordinary citizen. He came from an aristocratic family who moved easily among nobility. His cousin, Gervase Helwys, had been knighted by King James in 1603 and later appointed lieutenant of the Tower of London. Thomas had been educated at Gray's Inn, one of the elite schools in London intended chiefly for the education of the sons of the nobility and gentry. He had seen Queen Elizabeth as she visited Gray's Inn, and some of his old school chums were in Parliament and other high places of government.

Thus, Thomas Helwys led his little Baptist congregation to the very walls of danger and was willing himself to stand before the king. Yet it was not to be. King James was absolutely determined to refuse dissent;

---

[4]Ibid., cxix. Roger Williams said, "I am sure Mr. Cotton hath made some use of those principles and arguments on which Mr. Smith and others went concerning the constitution of the Christian church."

therefore, Thomas Helwys had to be content to open the cover of his book, *The Mistery of Iniquity,* and pen his appeal to the king:

> The King is a mortall man and not God, therefore hath no power over ye immortall soules of his subjects to make lawes and ordinances for them and to set spirituall Lords over them.
>
> If the King have authority to make spirituall Lords and lawes, then he is an immortall God and not a mortall man.
>
> O King, be not seduced by deceivers to sin so against God whom thou oughtest to obey, nor against thy poor subjects who ought and will obey thee in all thinges with body, life and goods or els let their lives be taken from ye earth.
>
> God save ye King.
>
> Tho. Helwys[5]

Such an appeal, as innocent as it appears today, was enough to have Helwys thrown into Newgate prison, where he died sometime before 1616. That cultured and courageous Baptist preacher never erected a great wall of separation between learning and piety; instead, like his colleague John Smyth, he addressed the head as well as the heart with the claims of the gospel.

Henry Jessey

Like Smyth, Henry Jessey was a Cambridge graduate; but unlike Smyth, he was a Calvinist in theology. That is, Jessey believed that salvation was intended only for the elect of God. He, therefore, was a Particular Baptist, as opposed to the General Baptists such as Smyth and Helwys, who believed that salvation was for all who would repent and have faith.

A convinced Baptist Jessey was; an uneducated Baptist he was not. For six years he studied at Cambridge, earning both the B.A. and M.A. degrees. In 1627 he was ordained a priest in the Church of England and

---

[5]See W. T. Whitley, "Thomas Helwys of Gray's Inn and Broxtowe Hall, Nottingham" (London: The Kingsgate Press, n.d.) for a good summary of Helwys's life. Walter H. Burgess, *John Smith the Se-Baptist,* has a more complete biography of Helwys. There are only four surviving copies of Helwys's book *The Mistery of Iniquity,* located in the Angus Library of Regent's Park College, Oxford; Trinity College, Dublin; the Dr. Williams Library; and the Bodleian Library at Oxford. A photographic facsimile, however, was made of the Bodleian copy and published for the Baptist Historical Society by the Kingsgate Press of London in 1935. For Helwys's argument on freedom of conscience see pages 37-83.

took his first post at East Riding, in his home county of Yorkshire. He continued his diligent study and became proficient not only in Hebrew and Greek, but also in Aramaic, so that much of his later ministry was devoted to making a new translation of the Bible.[6] His study of the Bible, however, led to problems with the Church of England. In 1634 he was dismissed from his church for his unwillingness to follow certain prescribed ceremonies from the Prayer Book. A year later he moved to London, where he became the pastor of a well-known Separatist congregation whose pastor, John Lathrop, had emigrated to America.

Jessey had entered a church that, like the nation as a whole, was in a state of transition. Before Jessey arrived, there had already been a secession by some who had come to Baptist views. A year after he became their pastor, six others came to Baptist views; in 1641 a larger number left for the same reason; and in 1643 even more concluded that the Baptists were correct. Jessey had great respect for many who had left, and he soon found himself seriously considering the twin questions of who should be baptized (infants or believers?) and how should they be baptized (sprinkling, pouring, or dipping?). By 1642 he became satisfied that immersion was the correct mode; thus he began to immerse babies brought to him for baptism. Two years later Jessey concluded that only believers should be baptized, and he therefore became a Baptist.

Jessey's decision was no small contribution to the struggling group of seven Baptist churches in the London area. He was not only well educated, but highly respected by the civil leadership of the country. His gifts in preaching and his generosity to the poor became well known. Not only did he preach regularly in his own church, but he also traveled throughout England inspiring and bringing some sense of unity to the struggling Baptist churches.

His intellectual labors resulted in continuous production of theological books throughout his sixty-three years of life.[7] Paramount in his intellectual life was the study of the Scriptures in the original languages. He carried both his Hebrew and Greek testaments with him constantly, and invited other biblical scholars of many denominations to work with him

---

[6]Thomas Crosby, *The History of the English Baptists*, 4 vols. (London: Printed for, and sold by, the Editor, 1738) 1:313.

[7]See a complete list of his writings in "Jessey or Jacie, Henry," *Dictionary of National Biography*, vol. 24 (London: Smith, Elder, and Co., 1892) 371-72.

on a new translation of the Bible, which was unfortunately never completed. At his funeral in 1663, Woodmongers Hall in London was filled with several thousand mourners of many denominations. Henry Jessey was a Baptist by conviction, but possessed broad sympathies and a depth of learning that won him the esteem of a large portion of the religious leadership of the nation.

Hanserd Knollys

Another Cambridge graduate who became one of the early leaders of the Baptists was Hanserd Knollys, who lived to the age of ninety-three and was described by his biographer as a man of "nobility, courage, insight, dedication, and Christian love."[8] To follow his life is to take a great adventure, to travel with him from London to America, back to London, to Holland and Germany, and back to London again. He was a preacher of renown, described by Thomas Crosby as "very much crowded after, having seldom less than a thousand hearers."[9] Such a following was rather embarrassing to the pastor of the St. Helen's parish church, which was located next door to Knollys' Baptist church. Some of the neighbors were so upset that a nonconformist preacher would regularly draw such large crowds that they became "hysterical,"[10] and eventually the congregation relocated more than once to escape persecution.

Such a dangerous life was far from the mind of the young Hanserd Knollys who entered Cambridge University in his teens. He intended to live a quiet life as an Anglican divine, but the same Puritan atmosphere that influenced Smyth and Jessey led Knollys to think seriously about the claims of the Separatists. By the time he had spent several years in his Anglican pastorate, he had decided to take the dangerous step: he broke with the established church and renounced his ordination. Persecution was soon at his heels and he fled with his family to New England, where he lived for about three years until his aged father requested that he return to England.

---

[8]Pope A. Duncan, *Hanserd Knollys: Seventeenth Century Baptist* (Nashville: Broadman Press, 1965) 51.

[9]Crosby, *History of English Baptists,* 1:336.

[10]B. R. White described them as "hysterical" in "Hanserd Knollys and Radical Dissent in the 17th Century," (London: Dr. Williams' Trust, 1977) 9.

Upon his return to London, Knollys joined the independent church led by Henry Jessey and was one of those who became convinced of the necessity of believer's baptism. He left Jessey's church in 1643 and became a Baptist. It was Knollys who played an important role in convincing Henry Jessey of his position on baptism, and it was Knollys who eventually baptized Henry Jessey, his former pastor.

Knollys was first of all an invincible evangelist. His impassioned pleas for conversion did not stop even when he was thrown into Newgate prison, where he preached daily to his fellow prisoners.[11] He was appointed by the Baptist churches in London to an evangelistic preaching tour of Wales. He was convinced above all that "if the sinner be willing to open the door of his heart, Christ will come in by his holy Spirit and He will communicate of his Grace to his soul."[12]

Along with his evangelistic spirit, however, Knollys steadily worked to raise the level of education among his fellow Baptist ministers. While pastor of his church, he was also a school teacher in order to supplement his income. Crosby said that he had "an extraordinary way of instructing youth . . . and many eminent persons, both for piety and learning, were trained by him."[13] In 1689 Knollys helped organize a meeting of representatives of over a hundred Baptist churches in London. The outcome of the meeting was the establishment of a central fund to support pastors and evangelists, and also to assist Baptist pastors in the study of the classical languages. Among his many published works were grammar books for the study of Greek, Latin, and Hebrew.[14]

As part of what may be termed the "Cambridge Connection," Hanserd Knollys played a vital role in shaping the life of the Baptist denomination. One of the leading scholars of early Baptist life in England has written that Knollys "represents a continuing concern for scholarship" in his denomination.[15] He helped set the course for the kind of evangelistic

---

[11]Duncan, *Hanserd Knollys*, 13.

[12]Hanserd Knollys, *The World That Now Is, and the World That Is to Come* (London: Printed by Thomas Snowden, 1681) 35-36. Quoted by Duncan, *Hanserd Knollys*, 18.

[13]Crosby, *History of English Baptists*, 1:339.

[14]See the complete list of Knollys' works in Duncan, *Hanserd Knollys*, 52-55.

[15]White, "Hanserd Knollys and Radical Dissent," 24.

preaching that took seriously the word of Christ to love God with the mind as well as the heart.

Henry Denne

In 1641, at a national gathering of Anglican ministers, the preacher chosen to speak on the occasion was Henry Denne, a fellow Church of England divine who had already established quite a reputation as "a more frequent and lively preacher than the generality of the clergy in those times."[16] His sermon that day was to be controversial, and he knew it. So it is no surprise that he prefaced his sermon by saying,

> My fear is . . . that I shall this day be mistaken; not that I fear the mistaking of my words, for that were to call your judgments into question; but I fear lest you should mistake the intentions of my heart.[17]

The intention of his heart, of course, was to proclaim the gospel as clearly as he knew how to such a learned congregation. What made him so anxious that day was not just the fact that he was about to preach the gospel, but that he intended to apply that gospel to the many abuses common to the clergy of that day. His sermon did not miss its mark. He made it clear that if the government had been as ardent in correcting the flagrant abusers within the Church of England as it had been in persecuting dissenters, then "surely by this time the church would have been as free from *them* [dissenters], as the land from *wolves.*"[18]

Such a sermon naturally caused a great uproar among the clergy, and so many attacks were printed against Henry Denne that he eventually had to publish the sermon in his own defense. From that day he became known as one of the best preachers in England, described by a contemporary as "the ablest man in England for Prayer, Expounding, and Preaching."[19] Thomas Edwards, an early historian who was not a dissenter himself and therefore not partial toward Denne, described Denne's emphasis on preaching that Christ died for all and quoted another as say-

---

[16]Crosby, *History of English Baptists*, 1:297.

[17]Ibid., 299.

[18]Ibid., 301.

[19]Quoted in Thomas Edwards, *Gangraene: or a Catalogue of Many of the Errours, Heresies, and Pernicious Practices of the Sectaries of This Time* (London: Printed for Ralph Smith, 1645-1646) 77.

ing that "this Denne delivered his Opinions . . . in such a manner, as if he had been an Apostle sent from Heaven."[20]

At that time, of course, Henry Denne was not a Baptist. He was indeed the young graduate of Cambridge University who had been ordained only eleven years earlier and showed such great promise as a leader in the established church. That was not to last, however. When civil war broke out in England in 1642, Henry Denne began to search the Scriptures, and he eventually concluded that infant baptism was without foundation. In 1643 he declared himself a Baptist and moved to London. When Henry Denne joined the ranks of the Baptists, that struggling denomination possessed one of the finest minds and most eloquent tongues in all of England.

It did not take long for the civil authorities to arrest Denne and place him in prison. His voice and reputation were too influential to allow him freedom to preach. Yet even in prison he bore witness to his faith. Every time he was released from prison he seemed to preach even more fervently, so that his life story is one of repeatedly going from jail to the pulpit and back to jail. On one occasion he was prevented from preaching in a particular church, and he therefore moved to the shade of a tree in the churchyard and "to the mortification of his opposers, a great number of the people followed him there."[21]

Throughout his life Denne remained one of the great preachers among the Baptists. His denomination looked to him as an evangelical scholar, one who could courageously defend their right to exist and explain their theological positions with precision. His death took place sometime after the restoration of Charles II in 1660.[22]

With these four remarkable preachers—John Smyth, Henry Jessey, Hanserd Knollys, and Henry Denne—Baptists benefited from the religious ferment taking place within the academic halls of Cambridge University in the seventeenth century. These, as an early Baptist historian wrote, were "men of the greatest learning and piety."[23] There was no academic standard required for a Baptist preacher; thus anyone who felt

---

[20]Ibid.

[21]Crosby, *History of English Baptists,* 1:304-305.

[22]See *Dictionary of National Biography,* vol. 14, 365-66.

[23]Crosby, *History of English Baptists,* 1:265.

called of God and had the support of a local church could preach. That ecclesiastical fact naturally opened the doors of the Baptist denomination to some who were not only ignorant, but in some cases wildly extravagant. Yet the strength of the denomination was found among those who took natural leadership positions, who held the esteem and confidence of the people, and who provided a preaching model that united both evangelism and scholarship.

BAPTIST PREACHING AND LITERATURE

In addition to those who had close connections with Cambridge University, there were some Baptist preachers who contributed to the store of English literature that has become the valued possession of all English-speaking peoples.

John Bunyan

The first to be mentioned is, of course, John Bunyan, whose *Pilgrim's Progress* stands among the greatest devotional classics of all time. In a sense, Bunyan embodies the Baptist faith, for while he was a man of the common folk, his deep piety and unreserved evangelistic spirit combined to produce literature that has blessed the whole world.

To read Bunyan's spiritual autobiography, *Grace Abounding to the Chief of Sinners,* is not only to experience one of the classics of Christian devotion, but to travel with Bunyan on a roller coaster of spiritual highs and lows. One wonders how anyone could be so morbidly concerned about things he considered grievous sins. Before he became a Christian, he said, "I had taken so much delight in [bell] Ringing, but my Conscience beginning to be tender, I thought such practice was but vain, and therefore forced myself to leave it, yet my mind hankered."[24] Still unable to stay completely away from bell ringing, he allowed himself to stand just outside the steeple door. If he had gone inside, he was afraid God might allow one of the bells to fall on him as punishment for his sin!

Bunyan's spiritual state fluctuated for years to the extremes of both highs and lows. "I could have spoken of his Love, and of his Mercy to me, even to the very Crows that sat upon the ploughed Lands before

---

[24]*Grace Abounding to the Chief of Sinners* (London: The Religious Tract Society, 1917) para. 33. Numbers cited hereafter refer to paragraphs.

me."[25] Yet hardly had he turned around before he wondered if he had committed the unpardonable sin: "Now I blessed the condition of the Dog and Toad, and counted the estate of everything that God had made far better than this dreadful state of mine."[26] Such radical shifts of mood he compared to the falling of "a Bird that is shot from the top of a tree, into great guilt, and fearful despair."[27]

Eventually Bunyan gained some spiritual stability: "Now remained only the hinder part of the Tempest, for the thunder was gone beyond me, only some drops did still remain, that now and then would fall upon me."[28] The little Baptist church of Bedford not only nourished him, but began to call out his extraordinary gifts. Some of the "most able among the Saints" began to urge Bunyan to speak before the church. With much "weakness and infirmity," he began to preach. Soon his preaching became more confident, and he was surprised to discover that people "received with rejoicing at the mercy of God to me-ward professing their Souls were edified thereby."[29]

The man who today is chiefly thought of as a great dreamer of dreams soon became one of the most exceptional preachers England had ever witnessed. Much of the revolutionary ferment in England during the seventeenth century can be traced to ordinary people's insistence on hearing the gospel in terms they could understand from preachers who knew their condition. Here was a man who came from the lower class: "my Father's House being of that Rank that is meanest and most despised of all the Families in the land," he claimed.[30] Yet John Bunyan was so endowed with natural gifts of speaking and imagination that, when united with a passion for the gospel, the common people heard him gladly. Such popularity cost him dearly. He spent twelve years in the Bedford jail, where he suffered not only for his own deprivations, but also for his wife and

---

[25]Ibid., 92.
[26]Ibid., 104.
[27]Ibid., 140.
[28]Ibid., 228.
[29]Ibid., 267.
[30]Ibid., 2.

children, "especially my poor blind Child, who lay nearer my heart than all I had besides."[31]

John Bunyan's ideal for the preacher can be seen in some of the vivid characters he portrayed in his famous allegory *The Pilgrim's Progress*. On the journey toward Mount Zion, Christian stops at the house of Interpreter, where is shown

> the Picture of a very grave Person hang up against the Wall, and this was the fashion of it. It had eyes lift up to Heaven, the best of Books in his hand, the Law of Truth was written upon his lips, the World was behind his back; it stood as if it pleaded with Men, and a Crown of Gold did hang over his head.[32]

Such a man, Interpreter explained to Christian, "is the only Man, whom the Lord of the Place whither thou art going, hath authorized to be thy Guide."[33] When, in the nineteenth century, a statue of Bunyan was erected in Bedford, the sculptor depicted Bunyan with his eyes lifted up to heaven, the best of Books in his hand, and as if he was pleading with all humanity to come to Christ. Thus, at least in the sculpture, Bunyan fulfilled his ideal of the preacher.

Such a vision of the preaching task was doubtless fulfilled in Bunyan's own life. His eyes were, indeed, lifted up to heaven: "When I have been in Preaching, I thank God, my heart hath often . . . with great earnestness cried to God that he would make the Word effectual to the Salvation of the Soul."[34] It was to God that Bunyan looked for his whole strength. He also had "the best of Books in his hand." His constant companion was the Bible, and Bunyan was careful not to become embroiled in doctrinal battles that were less than absolutely essential to the faith. "I never cared to meddle with things that were controverted and in dispute," he wrote. Instead, "it pleased me much to contend with great earnestness for the Word of Faith and the Remission of Sins by the Death and Sufferings of Jesus."[35]

---

[31]Ibid., 327.

[32]*The Pilgrim's Progress* (Oxford: Clarendon Press, 1925) 29.

[33]Ibid.

[34]*Grace Abounding*, 280.

[35]Ibid., 284.

The vision was embodied further in the fact that "the law of truth" was "written upon his lips." Throughout his life Bunyan preached and wrote about things that were real to ordinary people. He was transparently sincere. One of the reasons that his writings became so classic is that they breathed the air of reality. Everyone could relate to his characters. Who has not met Master Worldly-Wiseman and Master Facing-both-ways as well as Master Greatheart and Master Faithful? Who has not climbed Hill Difficulty and suffered in the Slough of Despond? His insights into the Christian life are permanent and universal.

The "World was behind his back" in the sense that Bunyan divorced himself from worldly ambitions and focused on a greater unseen world, which became clearer to him as he continued his preaching. He stood as if he "pleaded with Men." He readily confessed that "I have really been in pain, and have . . . travailed to bring forth Children of God; neither could I be satisfied unless some fruits did appear in my Work."[36] Finally, like the man in his vision, Bunyan did indeed have a "Crown of Gold" over his head—a crown not made with hands: "I counted myself more blessed and honored by this [preaching] than if he had made me the Emperor of the Christian World, or the Lord of all the Glory of the Earth without it."[37]

John Bunyan stands tall as a Baptist preacher and as a contributor to the world's great literature. Dean Arthur Stanley, who was a recognized church historian as well as the dean of Westminster Abbey from 1864 to 1881, said of Bunyan's *Pilgrim's Progress* that "it is one of the few books which act as a religious bond to the whole of Christendom; that it is, perhaps with six others, and equally with any of those six, the book which, after the English Bible, has contributed to the common religious culture of the Anglo-Saxon race."[38] Thus, it is no surprise that John Bunyan is one of only two Baptists memorialized in Westminster Abbey.[39]

---

[36]Ibid., 290.

[37]Ibid., 286.

[38]See John Brown, *Puritan Preaching in England* (New York: Charles Scribner's Sons, 1900) 151. It was from Brown's treatment of John Bunyan that I got the idea of tracing Bunyan's ideal of the preacher in his allegorical characters.

[39]One may see the beautiful stained glass window dedicated to John Bunyan. The other Baptist memorialized in the Abbey is William Carey.

Benjamin Keach

The year was 1664, and the young man standing before the judge for sentencing was a Baptist minister named Benjamin Keach, only twenty-four years old. A few weeks earlier he had published a little book, entitled *The Child's Instructor; or, a New and Easy Primer,* to be used for the religious instruction of children. Copies of the book had sold rapidly, and one had fallen into the hands of the local justice of the peace. Horrified by Keach's printed statement that "believers, or godly men and women only, who can make confession of their faith and repentance," were the only fit subjects for Christian baptism, the justice of the peace had Keach seized and jailed until a speedy trial could be arranged. The evidence had been placed before the jury and he was soon found guilty. Thus Benjamin Keach was called to the bar, and the judge passed sentence as follows:

> Benjamin Keach, you are here convicted, for writing, and publishing, a seditious and schismatical book, for which the court's judgment is this, and the court doth award: That you shall go to gaol for a fortnight without bail or mainprize; and the next Saturday, to stand upon the pillory at Ailsbury, in the open market, for the space of two hours, from eleven of the clock to one. . . . And the next Thursday, to stand in the same manner and for the same time, in the market of Winslow; and there your book shall be openly burnt, before your face, by the common hangman, in disgrace to you and your doctrine.[40]

The sentence was carried out to the letter, but to the judge's surprise, young Keach used his time in the pillory to preach to the throngs in the marketplace. When he was forced to stop speaking by the sheriff, his young wife stood beside the pillory and continued her husband's sermon.

Such was the determination of Benjamin Keach, who for forty-six years was for the Baptist denomination an able preacher, a prolific biblical scholar, and an imaginative writer. It is not surprising that soon after his two experiences in the pillory, he moved to London to become the pastor of a tiny congregation of Baptists meeting from house to house in Southwark, "the better to conceal themselves from those that persecuted them."[41] Such secrecy, however, was soon to end. The Act of Toleration passed in 1689, just a few years after Keach arrived in London,

---

[40]Crosby, *History of English Baptists,* 2:202-203.
[41]Ibid., 4:272.

opening the door for Baptists to come out of hiding. Keach's congregation, some of whom were well-to-do, soon built a meeting house in Horselydown, and from a handful of members under Keach's leadership the church quickly grew to accommodate nearly a thousand people for worship.

Keach's renown as a preacher gradually became matched by his reputation as a writer. A complete list and description of his works would take up far too much space, but to mention a few of them is to reveal his depth of understanding and his passion for the gospel. Like Bunyan, Keach had a fertile imagination, which took the published form of an allegory. *The Travels of True Godliness* is the story of one who is "the great and glorious Offspring of the Lord Jehovah,"[42] known variously as "True Godliness" or just plain "Truth," who travels "from the Beginning of the World, to this present Day" trying to find someone who will take him in. True Godliness meets all sorts of people such as Mr. Legalist, Mr. Formalist, and Mr. Belly-god, but finally finds a home with Mr. Thoughtful Christian, who embraces True Godliness as a member of his own family.[43] Keach's allegory went through many editions and enjoyed wide popularity as a book of devotion, but since it did not possess the genius of Bunyan's *Pilgrim's Progress, True Godliness* failed to become a spiritual classic. Yet the work of Keach is full of adventure and contains deep insight into the lives of ordinary people. Keach himself warned any potential reader of his book what to expect: "If thou art a believer, read with delight, but if thou art an Enemy to true Godliness, read and tremble, for the great Happiness of the one, and the miserable Condition of the other, is here laid open before your Eyes."[44] Perhaps one reason for Keach's failure to match Bunyan's allegory in popularity was the total lack of subtlety in *True Godliness*. Keach, at times, seems to be unable to decide whether to tell a story or to preach directly to his readers.

Of far more significance for the church was Keach's massive (980 pages) reference work entitled *Tropologia: A Key to Open Scripture Metaphors,* first published in 1682. It is hard to imagine that Keach was able

---

[42]Benjamin Keach, *The Travels of True Godliness* (London: Printed by I. Dawks, 1708) 9.
[43]Ibid., 176ff.
[44]Ibid., preface facing p. 1.

to complete such a project by the age of forty-two, for its value to anyone who studied the Scriptures was immeasurable. With a steady realism that flew into the face of some current wild allegorical preaching, Benjamin Keach provided an extended explanation of every metaphor and simile found in the entire Bible. Almost a century after its original publication John Ryland, the well-known Baptist educator, could write of *Tropologia* that "nothing can be imagined more adapted to inform the Understanding, in point of Knowledge, and at the same Time, to please the Imagination, enrich the Memory, and raise the Affections to Christ."[45]

Thomas Crosby, the first Baptist historian, was also Keach's son-in-law. Thus from his evaluation of Keach one can hear both a historian and a friend.

> Preaching the Gospel was the very pleasure of his soul, and his heart was so engaged in the work of the ministry, that from the time of his first appearing in public, to the end of his days, his life was one continued scene of labor and toil. His close study and constant preaching did greatly exhaust his animal spirits, and enfeeble his strength, yet to the last he discovered a becoming zeal against the errors of the day; his soul was too great to recede from any truth that he owned, either from the frowns or flatteries of the greatest. He, with unwearied diligence, did discharge the duties of his pastoral office.[46]

Baptists in England during the seventeenth century had an extraordinary number of evangelistic and learned leaders. Benjamin Keach was among the most well-known, and his influence is still with us. Keach's son Elias came to America and exerted strong and lasting leadership among the early Baptists in Pennsylvania. Perhaps the most highly publicized contribution of Benjamin Keach to the church was his early advocacy of hymn-singing, which produced the first hymnbook in England.[47] Keach's greatest contribution to his denomination is found, not in his many controversies and writings, but by his leadership in providing a model for an intelligent and evangelistic preaching ministry. Keach himself once wrote that "no Clas [*sic*] of Men have more need of Learning than the Ministers

---

[45]See the recommendations in Benjamin Keach, *Tropologia: A Key to Open Scripture Metaphors, in Four Books* (London: Printed by J. W. Pasham, 1779).

[46]Crosby, *History of English Baptists,* 1:304.

[47]See William J. Reynolds, "Our Heritage of Baptist Hymnody in America," *Baptist History and Heritage,* (October 1976):204ff. Keach published a hymnbook in 1691, seven years before Isaac Watts published his first book.

of the Gospel, because their Employment is of the highest Concern, viz. rightly to divide the Word of Truth."[48]

CONCLUSION

Some Baptists have speculated that the famous John Milton was a Baptist preacher. That is indeed stretching the truth, but it remains true that Milton's theological positions were in many ways sympathetic to Baptist views. Some parts of his *De Doctrina Christiana* could pass as Baptist tracts. His section on the local church, for example, clearly states his position that "a particular church is a society of persons professing the faith, united by a special bond of brotherhood."[49] Above all, he advocated believer's baptism as "the rite appointed for the admission of all persons, that is, of all adults, into the church."[50] Yet Milton never united with a Baptist church, even though his wife did after his death. All that can be said positively is that John Milton, though not a Baptist, was sympathetic to many theological positions that Baptists hold dear.

The Act of Toleration in 1689 marks a watershed in Baptist preaching. Baptists and other dissenters, as the very name of the act indicates, were *tolerated*—not given religious freedom. Dissenters were still required to pay tithes to the established church and to register their meetings with the local Anglican bishop. No Dissenter could hold public office. Thus while Baptists and others were relieved from active persecution, they were still restricted to some extent and there was still a favored Church in England.

When persecution is no longer tolerated, churches historically lose some of their original vitality. Without the necessity of defending their existence, Baptists entered a period when, on the whole, preaching became tepid. There were, however, some bright exceptions that pointed to a great renewal of Baptist preaching.

---

[48]Keach, *Tropologia*, iii.

[49]John Milton, *De Doctrina Christiana*, vol. 17 of *The Works of John Milton* (New York: Columbia University Press, 1934) 285.

[50]Ibid., 323.

Chapter 2

FREEDOM TO PREACH
Baptist Preaching in the Eighteenth Century

. . . the authority of Christ, and the Respect and Obedience we owe to His Commands, shou'd counter-balance all other Considerations.
John Gale, 1711

As far as Baptist history is concerned, a new century really began in 1689 when the Act of Toleration was passed. At last Baptist preachers could exercise their gifts without fear of arrest and imprisonment. Even though there were certain restrictions on their freedoms, such as registering their services with the local bishop, Baptists were free to preach.

Logic tells us that Baptists would take advantage of this new freedom and enter a period of renewed evangelism and expansion, but reality intrudes to say that such was not the case. During the first half of the eighteenth century Baptists joined others in a slow trudge through the bogs of theological controversy. The debate over baptism continued to rage between Baptists and non-Baptists. Within the Baptist ranks, internal struggles sapped the energy and narrowed the minds of many who would otherwise have seen beyond the horizon of their own theological vision. To some extent Baptists joined the Anglicans and Presbyterians in wrangling over their understanding of the Trinity. The General Baptists tended to drift toward Unitarianism; the Particular Baptists sometimes became entrenched in a hyper-Calvinism that claimed that God determined everything that ever happened.

Such a condition seems to be barren ground for an outbreak of evangelism. Yet this was the century of Whitefield and Wesley, and at the end of the century a cobbler named William Carey transformed hyper-Calvinism into the Baptist Missionary Society in 1792. How could great preaching survive among Baptists and then flower into the mission movement inaugurated by Carey? And what about an educated ministry, especially when dissenters like Baptists were barred from the great English universities? Such a condition prompted Baptist historian W. T. Whitley to claim that "the denomination was uncultured, and had no aspiration after culture. The fallacy gained ground that God set a premium on ignorance, that piety and education were barely compatible."[1] Yet like the ancient Hebrew remnant, there remained a remnant of great Baptist preaching that looked beyond the controversies to a greater and more expansive preaching ministry.

JOHN GALE

At the turn of the eighteenth century John Gale returned home to London after a brilliant university career in Holland. At the age of nineteen, he had been the youngest person in the history of the University of Leyden to receive a Doctor of Philosophy degree. His professor had written to Gale's father to say that "it has happened to no body that I know of, to gain such a knowledge of things which are to be trac'd out of natural reason . . . that before the expiration of the nineteenth year of his age, to be judg'd worthy to be adorn'd with the highest honours in a solemn ceremony."[2] He had mastered the Latin, Greek, and Hebrew languages to the extent that he could speak and write them fluently. He had so quickly shown an understanding of the ancient philosophers, as well as the Scriptures and the church fathers, that one of Gale's professors called him a genius.[3]

Added to his genius was a pleasing personality, a capacity for great friendship, and a humility that surprised even his friends. Said a colleague about Gale, "he always appeared humble and modest, mild and courteous, and was so far from having a vain and proud conceit of his own endowments, that he knew how (without the affected vanity of lessening his own qualifications) to esteem others better than himself."[4]

---

[1] W. T. Whitley, *A History of British Baptists* (London: Charles Griffin and Company, Ltd., 1923) 184.

[2] Anonymous, in "An Account of his Life," in John Gale, *Sermons Preach'd Upon Several Subjects*. (London: Printed by J. Darby and T. Brown, 1726) 1:v.

[3] Ibid., vii.

[4] Anonymous, "Funeral Sermon on the Death of John Gale," Pamphlet Collection, Andover-Harvard Theological Library, Harvard University. The author of this pamphlet is almost surely "the learned Dr. Kinch," who preached Gale's funeral sermon on 31 December 1721. Crosby, in *History of English Baptists*, 4:370ff., quotes from the sermon and names Kinch as the author.

Thus endowed with extraordinary gifts and education, John Gale returned to London, not sure what he wanted to do with his life, but aware of his potential to make a great contribution in whatever field he chose. Due to his father's wealth, Gale was able to postpone his decision, and he plunged into an even deeper study of ancient literature. If his father was frustrated over his son's indecision, we know nothing of it. His studies, indeed, were preparing him for an important work that began to take shape when William Wall, an Anglican clergyman, published *An History of Infant Baptism* in 1705. Wall's two-volume work was the most complete and influential defense of infant baptism ever published at that time. It was to young John Gale, not yet twenty-seven years old, that the Baptists turned to offer a learned and reasoned reply to Wall's book.

Gale's *Reflections on Mr. Wall's History of Infant Baptism* was published in 1711, and it immediately became the standard by which everyone involved in the controversy over baptism had to test his work. Several Anglican bishops, although differing with Gale on the subject of baptism, held him in great esteem after reading his book. Gale indeed became friends with religious leaders of many denominations because his insights into the gospel and his understanding of Scripture transcended denominational differences. No Baptist at that time did more to calm the ruffled feathers of religious controversy than did John Gale. Even writing the reply to Wall's work was repugnant to him if it meant that he must join the spirit of religious controversy. "Rage and Fury," he claimed, "are inconsistent with Christianity; and where these govern, that can find no place: For, what Agreement can there be between a persecuting Temper, and the peaceful Spirit of Christ our Lord?"[5]

Thus Gale very calmly and reasonably reflected on every point made by Wall and concluded that until more convincing arguments for infant baptism could be put forward, "I must desire you to allow me to continue my Separation from the National Church, and religiously adhere to that more despis'd one, of which, I hope, I shall never be asham'd or afraid to own my self a member."[6]

---

[5] John Gale, *Reflections on Mr. Wall's History of Infant Baptism* (London: Printed by J. Darby, 1711) 3.

[6] Ibid., 6-7.

When in April 1706 Gale was called to preach at the Barbican Baptist Church, London, it was a great day both for Gale and the Baptists. Gale found that he was preaching every week before what W. T. Whitley called "the most learned, the wealthiest, the most progressive of the London Particular Baptist Churches, with a fine library and the first baptistry north of the Thames."[7] Although Whitley implies that Gale was partly responsible for the Barbican Church becoming Arian in theology (the denial of Christ's divinity) a generation later, there are no such tendencies in Gale's published sermons. He was challenged to study and preach to his intellectual and spiritual limit. The happy result was that in John Gale the Baptists of England possessed a preacher who embodied the best of both piety and learning.

Although he urged the use of reason in the Christian faith, he was far from those who advocated the rejection of anything that could not be rationally understood. On the contrary, Christianity, he believed, was the most rational of all faiths when certain basic presuppositions were accepted. He stood, for example, on the authority of Scripture as "enough to determine the Things, which really are, and ought to be accounted necessary or not necessary by us; for no power can alter what our Lord has there establish'd."[8] He stood on the belief that God is all-powerful and that miracles and unusual events are natural results of God's dealings with humanity. Thus, Gale could accept the fundamental doctrines of the Christian faith and still appeal to the use of reason.

> For all the real great doctrines of the Christian religion, are believ'd very confidently with reason, and without putting the least strain or difficulty upon it. How easy and reasonable is it to believe . . . that the Son of God himself should come and lead a poor humble life here upon earth, and then become an offering for sin; that he should die a painful and ignominious death for us, to redeem and purchase us with the great price of his own blood; that he should be rais'd again to life the third day, and carried above the heavens, and seated at the right hand of the Majesty on high . . . when reveal'd to us, reason can make no objection to them.[9]

That is definitely not the preaching of one with Arian tendencies! Time

---

[7]Whitley, *History of British Baptists*, 201.

[8]Gale, *Reflections*, 62.

[9]John Gale, *Sermons Preach'd Upon Several Subjects* (London: Printed by J. Darby and T. Browne, 1726) 1:137.

and again in his published sermons he magnified Christ: "Christians ought to receive their Christianity from Christ alone. . . . a Christian means a follower and disciple of Christ, one who receives and professes to believe his doctrines as true, and submits to his commands. . . . I profess my self to be a Christian, I profess to hold those doctrines which Christ has taught, and no other, under that character, as a Christian."[10] Those are definitely not the words of a heretic.

Why, then, is the name of John Gale not more familiar to students of Baptist history and preaching? The answer lies in his early death, which snuffed out a great and promising light among the Baptists. Just before his death at the age of forty, John Gale was planning to preach through the entire New Testament and later publish the results as an exposition of the Scriptures. "My whole plan," he said to his congregation, "shall be to lay before you the most sacred and awful rule of our faith and practice, without any partial disguises, and to the utmost of my power assist you in opening your minds, to receive and own those great truths which are able to make you wise unto salvation."[11] This monumental and helpful work was never accomplished. He contracted a disease called "slow fever" and continued to worsen over a period of three weeks until he finally died. What might this brilliant Baptist preacher have accomplished had he lived to old age. Yet to bring him to attention is to resurrect him, in a sense, for he stood at the beginning of a new century as a sign of things to come.

THE HORSELYDOWN CHURCH

Some churches and pastors seem to exercise such a mutual gift of strength that both pastor and congregation are raised to a higher level of esteem as generation follows generation. No one can say whether it is the pastor who makes the church great or the church that makes the pastor great. Each seems to draw the best from the other, so that over a period of years the name of the pastor and the church become linked, as if they always belonged together as proper names. In the nineteenth century that happened with well-known preachers like Robertson of Brighton, Dale of Birmingham, and Maclaren of Manchester. Yet it also

---

[10]Ibid., 27-28.
[11]Anonymous, "An Account of His Life," xiv-xv.

happened in the eighteenth century—this time with a series of ministers who served successively in one church.

Benjamin Stinton

The Horselydown Baptist Church was located in Southwark, just across the River Thames south of London. The first of the great preachers to bring luster to the church was Benjamin Keach. Keach's son-in-law, Benjamin Stinton, succeeded Keach as pastor in 1704 and served the church and his denomination well until his early death in 1718.

Stinton, from all accounts, was an excellent preacher and leader, but he lacked the intellectual depth of his predecessor. Yet Keach must have considered Stinton to be well qualified for the post, for while on his deathbed he charged his son-in-law not to reject the call from Horselydown if it should come his way, "telling him with earnestness, that in so doing, he would reject the call of God, and could not expect his blessing to attend him"[12]

Stinton considered the dying words of Keach and the pressing of the church to accept its call as a summons from God. The result was that he plunged into that important pastorate with an enthusiasm and determination that helped cancel out his lack of training. While bearing all the duties of the pastorate, Stinton was determined to learn Greek and Hebrew, as well as to acquaint himself with great literature.

Early in his pastorate Stinton led in organizing one of the most innovative programs ever conceived among dissenting churches. Along with leaders of other dissenting denominations, Stinton helped found the first charity school for poor children to be established outside the control of the National Church. In the context of all the theological debate raging over the subject of baptism, it was a giant leap forward when an ecumenical catechism that omitted any reference to baptism was prepared for the school.[13] Forty poor children were maintained with food, clothing, and education, and not one bit of money was asked of their parents. When old enough to be apprenticed, the children were placed in positions that would allow them gainful employment. The Baptists of London, and par-

---

[12]Thomas Crosby, *The History of the English Baptists,* 4 vols. (London: Printed for the author, 1740) 4:348.

[13]See ibid., 117-22 for the formal rules on which the school was established.

ticularly the Horselydown Church under Stinton's leadership, were heavily involved in the charity school project.

The Baptists of London learned to trust the leadership of Benjamin Stinton. He was asked to compile a history of the Baptists, which he began to collect before his untimely death in 1718. Stinton's brother-in-law, Thomas Crosby, completed the task and published his *History of the English Baptists* in four volumes between 1738 and 1740.

John Gill

Forty years after the death of John Gill, a printer in Philadelphia began to explore the possibility of issuing a reprint of Gill's *Exposition of the New Testament*. From Charleston, South Carolina, came a letter of support for the project.

> Dear Sir,
>
> The very learned, copious, and evangelical *Exposition of the Sacred Scriptures,* by the Rev. Dr. John Gill, has been long held in high and deserved estimation by the most enlightened friends of religion.[14]

The letter was signed by Richard Furman and represents the extent to which the influence of John Gill traveled even long after his death.

The Horselydown Church called John Gill to succeed Benjamin Stinton as pastor in 1720. Gill was only twenty-one years old, but his commitment to Christ and his already extensive learning and preaching ability convinced the members of Horselydown that in John Gill they had found an able successor to Keach and Stinton. They were not mistaken. In spite of some who complained of his youth and his fervor, the church quickly began to grow, and conversions were numerous during his entire fifty-one-year pastorate.

Few Baptists of any age have attained the wealth of learning John Gill not only possessed but also shared in his voluminous writings. Because he had been raised as a Baptist, the English universities were closed to him, but Gill possessed an insatiable appetite for learning that would be satisfied even without the help of a university. By the age of eleven Gill had read the principal Latin classics and had become proficient in Greek. His parents were unable to afford the cost of sending Gill to one of the dissenting academies in London; thus on his own he studied logic, rhet-

---

[14]See "Recommendations" in John Gill, *An Exposition of the New Testament,* (Philadelphia: Printed by and for W. Woodward, 1811) vol. 1.

oric, philosophy, and Hebrew. His special interest became the Old Testament and how it helped one understand the New Testament Scriptures. He collected everything he could find that had bearing on the Old Testament until one historian commented that "no man in the eighteenth century was as well versed in the literature and customs of the ancient Jews as John Gill."[15]

What Gale had been unable to complete a generation earlier, John Gill fulfilled in a lifetime of work. His *Exposition of the Holy Scriptures* utilized his extensive research into ancient Jewish customs and rabbinical learning. The New Testament portion appeared in three volumes in 1746-1748; the Old Testament, in six volumes, was completed in 1766. For his brilliant work in biblical exposition the University of Aberdeen conferred upon him the honorary degree of Doctor of Divinity.[16] Many other works came from his prolific pen, including *A Body of Doctrinal Divinity* in 1767 and *A Body of Practical Divinity* in 1770.[17] His staunch Calvinistic orthodoxy reflected in his writings was characteristic not only of Particular Baptists in England, but also the early theology of the Philadelphia Association of Baptists in America, which exerted a profound influence upon the spread of Baptist principles in the New World.

Blessed with profound intellectual gifts, Gill also possessed the gift of preaching. Most of his published works, in particular his biblical expositions, had their origins in sermons. His language in the pulpit was described as "plain and expressive." As to content, his sermons were "substantial, clear and consistent, well digested, and delivered with great fluency and accuracy, which failed not to command and fix the attention of his hearers."[18]

A large collection of his sermons and addresses has survived the centuries. They all find their center in Jesus Christ, exemplifying Gill's own statement that just as Christ is the "alpha and omega of the scriptures,

---

[15]William Cathcart, ed., *The Baptist Encyclopedia* (Philadelphia: Louis H. Everts, 1811) 453.

[16]See "Memoirs," in John Gill, *A Collection of Sermons and Tracts* (London: Printed for George Keith, 1773) 1:xxiii.

[17]A complete list of his writings can be found in the *Dictionary of National Biography* (London: Smith, Elder, and Co., 1890) 21:355.

[18]"Memoirs," xxix.

so he should be of all your discourses and sermons."[19] He did not use a large number of illustrations, and those he did use tended to come from the Scripture. "When a man preaches the whole gospel of Christ," he said, "then may he be said to do the work of an evangelist, and to make full proof of his ministry."[20]

Gill urged younger ministers to take their gifts seriously and to improve them. A pastor who refuses to give himself up wholly to "frequent prayer, constant meditation, and in daily reading the scriptures and the writings of good men is nothing less than idle and lazy. He must even guard himself from too frequent visiting of church members as an excuse to neglect his studies."[21] "He who would be a preacher of the gospel to others," claimed Gill, "ought so to study the scriptures, and learn the doctrines of grace . . . that he may be able to speak them boldly, as they ought to be spoken."[22]

John Gill was, in every respect, an able representative of the kind of preaching that joined intellectual rigor to the preaching of the gospel. When he died at the age of seventy-four, the inscription placed on his tombstone said in part,

John Gill, D.D.
A man unblemished in life;
An ingenuous Disciple of Jesus:
A distinguished preacher of the gospel;
And, of the Christian faith, a strenuous
   defender;
      who
Embellished with mind, learning, and
   devotion,
      and
Ever unwearied amid the severest
   labours,
More than fifty years
   Strove

---

[19]John Gill, "The Work of a Gospel Minister Recommended to Consideration," in *A Collection of Sermons and Tracts* (London: Printed for George Keith, 1773) 2:17.

[20]Ibid., 19.

[21]John Gill, "The Duty of a Pastor to His People," in *A Collection of Sermons and Tracts,* 2:5.

[22]Ibid., 11.

With a zeal perpetual and glowing,
To fulfill the precepts of the Lord,
To advance the prosperity of the Church,
and to seek the salvation of men.[23]

THE BROADMEAD CHURCH

London was not the only home of great Baptist preaching in eighteenth-century England. The Broadmead Baptist Church in Bristol became synonymous with a great tradition of an educated and evangelical preaching ministry. Broadmead's influence far exceeded its size, for through the graduates of the Bristol Baptist College the church reached, and still reaches, remote parts of the world with the gospel.

Eighteenth-century Baptists were far from being of one mind on the value of an educated ministry. Some still held the sentiments of Thomas How, the London Baptist preacher who in 1639 wrote a pamphlet with the lengthy title "The Sufficiency of the Spirit's Teaching without Humane Learning: or, a Treatise Tending to prove Human Learning to be No Help to the Spiritual Understanding of the Word of God."[24] Broadmead Church, however, joined the growing number of Baptist churches that insisted on their ministers being well educated.

Broadmead became firmly rooted in support of an educated ministry through the generosity of Edward Terrill, who in 1679 willed to his church a substantial sum of money to be used, after his death, for the perpetual support of a minister at Broadmead who was capable of reading Hebrew and Greek and who, in addition to his pastoral responsibilities, would train young Baptist ministers. With that modest beginning there developed an outstanding dissenting academy at the Broadmead Church that flowered in the eighteenth century under a succession of able ministers.[25]

Bernard Foskett

Bernard Foskett came to Broadmead as an assistant to the pastor. He was thirty-five years old and served primarily as a teacher to the

---

[23]Gill was buried in Bunhill Fields, London. A copy of the inscription may be found in "Memoir," in *An Exposition of the New Testament,* 1:xxxii.

[24]See W. T. Whitley, *A Baptist Bibliography* (London: The Kingsgate Press, 1916) 1:10.

[25]See John Rippon, "A Brief Essay Towards An History of the Baptist Academy at Bristol," in John Rippon, *The Baptist Annual Register for 1794-1797* (n.p., n.d.) 413-56.

theological students until he became senior pastor seven years later, when the full work of the ministry fell upon his shoulders. Not only did he preach every week and attend to the pastoral care of the church, he also supervised the training of the young ministers who came to receive their education under his care. He was not known for his gentleness; rather, he was a stern taskmaster who gained the respect if not the love of his students. One student wrote in his diary, "This day when with Mr. Foskett he chid me exceedingly—and spoke some Severe Words which make a lasting impression on my Soul." The next day, however, the same student recorded, "Mr. Foskett was in a good temper and us'd us kindly."[26]

Yet Foskett was both a skilled administrator and an effective preacher, and for thirty-eight years he led both the Broadmead Church and the Bristol Academy to grow both in numbers and in depth. Another of Foskett's students (who later became his successor), Hugh Evans, described Foskett in a more favorable light.

> In the office of a tutor he failed not to pursue the same ends, which animated his profession as a Christian, and his public labours as a Minister. He was always studious to promote the real advantage of those under his care, endeavoring to lead their minds into a general knowledge of the most beneficial and important branches of literature. And though he judged a superficial education best suited to the years and capacities of some; yet he encouraged and assisted others in the pursuit of a more finished one, conforming himself on the whole to the professed design of the founder of this institution.[27]

Foskett himself was broadly educated. Although he was considered a skillful physician and sometimes prescribed remedies for his church members and students, he concentrated his attention on the Christian ministry. To his students he lectured on philosophy and psychology, logic, ethics, music, and politics. He supervised the study of five languages—English, Latin, Greek, Hebrew, and French—and taught preaching, church history, and geography. In his preaching classes he urged his students to prepare their sermons with such care that they would avoid what he called "barbarisms in the pulpit." "Words are to the preacher," claimed

---

[26]John Collett Ryland, "An Essay Towards an History of the Baptist Academy at Bristol," in H. Wheeler Robinson, *The Life and Faith of the Baptists* (London: Methuen and Co., Ltd., n.d.) 62-63.

[27]Hugh Evans, "Biographical Sketch of Rev. Bernard Foskett," in *Rippon's Register*, 2:427.

Foskett, "what tools are to a mechanic; and if a mechanic has not his tools in good order will he not be a botch after he has done his best?"[28]

Under Foskett's leadership, Bristol Baptist College became a "school of the prophets" to which Baptist churches looked for competent pastors and teachers. Some of the most eminent Baptist ministers of that century were trained under Foskett's direction and care. Among his students was a young Welshman named Hugh Evans, his successor as pastor of the Broadmead Church.

Hugh and Caleb Evans

It is not often that one finds a father-son team serving as co-pastors of any church, and much less frequently that they would serve harmoniously. Such was the case with the Broadmead Church when Hugh Evans succeeded Foskett in 1758 and a year later called his son Caleb to be his assistant. For eight years the son assisted the father, until in 1767 Caleb was ordained and became co-pastor with his father. For twenty-three years they served as a team, well received by the large and flourishing church and working as colleagues in the preaching and teaching tasks of the church and college. "The influence of his father was apostolic," wrote a student, "the popularity of the son proverbial, and every thing in the Church and Academy was approximating to perfection."[29] Even granting some latitude for an exuberant student to exaggerate, it is clear that the mid-eighteenth century found a growing and healthy body of Baptists in Bristol.

There are several reasons for the great success of their joint ministry. For one thing, Hugh and Caleb came from a Welsh family deeply embedded in the Baptist ministry. Hugh's grandfather had become a dissenting preacher in 1660, and his father had been an influential Baptist pastor in Pentre, Wales. Hugh came to Bristol to stay with some relatives while he received medical help (possibly from Bernard Foskett) for an ailing foot. We do not know if the foot problem was solved, but we do know that Foskett baptized Hugh Evans and nurtured him in the Broadmead Church. When Hugh became pastor upon the death of Foskett, he already had become a welcome part of the fellowship. Thus, the transi-

---

[28]Quoted by Morgan Edwards, in "Materials Towards a History of the Baptists in Delaware State," in *The Pennsylvania Magazine of History and Biography* 9 (1885):58.

[29]Rippon, "A Brief Essay," 441.

tion from Foskett to Evans was not only smooth but enthusiastic: one hundred and twenty-nine members signed the invitation for Hugh Evans to become senior minister.

Both Hugh and Caleb shared an approach to the ministry that contrasted with the sternness of Bernard Foskett. Even their portraits show the difference. The rugged features of Foskett tend to make one want to sit up straighter and make sure one's deportment is correct. The faces of Hugh and Caleb, however, are kinder, more gentle, as if they are holding back a smile with the greatest difficulty. John Rippon, who was a student at the time, said of Hugh Evans that "he possessed the assiduity without the severity of his immediate predecessor, and led his disciples into the fields of science by a method, in which hourly acquisitions brought new pleasures, and enabled us to pursue thought from thought, with tranquility and delight."[30]

Perhaps the most important reason for their great acceptance as a team was their gifts in preaching and leadership. "Their aim," said a modern historian, "was to prepare able and evangelical ministers, and this was possible because they were both able and evangelical."[31] They served in Bristol at mid-century, a time when old doctrinal debates were beginning to make way for greater evangelism. Their superior gifts in preaching and teaching endeared them to both the church members and their students. What Rippon said about Hugh would eventually become true also for Caleb: "Everyone who sat at his feet recognized him as a friend and a father."[32]

> *The Sire and Son the muse had long enjoy'd*
> *As bosom friends, in friendly deeds employ'd:*
> *Ah, lovely Pair! their virtues still arise*
> *in beauteous forms before her pensive eyes.*[33]

The preaching of the father was clear and striking. Caleb said that "only as a youth I beheld with admiration my father in the pulpit, and was

---

[30]Ibid., 436.

[31]Norman S. Moon, "Caleb Evans, Founder of the Bristol Education Society," *Baptist Quarterly* 24 (1971): 175.

[32]Rippon, "A Brief Essay," 436.

[33]Benjamin Francis, "An Elegy on the Death of the Rev. Caleb Evans, D.D.," in John Rippon, *The Baptist Annual Register for 1790-1793* (n.p., n.d.) 246.

delighted with the heavenly sounds which flowed from his lips."[34] Hugh was particularly gifted in being able to take a large, comprehensive, and masterful view of a subject. When he preached he virtually captured his congregation and would not let them go without "kindling all their noblest passions into a blaze of devotion."[35] Caleb inherited the same style of preaching and thus elicited the following lines from one poet who heard him preach:

> *His eloquence flow'd like a copious stream,*
> *And his whole soul flam'd in his mighty theme,*
> *A theme important, great, and well design'd*
> *To wound the proud and heal the humble mind.*
> *Old Sinai's thunder seemed to roar anew,*
> *The audience felt as if the lightning flew,*
> *While, as he pointed to the gaping tomb,*
> *He utter'd forth the sinner's awful doom;*
> *. . . . . .*
> *But wrath divine was not his favorite theme,*
> *He dwelt with joy on the melodious Name*
> *Ador'd by all the heavenly host above,*
> *The King of glory and the God of love. . . .* [36]

When Hugh Evans died in 1781, his son Caleb continued his ministry at Broadmead for ten more years until he died at the age of fifty-four. He left an active church that had greatly benefited from the association with either Caleb or his father for sixty-one years. It is no wonder that in the sermon at Caleb's funeral it was said that "it pleased God to crown the word thus preached with great success, as appears from the present flourishing state of his numerous congregation."[37]

> *Jesus, whose hands the universe control,*
> *He lov'd, he preach'd, he serv'd—with all*
> *   his soul.*[38]

---

[34]Quoted by Moon, "Caleb Evans," 176.

[35]Rippon, "A Brief Essay," 435.

[36]Francis, "An Elegy on The Death of the Rev. Caleb Evans D.D.," 250.

[37]Samuel Stennett, "Memoir of the Late Rev. Caleb Evans, D.D. Extracted from his Funeral Sermon," in *The Baptist Magazine for 1817* (London: Printed by J. Barfield, 1817) 321-22.

[38]Francis, "An Elegy on the Death of the Rev. Caleb Evans, D.D.," 251.

One of the most significant and far-reaching organizations for the promotion of intelligent evangelical preaching was formed in Bristol during the ministry of Hugh and Caleb Evans. The Bristol Education Society was organized at the Broadmead Church in 1770 out of the need for Baptist churches to have a larger number of able evangelical preachers. Baptists in England were still suffering from their exclusion from the great universities, and there was a growing number of Baptists who wanted to provide a larger number of preachers with the opportunity to obtain liberal education than just one church such as Broadmead could support. Thus, Hugh and Caleb Evans wrote all the Baptist churches in England and Wales, calling for the formation of the Society "for the enlargement of the number of students in this seminary, and their more effectual and permanent support."[39]

The Bristol Education Society was indeed formed with generous support both from churches and individuals, but the resistance to an educated ministry was still strong in some quarters. Human learning, claimed some, dishonored the work of the Holy Spirit; a preacher needed only a call from God and nothing else. One association, in its annual meeting, had gone on record asking the question (with its obvious implication), "Whether it be not a dishonour to the Holy Spirit to raise up a ministry of human learning, or to send them to school who have gifts to preach the Gospel?"[40] Thus, it is no surprise that Hugh and Caleb Evans wrote and published a statement in defense of an educated ministry.

They admitted readily that "all the learning in the world is, of itself, by no means sufficient to complete the ministerial character." They affirmed the prior necessity for a preacher to be called by God into the ministry and furnished with native gifts to fulfill that calling. Yet they forcefully asserted the absurdity of expecting a preacher to be fully equipped for the ministry without any effort to improve and develop those native gifts. Then they turned to the history of the church to support their argument. "Consult the history of the Church," they claimed, "and you will uniformly find through every period of it, with very few exceptions, that

---

[39]The entire letter is included in Stephen A. Swaine, *Faithful Men* (London: Alexander and Shepheard, 1884) 70-71.

[40]Josephy Ivimey, *A History of the English Baptists* (London: Isaac Taylor Hinton, 1830) 4:264.

those ministers who have been the most laborious and successful in their work, have been as eminent for sound learning as for substantial piety."

They then proceeded to list and describe the courses they required young ministers to take while under their care and direction. The most striking characteristic of their required studies was not the usual demands for theological competency, which would naturally be expected in such a program. What really stood out was their insistence that Baptist ministers not be blind to the great currents of scientific and philosophical thought that were sweeping their world and changing the whole approach to reality for their generation. During their ministry at Broadmead there was an intellectual ferment in the national life: Matthew Tindal's *Christianity not Mysterious,* the so-called "Bible of Deism," had appeared seven years before Caleb's birth; David Hume's *Natural History of Religion* was published when Caleb was twenty; Edward Gibbon's *Decline and Fall of the Roman Empire* and Thomas Paine's *Common Sense* were published in 1776. They ministered during a time of radical politics in America, which led to the independence of the colonies. In addition, their world view was expanding with the discoveries of men like Captain Cook, who explored the South Sea islands and set foot in Australia in 1770.[41]

Such a mind-expanding time sent some churches running for the protection and security of the old days, but not Broadmead. Unafraid of the new knowledge and certain that God was still over all, Hugh and Caleb Evans led their students into the realm of modern thought. Geography, astronomy, natural science, and philosophy were all part of the curriculum for young ministers.

The Bristol Education Society was not only a success; it was a permanent and lasting influence on the quality of preaching among the Baptists. Many promising ministers, who otherwise would have spent their lives preaching upon the shaky foundation of ignorance and emotionalism, were able to receive a sound theological education in Bristol under the influence of the Broadmead Church. One of Caleb's students, William Staughton, later emigrated to America and founded the Philadelphia Education Society along the same lines and thus promoted an able and evangelical preaching ministry among Baptists in America.

---

[41]See Moon, "Caleb Evans," 182-83.

ROBERT ROBINSON

Before leaving the eighteenth century, the name Robert Robinson must be mentioned. He served the Baptist church in Cambridge for nearly thirty years (1761-1790). In that stimulating university setting, where Baptists were anything but respected, Robinson maintained a preaching ministry that consistently attracted crowds of six to seven hundred people two and sometimes three times each Sunday. He soon became one of the most highly respected and sought after preachers of his time. Those who knew him testified that his power over an audience was complete and that he had an uncommon ability to sway a congregation as easily to tears as to sustained laughter. Perhaps the greatest compliment to his preaching came from Robert Hall, the pulpit genius who succeeded Robinson at Cambridge. "He had a musical voice," said Hall, "and was a master of all its intonations; he had wonderful self-expression, and could say *what* he pleased, *when* he pleased, and *how* he pleased."[42]

Just what was it that made Robert Robinson so appealing as a preacher? As with all successful speakers, the answer lies in a combination of his personality and his method of preparation and delivery. As to the former there were many who testified that he was a down-to-earth, unvarnished sort of man who tried to present the gospel in simple, but not simplistic, terms. This was true in all his sermons, but especially the "village discourses," which he preached during mid-week excursions among the villages near Cambridge.[43] Robinson consistently lived up to a later description of him: "his mode of address was simple and insinuating, his eloquence easy and natural, his tone modest and unassuming."[44] This, of course, was not an unconscious approach to preaching for Robinson. He believed that dissenting ministers should be careful never to "affect the dignity of priesthood" or to "affect show and parade in reli-

---

[42]Olinthus Gregory, *The Works of Robert Hall* (London: Holdsworth and Ball, 1882) 6:21.

[43]See, for example, the sermon entitled "The Christian Religion Easy to Be Understood," in Robert Robinson, *Seventeen Discourses on Several Texts of Scripture; Addressed to Christian Assemblies, in Villages Near Cambridge* (Harlow: Benjamin Fowler, 1805) 1-18.

[44]George Dyer, *Memoirs of the Life and Writings of Robert Robinson* (London: G. G. and J. Robinson, 1796) 175.

gion."[45] He pleaded with younger ministers to preach clearly and plainly, stating the facts of the gospel in their "native purity and perspicuity."[46]

Robinson's simplicity was combined with an irrepressible sense of humor which sometimes shocked his graver brethren. When a fellow minister remarked that he had never heard Robinson preach on the Trinity, Robinson quipped that he would gladly do so as soon as he understood it.[47] It must have been refreshing to the Cambridge academic community, frequently burdened with philosophical speculations, to witness a man who was obviously brilliant, but who nevertheless abhorred the pomposity and assumed gravity sometimes associated with academic circles. He even refused to be called "Reverend," a title he believed could be ascribed only to deity. Thus his warm spirit, keen wit, facile mind, and love of conversation won him many warm and lasting friendships.

Robinson's engaging personality was united with a definite method of sermon preparation and delivery. Like most preachers, he initially had a pulpit hero whom he naturally tried to emulate. For Robinson the model was George Whitefield, but Robinson's preaching soon evolved its own style which, in a later generation, others tried to emulate. His early sermons were usually extemporaneous, and all his biographers delight in telling the story related in his diary about one occasion when he remained undecided about a sermon topic until the last verse of the hymn preceding the sermon. Then, by some supernatural intervention, he believed, a verse came to him from the Song of Solomon (2:5): "Comfort me with apples, for I am sick of love." He preached on the text, and one can only wonder what he did with it.[48]

The rigors of the Cambridge pastorate, however, soon changed his approach to sermon preparation. He became a student of preaching, and through the years he developed definite ideas on how one should go about the task. Fortunately, he wrote and published his principles in voluminous notes to his translation of John Claude's *An Essay on the Composi-*

---

[45]Robert Robinson, "The Kingdom of Christ Not of this World; a Sermon, Preached at Broadmead, Bristol, August 28, 1781, Being the Day of the Annual Meeting of the Education Society" (Bristol: William Pine, 1781) 16.

[46]Ibid., 7.

[47]Graham Hughes, *With Freedom Fired* (London: The Carey Kingsgate Press Ltd., 1955) 80.

[48]Dyer, *Memoirs of The Life and Writings of Robert Robinson,* 26.

tion of a Sermon: or, the Beauties and Defects of Preaching. Claude stood at the heart of the reformers in France during the seventeenth century and found an agreeable place of refuge at The Hague, where he preached before nobility and foreign ambassadors. Robinson translated Claude's lengthy essay while he was recuperating from a sprained ankle and added so many of his own comments that his footnotes literally took more space than the essay.[49]

Robinson belived that preaching should follow its own rules and that it was as important a field of study as languages and theology. He saw little good in a minister who had a good understanding of sound doctrine but was unable to preach these doctrines effectively. "A man may be a good *lawyer*," he claimed, "and yet not a good *pleader;* so he may be a good *divine,* and yet not a good *preacher.*" He scorned universities that took great pains in teaching their divinity students the fundamentals of theology while disregarding their application from the pulpit. "They presently think themselves fit for the pulpit without any further enquiry," he chided, "as if the gift of preaching and sacred oratory was not a distinct art of itself."[50]

Robinson early emphasized the simplicity he considered vital to a strong pulpit ministry. A sermon should be so clear and simple that it should "reach even the most inattentive; like as the sun strikes our eyes without our thinking of it, and almost in spite of us."[51] He encouraged his readers to preach in the idiom of the people, reminding them that the only way to reach the minds of the people was to speak in terms they would understand. In the preface to the volume of his village sermons, he wrote at length on the problem of adapting one's language to the listeners. For Robinson, the matter boiled down to common respect for people and a genuine desire to communicate the gospel.[52]

Above all, he claimed, a sermon should not be dull. By his emphasis on making sermons interesting, Robinson implied that the unforgivable

---

[49]Robert Robinson, trans., *An Essay on the Composition of a Sermon: or, the Beauties and Defects of Preaching,* by John Claude, 2 vols. (London: Scatcherd and Whitaker, 1778-1779).

[50]Ibid., 1:2-3.

[51]Ibid., 1:12.

[52]Robinson, *Seventeen Discourses,* vi-vii.

sin in preaching was dullness: "Such preaching, like the passing bell at a funeral, tolls us into the land of darkness and the shadow of death."[53]

Perhaps as a result of his own experience of extemporaneous preaching early in his ministry, Robinson repeatedly stressed *"purity of heart, prayer to God, and diligent study."* Each is essential, he believed, for a good preacher, as diligent study "will distinguish him from those enthusiasts who pray; but who do not study, because they trust to immediate suggestions and expect new revelations."[54] He advised preachers to study until they thoroughly understood the subject of the sermon, then to retire for ten minutes before preaching, and in fervent prayer to prepare themselves before God. Then, as Robinson wrote, "they go from prayer to the pulpit, as Moses went down from the mount from God to speak to the people."[55]

Robert Robinson stands tall among eighteenth century preachers as an excellent example of one who helped demonstrate the fact that Baptists stood on more than emotion. Educated people who had been repelled by the pious platitudes of many illiterate preachers of the time felt drawn to this Baptist preacher whose evident learning, keen mind, and powerful appeal helped convince people that dissenting churches could represent a formidable power for good and command their utmost respect.

CONCLUSION

The close of the eighteenth century marks a turning point in Baptist preaching. Worldwide events would profoundly alter the course of the Baptist denomination. The dreams of an humble yet brilliant cobbler named William Carey began to take shape. A theological movement called "the new evangelical Calvinism" gradually began to take hold of Baptist leaders. Its effect on Baptist preaching was profound and lasting.

---

[53]Robinson, *An Essay on the Composition of a Sermon,* 1:15.
[54]Ibid., 1:97.
[55]Ibid., 2:466-67.

Chapter 3

LIFTING THE LIMITS
The Emergence of the New Evangelical Calvinism

. . . the commission is a sufficient call . . . to venture all, and, like the primitive Christians, go everywhere preaching the gospel.

William Carey

The character of the preaching of an age, contributes, more than most other things to give character to the Christians of that age.

Andrew Fuller

This is the story of four men. They lived for the most part in rural places, serving churches that were relatively small by their standards and tiny by today's standards. They never attended great universities, but their work has been the subject of university studies. They and their theological colleagues could virtually be counted on the fingers of two hands, but they inaugurated a new movement in preaching that circled the globe within their lifetimes. Consciously or unconsciously, every Baptist preacher must take seriously their views on preaching and ask a fundamental question: Shall I or shall I not unite with these four men in their understanding of what preaching the gospel is all about?

The names of these four men are familiar to anyone versed in Baptist history: William Carey, Andrew Fuller, John Ryland, and Robert Hall. The first three men (along with John Sutcliff) are remembered as the prime movers of the modern mission movement because they were among the small group who formed the Foreign Mission Society in 1792. The last of the four, Robert Hall, was the youngest by nearly a generation, but as a preacher he did more to further the Baptist adoption of the new kind of preaching than anyone else in his era.

Just what was this new preaching, and what made it lift the limits? To answer this question we must carefully describe what the limits were. Decades of theological controversy had pushed a large number of Baptist preachers into the corners of dogmatic theological extremes. The General Baptists, with their Arminian theology, became so enamored of open-mindedness and freedom from all constraints that they drifted toward Arianism and Unitarianism—denying the divinity of Christ and the doctrine of the Trinity. Their preaching tended toward dry intellectualism without any sense of urgency or warmth. As a reaction, Dan Taylor organized the New Connexion of General Baptists in 1770 along more evangelistic lines.

The Particular Baptists, on the other hand, drifted toward hyper-Calvinism, which became more "Calvinistic" than John Calvin himself. If Calvin believed that the elect would be saved, the hyper-Calvinists went a step further and believed that preaching for repentance and faith was futile. If God were going to save some and damn others, why should anyone interfere by inviting a sinner to repent?

A good example of a hyper-Calvinistic Baptist was John Brine, who was a leading pastor in London for thirty-five years until his death in 1765. Brine was described by one historian as "the most influential leader in the Baptist denomination" next to John Gill.[1] Brine's preaching was Christ-centered, but he emphasized the merits of Christ's sufferings to such an extent that he left no room for human response in obedience: "it is clear," he wrote, "that our Right to Impunity springs not from our Acts of Obedience; but results absolutely, and alone, from the infinitely meritorious Sufferings of the Blessed Jesus."[2] Anyone may believe the doctrines of salvation, he taught, but only those whom God chooses will be saved. One can imagine what such a belief did to evangelism. Brine himself made it clear:

> A minister is not to make inquiry after, nor trouble himself about, those secrets of the eternal mind of God, viz. whom he purposeth to save, and whom he hath sent Christ to die for in particular: it is enough for them to search his revealed will; and thence take their directions from whence they have their commissions.[3]

The hyper-Calvinists preached an evangelical gospel, but it was limited

---

[1] See William Cathcart, ed., *The Baptist Encyclopedia* (Philadelphia: Louis H. Everts, 1881) 134-35.

[2] John Brine, "Animadversions Upon the Letters on Theron and Aspasio" (London: J. Ward, 1758) 36.

[3] From John Brine, *Death of Death*, book 4, ch. 1, quoted in Andrew Fuller, *The Gospel Worthy of All Acceptation: or, the Duty of Sinners to Believe in Jesus Christ*, 3d ed. (Philadelphia: Charles Cist, 1805) 111.

only to those who were among the elect. As to the rest of the world, they applied the words of the apostle Paul to the Corinthians: "But the natural man receiveth not the things of the Spirit of God: for they are foolishness unto him: neither can he know them, because they are spiritually discerned" (1 Corinthians 2:14 KJV). If Paul was correct, they reasoned, why should preachers go to the trouble and expense of proclaiming the gospel to the "natural man"? If God wanted to save the world, He would do it in His own time and use His own methods. They believed that the best thing preachers could do was stay out of God's way.

For some Particular Baptists, such hyper-Calvinism was not the way of the gospel. They remembered another Baptist preacher, John Bunyan, who a century earlier had offered God's salvation to anyone who, like Christian in the famous allegory, would travel toward the Light.[4] They had read the exciting accounts of John Eliot and David Brainard, who freely offered the gospel to the American Indians. They read the accounts of New England religious revivals written by Jonathan Edwards. They witnessed the great preaching of John Wesley and George Whitefield, both of whom called for decisions for Christ. But most of all, they searched the Scriptures until they came to the conclusion that repentance and faith were the duty of every person who heard the gospel preached and that therefore it was the responsibility of Christians to preach the gospel to everyone. They did not reject their Calvinism and become General Baptists; rather, they rejected what they believed to be an abberation of true Calvinism. Andrew Fuller explained their view:

> Neither Augustine, nor Calvin, who each in his own day defended predestination, and the other doctrines connected with it, ever appear to have thought of denying it to be the duty of every sinner who has heard the gospel, to repent, and believe in Jesus Christ.[5]

Thus what has come to be known as the New Evangelical Calvinism was born. Without rejecting their Calvinistic theology, these ministers changed the course of Baptist preaching by lifting the limits of preaching. No longer was the gospel to be preached only to the elect. The way was cleared for the world preacher.

---

[4]They remembered that Evangelist, in Bunyan's allegory, offered directions for salvation to Christian while still a sinner. See *Pilgrim's Progress* (Oxford: Clarendon Press, n.d.) 12-13.

[5]Fuller, *The Gospel Worthy of All Acceptation*, 94.

The birth of evangelical Calvinism was not sudden. Several generations of Particular Baptist preachers had been toying with the idea of offering God's salvation to everyone. Bristol Academy, in particular, had enjoyed a series of thoughtful principals who at the same time served as pastor of the Broadmead Church. Bernard Foskett, and his successors Hugh and Caleb Evans, had all preached more evangelistic sermons than the hyper-Calvinists. Caleb, in the statement of faith he submitted at his ordination in 1767, affirmed the Calvinistic doctrines of total depravity and divine election, but went on to speak of the atonement of Christ as "an effective way opened for a happy union between God and every believing soul." Then he used a phrase that would later be made famous: "I receive, therefore, this glorious, heart-cheering doctrine as well *worthy of all acceptation.*"[6] Whether Evans influenced Andrew Fuller or not is unknown, but when Fuller published his book entitled *The Gospel Worthy of All Acceptation* in 1785, the New Evangelical Calvinism was born.

ANDREW FULLER: THE THEOLOGIAN

Perhaps Fuller, more than any of his close friends, had the best reasons for wanting to work out a theological rationale for the new evangelical Calvinism. He had been raised in a strict Calvinistic home and went with his parents to a Baptist church where he heard sermons that were theologically correct, but had little appeal to the unconverted. "The preaching upon which I attended," he later wrote to a friend, "was not adapted to awaken my conscience, as the minister had seldom anything to say, except to believers; and what believing was, I neither knew, nor was I greatly concerned to know."[7] During his early adolescence, however, he began to have periods of deep thought and struggle over the meaning of salvation. Sometimes those periods surfaced in great emotional crises. At times he thought that he would just as soon not be bothered with thoughts of God so that he could all the more enjoy those times

---

[6]See Norman S. Moon, *Education for Ministry* (Rushden, England: Stanley L. Hunt, Ltd., 1979) 20.

[7]A series of five letters written by Andrew Fuller relating his conversion is included in John Ryland, *The Work of Faith, the Labour of Love, and the Patience of Hope, illustrated; in the Life and Death of the Rev. Andrew Fuller* (Charlestown: Printed by Samuel Etheridge, 1818) 1-25. In the edition I used the pagination was very confusing. Chapter 1 proceeds with pages 1-8, then begins again at page 1 and continues to the end of the chapter. The quotation above is found on the *second pages 1-2.*

spent with his friends. Yet the struggles became more frequent until he concluded that he would separate himself from all his known sins in order to "qualify" for salvation. He continued to relapse repeatedly, however, until in near despair he made the fundamental discovery that God did not require *qualifications* for salvation, but rather offered a *warrant* to come to Christ. The warrant was based purely on divine mercy and not on human qualifications. Thus in the autumn of 1769, at the age of sixteen, Andrew Fuller drank in salvation "as cold water is imbibed by a thirsty soul."[8] The following spring he was baptized and became a member of the Baptist church in Soham, Cambridgeshire.

His bent toward theology was tested when the church at Soham split in the midst of theological controversy. When the pastor left in 1771, Fuller was called on to lead the church as an interim measure, and four years later the church officially called him as its pastor. Without any formal theological training, Fuller was cast into the unenviable position of reuniting a divided church in which emotions had run hot and to which theological controversy was no stranger. He learned his theology as a soldier learns to fight in the midst of a battle. Yet it was to his years at Soham that he credited many of his ideas, which were later published.

> But though, during these unpleasant disputes, there were many hard thoughts and hard words on almost all hands, yet they were, ultimately, the means of leading my mind into those views of divine truth which have since appeared in the principal part of my writings. They excited me to read and think and pray, with more earnestness than I should have done without them: and, if I have judged or written to any advantage since, it was in consequence of what I then learned by bitter experience, and in the midst of many tears and temptations. God's way is in the deep.[9]

In 1782, at the age of twenty-eight, Fuller was called to the Baptist church in Kettering, Northamptonshire, where he served as pastor for thirty-three years until his death at the age of sixty-one. Two things happened within the first few years of his Kettering pastorate that ultimately had momentous influence both on preaching and on the Baptist denomination to this day. The first was his writing and publication in 1785 of his *The Gospel Worthy of All Acceptation*. A modern Baptist historian has said that Fuller's book "finally released the denomination from hyper-Calvin-

---

[8] Ibid., 9.
[9] Ibid., 14-15.

ism and paved the way for the foundation of the Baptist Missionary Society, and for evangelism at home."[10] If Fuller's work did indeed release the denomination from hyper-Calvinism, the release came in stages. But the book did make public, in a logical and consistent manner, an interpretation of the gospel that called for repentance and faith on the part of all who heard it. Those who had formerly harbored such feelings now had a standard to which they could refer. The door was opened for the kind of preaching that lifted the limits of proclamation so that not a person in the world, regardless of how remote and savage he might be, was beyond the limits of gospel preaching. Not even Fuller, in 1785, realized to what extent such a theology might lead. He simply lifted the standard when he said that "trusting in Christ, no less than crediting his testimony, is the *duty* of every sinner to whom the revelation is made."[11]

There is more: not only did Fuller publish an influential book; he also made some influential friends. One of the mysterious facts of Baptist history is the amazing grouping of ministers in Northamptonshire and Leicestershire in the late eighteenth century. They each seemed destined to play a particular and important role in the ensuing drama. In the village of Moulton was a young cobbler named William Carey, employed by one of Fuller's own church members to make shoes and deliver them in Kettering. At the same time he was faithfully serving as pastor of the Baptist church in Moulton. When Fuller first met Carey in 1788 he was so impressed with his linguistic abilities that he convinced Carey's employer to release the young man from his duties as a cobbler and to continue paying him his full salary while he devoted his time to the study of languages. Their friendship was cemented, and only Fuller's death would eventually break their lifelong ties. "I loved him," wrote Carey. "There was scarcely any other man in England to whom I could so completely lay open my heart."[12]

At Olney was John Sutcliffe, two years older than Fuller and one who would become his friend and colleague in the administration of the Baptist Missionary Society. At Northampton was John Ryland, who in 1781

---

[10] Moon, *Education for Ministry*, 19.

[11] Fuller, *The Gospel Worthy of All Acceptation*, 26.

[12] Quoted in S. Pearce Carey, *William Carey* (New York: George H. Doran Co., 1923) 313.

became co-pastor of the Baptist church, serving with his father, John Collett Ryland. Five years later he became its sole pastor when his father moved to London. Fuller and Ryland had become acquainted as early as 1775, and their friendship soon cemented into a lifelong affection crowned when Ryland years later was asked to preach at Fuller's funeral. Ryland eventually wrote a biography of Fuller in which he said in the preface, "Most of our common acquaintance are well aware, that I was his oldest and most intimate friend."[13]

At Arnsby was Robert Hall, Sr., who served the Baptist church there for thirty-eight years. It was there that Robert Hall, Jr., was born in 1764—the youngest of fourteen children. Thus the younger Hall, who was later to become one of the greatest English Baptist preachers, was raised in the climate of the new evangelical Calvinism. These friends joined Fuller to change the whole complexion of Baptist preaching: "In them," wrote Fuller to a friend, "I found familiar and faithful brethren; and who, partly by reflection, and partly by reading . . . , had begun to doubt of the system of False Calvinism."[14]

The Baptist Missionary Society

Fuller's leading role in the formation and support of the Baptist Missionary Society is not as well known as it should be. Doyle L. Young's assessment was to the point when he wrote that "Fuller played an even more significant role than Carey in the Society's early development."[15] Fuller not only hosted the meeting in which the Society was organized, but literally gave his life as a result of his sheer exhaustion from traveling all over Great Britain to raise funds for the missionary cause. Carey's role as the first missionary sent out by the Society deserves its renown, but Fuller's indispensable role, though less apparent, deserves equal acclaim.

It was Fuller's theological writing that laid the foundation for the Society. In May of 1792, when the Northamptonshire Association met in

---

[13] Ryland, *Work of Faith*, viii.

[14] Ibid., 22.

[15] Doyle L. Young, "Andrew Fuller and the Modern Mission Movement," *Baptist History and Heritage* 17 (October 1982): 17. See also his 1981 Ph.D. dissertation from Southwestern Baptist Theological Seminary, "The Place of Andrew Fuller in the Developing Modern Missions Movement."

Nottingham, Carey had pressed for a resolution to form a missionary society. Fuller, like many of the others present, was not quite sure they should take such a daring leap of faith, even though his own theology led inevitably to such a conclusion. Just when Carey's proposal was about to be tabled, Carey gripped Fuller's arm and cried, "Is there nothing again going to be done, sir?" That instant was indeed, as Carey's finest biographer calls it, "a creative moment in the history of Christ's Kingdom."[16] Fuller interceded and Carey's motion passed. With Fuller on his side, the rest of the men had to pay attention to young Carey. If they thought Carey was a "hare-brained enthusiast" when he spoke alone, they could not think the same when Fuller stood with him. That historic moment led the following October to the famous meeting in the home of Mrs. Beebe Wallis, the widow of one of Fuller's deacons, where the Foreign Missionary Society was organized.

Fuller was immediately elected the first secretary of the Society. While Carey and his colleagues labored in India, Fuller spent up to a fourth of his time preaching in all parts of the country to raise funds for their support. He visited Scotland five times, and made several trips to Wales, one to Ireland, and numerous preaching visits to all parts of England. His goal was to raise one pound for every mile he traveled. When Parliament tried to kill the mission movement on the grounds that Carey and his friends were disturbing the domestic peace of India, Fuller made repeated trips to London where he petitioned Parliament and personally urged the prime minister to allow the missionaries to remain at their stations. He was successful in his attempts to persuade Parliament, but the exhaustion caused by his labors led to his death in 1815.

Fuller's Preaching

Throughout all his labor for the Foreign Missionary Society, Fuller was first and foremost a pastor and preacher. He had not the eloquence of Hall, the education of Ryland, or the linguistic skills of Carey, but he had a deep-running pulpit style that maintained steady growth in his Kettering church throughout his ministry. The membership more than doubled under Fuller's leadership, but perhaps of greater significance, the number of "hearers" (not official members) grew to well over a thousand, requiring several additions to the sanctuary.

---

[16]S. Pearce Carey, *William Carey*, 84.

With his great pulpit appeal, it is surprising to find frequent entries in his diary that reveal his low opinion of his own preaching. Most preachers today can sympathize with this Saturday night entry:

> Alas! with what can I go forth tomorrow? My powers are all shackled, my thoughts contracted. Yesterday and this morning, I seemed to feel some savour; but now all is gone, like the seed by the way-side, which the fouls of the air devoured.[17]

On another occasion he lamented his lack of time for visitation and concluded that his preaching would be more effective if he conversed more frequently with his members and hearers.[18] His sensitive spirit was always ready to lay any success in preaching at the feet of his Lord and any failure to his own pride: "if I am praised at any place as a preacher, how prone am I, at that place to keep pace with their esteem, if not to outgo it, in the estimation of myself!"[19]

At the center of Fuller's preaching was the atonement of Christ and free grace. Not only was he an ardent defender of the theological principles underlying the new evangelical Calvinism, he was also heart and soul a preacher of God's invitation for all to repent and come in faith to Christ. Upon his return from a preaching mission to Ireland, Fuller declared "The doctrine of the cross is more dear to me than when I went. I wish I may never preach another sermon but what shall bear some relation to it."[20] He was very direct in his appeals, often using the word *you* far more than the word *we*.

> *You* are, whether *you* know it or not, a lost sinner. . . . if *you* could resist his power, escape his hand, or endure his wrath, *your* unconcernedness might admit of some kind of apology. . . . But whether *you* will hear, or whether *you* will forebear, I will declare unto *you* the only way of salvation. That which was addressed to the Philippian jailor, is addressed to *you* [italics mine].[21]

---

[17]Ryland, *Work of Faith*, 56-57.

[18]Ibid., 58.

[19]Ibid., 65.

[20]Ibid., 276.

[21]Andrew Fuller, "The Great Question Answered" (London: W. Button and Son, 1803) 13-17.

It was so vitally important to Fuller that people actually experience the gospel that he repeatedly advised young preachers of the fact that it was possible for them to preach without any theological errors and yet still "be aside from the doctrine of the cross."[22] He insisted that a sermon could be ingenious and yet miss the gospel altogether. During a time of theological controversy, one can understand why he continually urged such advice upon his fellow preachers. Debates over predestination and free grace became so heated during his lifetime that the gospel was often overlooked in favor of orthodoxy. Once Fuller commented that some folk "almost make the *definition* of faith the very *object* of faith."[23]

Yet, like other great Baptist preachers, Fuller warned repeatedly against frothy, unsubstantial emotionalism in preaching. He recognized that preachers with little or no formal theological education, like himself, were prone to depend upon emotional appeal alone, and he warned himself in his diary not to allow that to happen in his preaching.[24] To make up for his own educational deficiencies, Fuller pored over theological books and set the pace for study among his colleagues. He was not immune to the particular malady that sometimes plagues preachers in their studies. A diary entry for 11 November 1780 reveals, "A gloomy day. The study, a prison; my heart as hard as the bars of a castle; my mind exceedingly dull and dark."[25] How can preachers feed others with knowledge and understanding, he asked, if they are destitute of it themselves? A preacher who depends solely upon his emotions is an unprofitable servant; but what is worse, he is unable to think for himself and is apt to sway with whatever sentiment he happens to meet. Fuller was not opposed to preachers' changing their sentiments on theological matters—he had done so himself. Rather he was disturbed by those who "have no sentiments of their own to change; they have only changed the sentiments of some one great man for those of another."[26]

---

[22]Andrew Fuller, "Ministerial Doctrine," in *The Last Remains of Rev. Andrew Fuller* (Philadelphia: American Baptist Publication Society, 1836) 359.

[23]Ryland, *Work of Faith*, 112.

[24]Ibid., 83.

[25]Ibid., 65.

[26]Andrew Fuller, "The Qualifications and Encouragement of a Faithful Minister," in *Three Occasional Sermons* (Boston: Manning and Loring, n.d.) 17.

Fuller was particularly concerned that preachers immerse themselves in the study of the Scriptures. When he accepted the call from the Kettering church in 1783, Fuller submitted a statement of his religious principles. Regarding God's special revelation he said,

> I believe the Scriptures of the Old and New Testament to be, without accepting [*sic*] any one of its books; a perfect rule of faith and practice.[27]

His entire ministry was built upon this presupposition. The best of writers, he reminded his hearers at an associational meeting, still viewed things only partially. Preachers cannot afford to obtain their knowledge of divine truth secondhand, else their truth will be what Saul's armor was to David: "we shall be at a loss how to use it in the day of trial."[28]

As fundamental as the Scriptures are to preaching, however, he was careful to warn preachers against the misuse of the Bible. He attacked the dreary business of dangling a string of widely separated texts before a congregation as proof for some favorite theological theory. Rather he implored his colleagues to "drink in the spirit" of the Scriptures to find their true meaning.[29] Of even greater current interest is the fact that before biblical criticism became well known, Fuller warned preachers to allow the Bible to speak authoritatively only in the field of religious faith and not in scientific disciplines.

> [Scriptures] were not given to teach us astronomy, or geography, or civil government, or any science which relates to the present life only; therefore they do not determine upon any of these sciences. These are things upon which reason is competent to judge, sufficiently at least for all the purposes of human life, without a revelation from heaven. The great object of revelation is, to instruct us in things which pertain to our everlasting peace.[30]

It was no dishonor to Scripture, he held, to hold the Bible within its professed end. Although the Bible does not offer a unified system of astron-

---

[27]Ryland, *Work of Faith*, 47.

[28]Andrew Fuller, "The Importance of Deep and Intimate Knowledge of Divine Truth," (n.p., n.d.) 16.

[29]Andrew Fuller, "Thoughts on Preaching," in *The Works of the Rev. Andrew Fuller* (New Haven: S. Converse, 1824) 316-17.

[30]Andrew Fuller, *The Gospel Its Own Witness: or, The Holy Nature, and Divine Harmony of the Christian Religion, Contrasted With the Immorality and Absurdity of Deism*, 3d edition (London: J. W. Morris, 1802) 182.

omy, it does encourage the study of the works of God. Thus Fuller, like many of his predecessors, was unafraid of the emerging new scientific knowledge, and he urged his colleagues to address the scientific world as fellow believers in the handiwork of God.

Fuller's preaching can be characterized by a statement he made in a letter to his close friend John Ryland, who had become pastor of the Broadmead Church and principal of Bristol Academy. Fuller was expressing his deepest longings for the young ministerial students: "I wish they could so believe and feel and preach the truth, as to find their message an important reality, influencing their own souls and the souls of others."[31] As a theologian who regularly put his theological convictions to the test by preaching them, Fuller was a worthy preacher of a worthy gospel.

WILLIAM CAREY: THE IMPLEMENTER

The story of any great missionary whose childhood nickname was "Columbus" and who had hated religion as a boy is anything but boring. William Carey's numerous biographies can easily fill a bookshelf, and rightfully so, for his story is a true fairy tale. And like all good fairy tales, one yearns to hear it again and again. He is the Ugly Duckling who grew up to become a swan; he is Peter Pan who flew away to Never Never Land where exciting things happen; but most of all, he is the tortoise who plodded to victory in a race with the hare. "I can plod," he once wrote. "That is my only genius. I can persevere in any definite pursuit. To this I owe everything."[32] From a poverty-stricken cobbler in a village hamlet to one of history's greatest linguists and the father of all Protestant missionaries is more than a jump—it is a giant leap! But Carey did it by plodding—plodding with an extraordinary faith in God and the truth of the gospel. Without retelling the story of Carey's life in any chronological order, I want to focus on Carey as a preacher and as one who influenced the preaching of Baptists.

Eventually, someone would have to do it. Someone would have to put Fuller's theological conclusions to the test. If the gospel was indeed "worthy of *all* acceptation," and if it was indeed the privilege of everyone

---

[31]Fuller, *Last Remains*, 358.
[32]S. Pearce Carey, *William Carey*, 23.

who heard the gospel to repent and believe, then there was a clear mandate to preach the gospel to all nations. This goal could not be reached by discussing the project or by writing books of theology—rather it could be attempted only by someone willing to leave family and friends to preach in a foreign land in a foreign tongue with little prospect of seeing England again. Carey did precisely that, with limited hope for adequate financial support from the newly formed Baptist Missionary Society and little encouragement from his family, his denomination, or his government. Indeed, his government was in direct opposition to his missionary work and would have sent him back home from India had he not been so strategic an interpreter of Bengali society and such a beloved university professor.

For one who in later life said that "preaching the gospel is the very element of my soul,"[33] memories of his early efforts in the pulpit must have been humiliating. Surely he never forgot that summer day in 1785 when at the age of twenty-four he attempted to preach in the village of Olney. He had hoped to be recommended by the Olney church to become the pastor of the struggling Baptist church in the hamlet of Moulton, just a few miles away. But his efforts in the pulpit that day were so pitiable that the church was unable to commend him and advised Carey to work on his preaching for another year. They agreed to hear him again the following summer. The next summer he preached again, later terming his effort "as weak and crude as anything ever called a sermon." Yet the church approved him—perhaps only to save him from embarrassment—and commissioned him to preach "wherever God in His providence might call him."[34] If they had only known where Providence would lead.

For seven years Carey preached, first at Moulton and later at Leicester. As season followed season, he heard a voice that refused to be silenced. His field was to be broader than the country village of Northamptonshire. His nickname may have been lost with his boyhood, but the spirit of Columbus lived on in the man. His reading was not confined to the Bible and books of theology; he stayed up late at night thrilling like a child to Captain Cook's *Voyages*. Here was a modern-day

---

[33]Ibid., 165.
[34]Ibid., 47.

Columbus whose descriptions of the South Sea islands struck a chord in Carey that would not be silent. He determined that God was calling him as a missionary to preach the gospel to those who had never heard it. But how? No Englishman since the Reformation had been sent out as a missionary. There were no organization, no funds, and even very little missionary sentiment in his denomination to give him the slightest hope of fulfilling his dream. So Carey kept preaching, but his preaching showed a decided missionary bent—so much so that not a few thought he had gone slightly crazy. He was the youngest minister in the Northamptonshire Association, shy by nature, and therefore hesitant to speak forcefully at ministerial meetings. But his pen was not shy. For years he had been working on "a piece," as he called it, which he entitled "An Enquiry Into the Obligations of Christians to Use Means for the Conversion of the Heathens." When it was published in 1792, it contained only eighty-seven pages, but Carey's words were distilled power, and they spoke eloquently to his hesitant colleagues.

Carey introduced the "Enquiry" with the bare facts: God had chosen to deal with the world's sin, not by another deluge or natural disaster, but by wooing people to the Savior through the preaching of the gospel. To accomplish this purpose, the apostles proclaimed the Good News near and far, but their zeal had since declined, and now preachers "love wealth better than the souls of their fellow-creatures."[35] Then Carey listed the chief criticisms against missions that he had long encountered. Carefully and clearly he answered each objection both with logic and the words of Scripture. Every sentence was calm and clear, but the calmness was like the stillness of a volcano before an eruption. Having answered the objections to missions, Carey reviewed the history of preaching the gospel, emphasizing in each paragraph the urgency of preaching to "all nations." Finally he became very detailed, providing in another section a series of tables showing the facts and figures of world population, comparing numbers of Christian and non-Christian people. Here he drew from his hobby of mapmaking to make one of his strongest points. He grieved over his statistics. To have to write "Pagan" over vast regions of population gave him great grief. His conclusions were tragic.

---

[35]William Carey, "An Enquiry Into the Obligations of Christians to Use Means for the Conversion of the Heathens" (Leicester: Ann Ireland, 1792) 5.

> The inhabitants of the world according to this calculation, amount to about seven hundred and thirty-one millions; four hundred and twenty millions of whom are still in pagan darkness.[36]

The statistics were overwhelming, but he advised no hesitation: "All these things are loud calls to Christians, and especially to ministers, to exert themselves to the utmost."[37] From that point, in very practical and concrete terms, Carey proposed a plan for the formation of a society to administer a foreign missionary program.

In the light of his day, Carey's proposal was more than bold—it was virtually ridiculous. But he would not keep silent, and to confound the opposition, the most respected pastors in the Association joined young Carey in support of his sentiments. The stage was set for what has been called "the deathless sermon."

If Carey had never preached another sermon in his life, he would have deserved a prominent place in the history of Baptist preaching because of his work on the morning of 31 May 1792 in Nottingham. In the very shadow of the castle where legendary Robin Hood had scorned overwhelming odds, this cobbler-turned-preacher ignited a worldwide mission movement with the simplest of sermons. Pulpit discourses of the day were normally long and complex, especially at associational meetings, where the congregation included fellow ministers who would doubtless be impressed by the preacher's homiletical skill. But Carey would have none of that. He threw aside conventional homiletics for the simplicity and appeal of his message. His sermon was based on the call in Isaiah 54:2-3:

> *Enlarge the place of thy tent, and let them*
> *Stretch forth the curtains of thine habitations.*
> *Spare not,*
> *Lengthen thy cords, and*
> *Strengthen thy stakes;*
> *For thou shalt break forth on the right*
>   *hand and on the left; and*
> *Thy seed shall inherit the Gentiles, and*
> *Make the desolate cities to be inhabited.*
> *Fear not.* (KJV)

---

[36]Ibid., 62.
[37]Ibid., 66.

Carey developed his sermon around two pungent watchwords: "Expect great things from God; attempt great things for God." He led his listeners to the mountaintop to view the promised land of world preaching and bid them to take the land without further hesitation.

It is difficult to reckon the effect of that sermon in modern terms. Its watchword lives on as a call to mission preaching, but its living spirit has swept through the two centuries since it was preached and encompassed Carey's own denomination and many more. It has animated many a preacher to renewed faith in the preaching task; it has provided a model for simplicity and earnestness. But perhaps most important, it broke the deadlock that had confined gospel preaching to the homeland and opened the door for Carey himself to become the first implementer of the new evangelical Calvinism.

For those enamored of crowds, it is worth noting that Carey preached his sermon at a tiny Baptist chapel that would barely seat over two hundred people. The local newspaper made no mention of it, but filled its pages with the sound and fury of the French Revolution, then reaching its height. For political and military exploits, the media had all eyes and ears, but to that "still small voice" in the Baptist meetinghouse, it was stone deaf.

A year later, when the events had transpired that enabled Carey to be on a Danish ship called *Kron Princess Marie* headed for India, he was commissioned primarily to preach the gospel. He wasted little time, but proceeded on shipboard to preach each Sunday. In a letter to Fuller he described his congregation as a mix of "Norway and Holstein men, Danes, English, Flemings, and French."[38] Such a mixture of cultures was a foretaste of what he would encounter in the years ahead. Throughout his busy years in India as a teacher, translator, and horticulturist, preaching the gospel remained his primary task. He mastered the Indian languages and dialects quickly, and his eventual settlement in the busy seaport of Serampore placed him in a strategic position to preach before many nationalities.

Even when for a time the government opposed all preaching in India, Carey remained committed to his task. Said a government official to him,

---

[38]See *Serampore Letters,* ed. Leighton and Mornay Williams (New York: G. P. Putnam's Sons, 1892) 33.

"Don't you think it is wrong, Dr. Carey, to try and make Indians Christians?" Carey's answer is a classic statement of the purpose of preaching:

> You mistake us, Your Lordship. We have no faith in makings. You can make hypocrites by compulsions: Christians never. We only solicit the right to present the truth to each man's intelligence and conscience, as our Master ordained.[39]

"To each man's *intelligence* and *conscience*"—intellectual rigor coupled with evangelistic warmth—William Carey remains both a pioneer and a model for great Baptist preaching.

JOHN RYLAND: THE EDUCATOR

For any great religious movement to succeed, there must be a theologian and an implementer, but for the future health of the new evangelical Calvinism there had to be an educator. John Ryland was ideal for the task. He had been raised in the home of an educator, for his father, John Collett Ryland, was not only a Baptist pastor but also conducted a private school which stood in high esteem among dissenters. Young Ryland had early tasted the satisfaction of diligent study. At the age of five he had been fascinated by watching his father's students learn Hebrew, and he asked if he, too, could study the language. Thus, before his sixth birthday he could translate the twenty-third Psalm.[40]

When he was six, his family moved to Northampton, where his father became pastor of the Baptist church and continued conducting his private academy. Devotion and learning were ingrained into the heart and mind of John Ryland from an early age. His later love for his students may have been rooted in the fact that two of his father's students were instrumental in his commitment to Christ and his subsequent baptism in 1767. He was not content with mere conversion—he determined to be like Christ and thus devoted himself to the Christian ministry before the age of fifteen. Soon he began to preach to small groups of willing friends, and in March 1771 his church endorsed his abilities to preach publicly. He was only eighteen years old, but thirty-six years later he referred to that occasion when he said, "From that time I have had very few silent sab-

---

[39] S. Pearce Carey, *William Carey*, 264.

[40] See Ryland's own account in *Pastoral Memorials, Selected from the Manuscripts of the Late Rev'd. John Ryland, D.D.* (London: B. J. Holdsworth, 1828) 2:3-4.

baths."[41] Ten years later the church invited young Ryland to join his father as co-pastor, and five years after that he became the sole pastor when his father moved to London.

Ryland's ministry in Northampton was blessed as the church grew and flourished under his ministry. His friendship with Andrew Fuller grew, and he became one with Fuller in rejecting the false Calvinism of his day. That was especially difficult for Ryland, for in doing so he turned from the sentiments of his own father.[42] Ryland's ordination sermon had been preached by none other than the venerated hyper-Calvinist himself, John Brine, who had charged Ryland in no uncertain terms to preach the human inability to respond in faith to the grace of Christ. Yet Brine made one mistake in his address. He charged young Ryland "to examine what Doctrine God hath revealed, and preach it, yea to preach it boldly."[43] Ryland was an independent thinker, and he took Brine's advice seriously. He eventually turned from hyper-Calvinism, declaring that it "would have annihilated at once the apostolic commission, by rendering it impossible to preach the gospel to any creature."[44] From that day on, Ryland's sermons bristled with urgent calls for repentance and faith, placing him in the front rank of the emerging movement of new evangelical Calvinism.

When William Carey began writing his *Enquiry*, it was to John Ryland's study in Northampton that he traveled to seek advice. Ryland read the manuscript and found nothing to correct or add—the young Carey had written well.[45] By the time Carey finished preaching his "deathless sermon" in May 1792, Ryland was almost in tears, so moved was he by Carey's forceful simplicity.[46] When the time came for the brave step of organizing the new missionary society, Ryland was a leader among the

---

[41]Ibid., 2:8.

[42]It was Ryland's father, John Collett Ryland, who allegedly told Carey, "Young man, sit down, sit down. You're an enthusiast. When God pleases to convert the heathen, He'll do it without consulting you or me." But John Ryland contradicted that story as an "ill-natured anecdote" and claimed that he had never heard of it until he saw it in print. See Ryland, *The Work of Faith*, 88n.

[43]John Brine, "The Solemn Charge of a Christian Minister Considered" (London: n.p., n.d.) 21.

[44]*Pastoral Memorials*, 2:14.

[45]Ryland, *The Work of Faith*, 123.

[46]Ibid., 125.

thirteen who met in the home of Mrs. Wallis in Kettering. His name headed the list of those who contributed from their own pockets for the initial financial support of the society.[47]

Carey boarded the ship for India on 13 June 1793. Scarcely had Carey left before Providence called John Ryland to the precise spot on earth where he could most benefit the interests of the new evangelical Calvinism. The twin positions of pastor of the Broadmead Church and principal of Bristol Academy were vacated upon the death of Caleb Evans in 1791. The church had searched unsuccessfully for a pastor, but in 1793 turned to John Ryland. His move to Bristol in December of that year marked the beginning of more than thirty years of ministry which, through his students, extended literally all over the world. Through Ryland, Bristol Academy became the center of training for the new evangelical Calvinism. Students were regularly sent on summer preaching missions in the surrounding villages and into Wales. The old emphasis upon doctrinal controversy receded into the background. The glad tidings of the gospel moved front and center, and thus preaching experienced a great renewal leading to a resurgence of life in the west country churches.

To a remarkable degree John Ryland combined an almost mystical piety with a rigorous and evangelistic preaching. His students found in him not only a teacher, but a model and a friend. "I never left any place with so much regret, " said a former student. "To the end of life, and most likely for ever, I shall retain a grateful and delightful remembrance of the inestimable benefits I derived from his tuition and friendship."[48]

People loved John Ryland foremost because of his transparent piety. No sham, no affectation, no pretense—he was aglow with the gospel. He considered himself to be an ambassador for Christ, an ambassador chosen not for his merit, but as a pardoned rebel "commissioned to go to those who have engaged in the same traitorous conspiracy against the God of the Universe."[49] His task was to appeal to his fellow rebels to lay down their weapons and accept the grace and pardon of the God they had wronged. Robert Hall said that Ryland's devotion was the principal ele-

---

[47]See S. Pearce Carey, *William Carey,* 92.

[48]*Pastoral Memorials,* 2:50.

[49]John Ryland, "The Difficulties and Supports of a Gospel Minister" (Bristol: Harris and Bryan, 1801) 12.

ment of his being. Simply to talk with him was to experience the presence of God. But his piety did not express itself in a profusion of religious talk. It rather appeared in its fruits: gentleness, humility, benevolence, and a steady and conscientious performance of duty.[50] He once wrote in his diary,

> I often think of that expression, "One sinner destroyeth much good." So may one lukewarm professor; and doubtless, my dullness may greatly injure others.[51]

Combined with his genuine piety was a commitment to rigorous intellectual development. He worked hardest in areas in which he was most deficient and urged his students to do the same. Study was never separated from prayer. For Ryland, the two disciplines meshed to such a degree that they were mutually dependent. He was a leader in placing learned as well as pious preachers in Baptist pulpits. Thus, he himself taught the subjects of Hebrew, Greek, Latin, theology, church history, sacred antiquity, rhetoric, and logic. Ryland used the seminar method in teaching, which was an extraordinary innovation in his day. Students remained at the academy for a full four-year course of study and left only upon recommendation of the committee (trustees), either to a church or to do graduate study at one of the Scottish universities, which were open to dissenters. Altogether twenty of Ryland's students went on to Scotland for further studies, and they provided a foundation of educated and evangelical ministers who helped inaugurate the period of great preaching that would climax the nineteenth century.

Ryland's preaching, although never to reach the oratorical heights of Robert Hall, was nevertheless vigorous, direct, and personal. During his lifetime he preached 8,691 sermons in eighty-six different places, often displaying the fervor of an evangelist and the simplicity of a child. His sermons are filled with yearning invitations for his hearers to come to Christ: "O my hearers! . . . I am sure I long for your salvation, for your eternal salvation. Numberless defects have attended my ministry; but I have laboured to recommend Christ to you."[52] His people heard him gladly be-

---

[50]Robert Hall, "A Sermon, Occasioned by the Death of the Rev. John Ryland, D.D." (London: Hamilton, Adams, and Co., 1826) 29-30.

[51]*Pastoral Memorials*, 2:54.

[52]Ibid., 2:52.

cause his life was the mirror of his message. When Ryland died in 1825, Carey had lost his two closest friends in England—Fuller and Ryland. The Broadmead Church had lost a greatly loved pastor, and Bristol Academy had lost an esteemed principal. "Our hands are weakened this day," said Robert Hall at Ryland's funeral, "and if the glory is not departed from us, it is at least eclipsed and obscured."[53] Little did Robert Hall know, when he spoke those words, that he himself would eventually succeed Ryland at Bristol, and through his great preaching, elevate the new evangelical Calvinism to new heights.

ROBERT HALL: THE PROCLAIMER

After hearing George Whitfield preach, Robert Hall could not describe it in words, for "it is impossible," said Hall, "to paint eloquence."[54] Precisely the same thing may be said of Robert Hall's preaching. His *Works* may be read—all six volumes of them—but written sermons are a poor substitute for Hall's rapid-fire delivery and flashing eyes that captivated an entire nation. Hall's moving eloquence in the pulpit was the inevitable result of the emergence of the new evangelical Calvinism pioneered by Fuller, Carey, and Ryland. The old hyper-Calvinism had no need or desire for such powerful preaching. For the old school, it was simply a matter of sticking to the facts. Doctrinal orthodoxy, dry as it could be, was far more important than religious experience. While the hyper-Calvinists were busy puttering around in their garden of orthodoxy, the little group from Northamptonshire watched a forest of faith grow, a forest not limited by oceans or contained by continents.

Hall's relationship to Fuller, Carey, and Ryland went all the way back to his childhood. His father was the pastor of the Baptist church in Arnsby, where the elder Hall was already of like mind with Fuller in turning away from hyper-Calvinism to a more evangelical gospel. Robert Hall, Sr., wrote a little book entitled *Help to Zion's Travellers,* whose aim was "to remove the stumbling-blocks . . . relating to doctrinal, experimental, and practical religion."[55] Young Carey, while still a cobbler, was deeply influ-

---

[53] Robert Hall, "A Sermon," 50.

[54] *The Works of the Rev. Robert Hall, A.M.,* ed. Olinthus Gregory (London: Holdsworth and Ball, 1833) 6:125.

[55] Robert Hall, Sr., *Help to Zion's Travellers* (Boston: Lincoln, Edmands and Co., 1833) 28.

enced by the book, and soon Robert Hall, Sr., became one of Carey's pulpit heroes. Through his father the young Robert Hall became acquainted with both Fuller and Carey as a young boy. At the age of eleven he entered John Collett Ryland's school in Northampton, thus becoming the friend of John Ryland. At the age of fifteen Hall entered Bristol Academy and studied under Hugh and Caleb Evans, later becoming an assistant to Caleb Evans at Broadmead. The relationships among the four men in this chapter ran deep, and Robert Hall, who was twelve years younger than Ryland, seemed to gather the best qualities of each and add to them a natural pulpit eloquence that has seldom been known before or since.

Olinthus Gregory, who was very closely related to Robert Hall as an adult, provided us with an amazing description of Hall's preaching, which, he said, was not unusual, but seen repeatedly whenever Hall preached.

> From the commencement of his discourse an almost breathless silence prevailed, deeply impressive and solemnizing from its singular intenseness. Not a sound was heard but that of the preacher's voice—scarcely an eye but was fixed upon him—not a countenance that he did not watch, and read, and interpret, as he surveyed them again and again with his rapid, ever-excursive glance. As he advanced and increased in animation, five or six of the auditors would be seen to rise and lean forward over the front of their pews, still keeping their eyes upon him. Some new or striking sentiment or expression would in a few minutes, cause others to rise in like manner: shortly afterwards still more, and so on, until, long before the close of the sermon, it often happened that a considerable portion of the congregation were seen standing,—every eye directed to the preacher, yet now and then for a moment glancing from one to another, thus transmitting and reciprocating thought and feeling:—Mr. Hall himself, though manifestly absorbed in his subject, conscious of the whole, receiving now animation from what he thus witnessed, reflecting it back upon those who were already alive to the inspiration, until all that were susceptible of thought and emotion seemed wound up to the utmost limit of elevation *on earth,*—when he would close, and they reluctantly and slowly resume their seats.[56]

If such a description is astounding, it is even more so when one considers that Hall, at the time, was preaching in the secular community of Cambridge University, and at an early point in his life. The universal sentiment among those who heard him later in life was that he improved with age.

---

[56]*Hall's Works,* 6:55.

What made Robert Hall so successful as a preacher? For one thing, he was endowed with unusual gifts for the task. He had an active mind that pondered a wide variety of subjects, both sacred and secular, which enabled him to think in wholes rather than in parts. He could see the large picture, and in any one sermon he could pull from his prodigious mind both pertinent facts and well-formed phrases that stabbed his listeners with new awareness and understanding. In addition, he had a full grasp of the evangelical gospel. He was the only one of the four—Fuller, Carey, Ryland, and Hall—who had been raised from birth in the exciting atmosphere of the new evangelical Calvinism. Unlike the others, Hall did not have to overcome his early training to embrace the new understanding of preaching. As a young man he had a few periods of rebellion when his orthodoxy was questioned by some, but after his father died in 1791, Hall became a champion of the orthodox evangelical gospel.[57]

There are other reasons for his success in the pulpit. He had the unique gift of feeling what he spoke to such an extent that his feeling was transferred to those who heard him. He communicated with feelings as much as with words, so that one worshiper said that upon hearing Hall he first "learnt the difference between one who feels while he is speaking . . . , and one who after he has spoken long and with apparent earnestness, still does not feel."[58] Hall's use of language was striking. With a thorough grasp of technical theological and biblical terminology, Hall deliberately chose to use the simplest words of Saxon origin in his preaching. Instead of *felicity* Hall chose the word *happiness*. Why? "Happiness is a better word," said Hall, "more musical and genuine English, coming from the Saxon."[59] Thus not only was he understood and appreciated both by the simple and the learned; he also stood in stark contrast to many popular preachers who were showy and admired orators. John Foster, well known in literary circles of the day as a successful essayist, described Hall's preaching as a series of thoughts that "seemed to take fire

---

[57]When Hall was invited to become pastor of the Baptist church in Cambridge, the liberal-minded church "could not but congratulate one another that their new pastor, a man of splendid talents, was *almost* as liberal and unshackled as they were." See ibid., 6:29.

[58]Ibid., 6:39.

[59]Ibid., 6:50.

in passing on, to end in a still more striking figure, with the effect of an explosion."⁶⁰

Still another asset to Hall's preaching ability was his pastoral fidelity. He paid careful attention to living books as well as printed books, and to know them well he readily left his study for the firesides of his members. He made it a habit to visit each family in his church once a quarter. He was an avid tea drinker, consuming as many as thirty cups a day, so when he visited his poorer members he carried along his own tea and sugar to keep from causing them unnecessary expense. He had a special sympathy for those who suffered, since he had suffered all his life with a back problem that rarely left him at ease and sometimes caused him great agony. For the last twenty years of his life he did not have a single night that was uninterrupted by back pain. When he died in 1831, his physician commented that "probably no man ever went through more physical suffering than Mr. Hall," yet he was known for his prevailing cheerfulness.⁶¹

Robert Hall held three strategic pastorates. In July 1791 he was called to the Baptist church at Cambridge and remained there for fifteen years. It was in the Cambridge University community that he became a renowned preacher. So many Anglican students were attending the Baptist services that at one point the university administrators considered the imposition of a new rule to prevent attendance of Hall's services. That measure was abruptly stopped when the influential head of Trinity College declared that he not only admired Hall's preaching, but that if he were not the Master of Trinity he would attend the Baptist church himself.⁶² Hall first came to national attention in 1793 upon the publication of a tract entitled "An Apology for the Freedom of the Press, and for General Liberty," written during a storm of national debate caused by the French Revolution.⁶³ His articulate championing of freedom of the press won him a host of friends who had never heard him preach. In 1801 Hall published a sermon entitled "Modern Infidelity Considered," which carried his fame

---

⁶⁰Ibid., 6:145.

⁶¹Ibid., 6:134.

⁶²Ibid., 6:67.

⁶³See ibid., 3:61-173. He called the French Revolution "the most splendid event recorded in the annals of history" (172).

throughout the country.[64] Two years later, when the threat of an invasion of England by Napoleon lay heavy on the minds of his congregation, he preached a sermon entitled "Sentiments Proper to the Present Crisis," copies of which were spread throughout England.[65] When the prime minister, the famous William Pitt, read it, he declared that "the last ten pages were fully equal in genuine eloquence to any passage of the same length that could be selected from either ancient or modern orators."[66]

With his reputation as a national preacher, the steadily increasing demands on Hall's time and energy led eventually to a mental breakdown in 1804. It was likely brought on by sheer exhaustion, for after a period of rest he became the pastor of the Baptist church in Leicester, where he served for twenty years until he succeeded his friend John Ryland as pastor of the Broadmead Church in Bristol in 1825.

Robert Hall, with all his natural eloquence, imbibed deeply into the mind of Christ. While his piercing intellect became so renowned that the University of Aberdeen conferred upon him an honorary doctorate in 1817,[67] his simple trust in Christ prompted one hearer to comment, "this man must have read much, thought much, and prayed much."[68] He read the Scriptures both devotionally and critically, and during a time when biblical criticism was a relatively new field, Hall could discuss with intelligence the findings of the leading critics. Yet he never displayed his knowledge of critical methodology from the pulpit. Rather he used the findings of biblical criticism to strengthen, not diminish, his faith. He even used a contemporary translation of the Gospels by one of the great biblical critics as the basis for his family devotions.[69] "The light of revelation," he declared to the students of Stepney Academy, " . . . is not opposite to the light of reason. . . . Revealed religion is not a cloud which overshadows reason; it is a superior illumination designed to perfect its exercise and supply its deficiencies."[70]

---

[64]See ibid., 1:13-78.

[65]Ibid., 1:125ff.

[66]Quoted in Cathcart, *The Baptist Encyclopedia,* 489.

[67]In spite of his receiving the degree, he never adopted the title of "Doctor" because of conscientious objections to such appellations.

[68]*Hall's Works,* 6:57.

[69]Ibid., 6:101.

[70]Ibid., 4:409.

How could intellectual rigor and warm evangelical faith both flourish so well in one man? The fundamental position on which Hall stood was that truth can never suffer from the most strenuous intellectual exertions, provided those exertions be submitted in reverence to God made known in Jesus Christ.

Hall's evangelical outlook and his renowned preaching were the natural outgrowth of the movement begun in rural Northamptonshire by his friends Fuller, Carey, and Ryland. Through those four men, the entire landscape of Baptist preaching was transformed. The limits were lifted. The way was clear for a succession of great pulpit masters who carried Baptist preaching in England to heights never before known.

Chapter 4

JOHN CLIFFORD
A Rigorous Gospel

When John Clifford died on 20 November 1923 the reaction was immediate and widespread. From the king and prime minister, the Archbishop of Canterbury and the Bishop of London, to say nothing of the ordinary and unrecognized masses in London and around the world, the unanimous sentiment was that John Clifford had been a national asset to England and a man of "stainless honour."[1] Lloyd George, the prime minister, said that his own sense of personal loss occasioned by Clifford's death "defies estimate and description."[2] The chorus of praise continued to reach Clifford's home from all parts of the world until a stranger might have thought that the object of such acclaim must have been some national military hero. But no, he was a simple Baptist preacher who never lost touch with his humble origin.

THE ROCK FROM WHENCE HE WAS HEWN

Morning dawned cold and rainy in the English Midlands, the kind of morning that sends chills through a boy's skin. "Up John! Get up!" The voice seemed to come from another world. "Time to get up, son!" Two big hands wrapped around the boy's scrawny middle and lifted him bodily out of bed, placing his feet squarely on the cold plaster floor. Rubbing the sleep from his eyes, the boy dressed and walked out into the cold with his father, where they made their way to the local lace factory for a normal sixteen-hour working day. The boy was John Clifford at ten years of age, and any idea that he would become one of the greatest Baptist preachers of his age or any age was as far from his mind as was rest from his body.

---

[1]The many tributes written at the time of Clifford's death could fill a whole volume, but one of the best collections of statements made at his passing may be found in a special supplement devoted to John Clifford in *The Baptist Times and Freeman*, 30 November 1923.

[2]Ibid., 829.

Yet one thing was not far from his mind, his books. He loved to read his Bible, and his Sunday school teacher had presented him with a copy of Emerson's *Essays*. These books always bulged from his pockets, and even while at work in the factory John would read a page or two in any spare moment. "Put that book away and get to work!" The command was from John's foreman, but at the age of thirteen John was old enough to defend himself: "I can produce just as much while reading!" So John was put to the test, proved his case, and was henceforth allowed to read at work.[3]

His Conversion

A large number of people and events join to lead a young person to a life-changing trust in Christ. In the case of John Clifford many months of soul-searching and agonizing prayer led to that momentous Sunday evening in a village Baptist chapel. The service was conducted as usual, but the words of the closing hymn especially spoke to him:

> *The soul that longs to see My Face*
> *Is sure My love to gain,*
> *And those that early seek My grace*
> *Shall never seek in vain.*

What happened to John Clifford in those moments defies rational explanation, but he could join the hosts before and after him and say that "the fetters seemed to be broken by one stroke, and into the liberty of the children of God I leaped as in an instant."[4]

Although John Clifford never regarded baptism by immersion as a prerequisite for becoming a Christian, he did ask to be baptized as a public declaration of his faith in Christ. At the age of fifteen on 16 June 1851, Clifford was immersed in the presence of the assembled congregation

---

[3] G. W. Byrt, *John Clifford: A Fighting Free Churchman* (London: The Kingsgate Press, 1947) 21.

[4] There are four biographies of John Clifford, all of which testify to his conversion experience. Two were written during Clifford's lifetime: Charles T. Bateman, *John Clifford, Free Church Leader and Preacher* (London: National Council of the Evangelical Free Churches, 1904) and Denis Crane, *John Clifford, God's Soldier and the People's Tribune* (London: Edwin Dalton, 1908). A year after Clifford's death Sir James Marchant wrote the longest of the biographies, *Dr. John Clifford, C.H., Life, Letters and Reminiscences* (London: Cassell and Company, Ltd., 1924). The most recent, and in my judgment the best of the Clifford biographies, is the work of G. W. Byrt, *John Clifford: A Fighting Free Churchman*. Byrt records the story of Clifford's conversion on pages 25-26.

which, along with his parents, had nurtured him for those fifteen years. Through all his years of ministry, Clifford annually marked that day in June, for on that day he always recalled, he later said, "that baptism into a quickening of the conscience, which set me, in full dependence upon God, to a full-hearted determination to obey Him."[5]

His Call into the Ministry

For a poor factory worker in Victorian England to enter the Christian ministry was quite a step, but John Clifford seemed to be drawn by an unseen hand toward his destiny. Clifford was willingly led, although his early attempts at preaching could not be counted among his greatest successes stories. Long before he was willing to speak before an entire church, Clifford met from time to time with several of his factory friends to "practice." Yet those practice sessions were taken as seriously as any of the world-renowned services he conducted in later years. His sermons were as crude as the old box the boys had used for a pulpit, but over two years Clifford received a great deal of encouragement, not only from his young friends but also from his pastor, who had inevitably heard of those "practice sessions."

By the age of nineteen John Clifford had been accepted as a student at the General Baptist Academy in Leicester, where he was like a great bird finally set free to soar in a higher atmosphere. Although as a student he was full of fun and a favorite friend of his colleagues, he was also deadly earnest in his studies. "He thought nothing," said a fellow student, "of twelve hours' hard labor."[6] On weekends he preached in nearby churches, and at the end of three years he had won prizes in Greek, Greek History, and Latin.

JOHN CLIFFORD THE PASTOR AND PREACHER

For John Clifford there was only one church. He never moved from church to church trying to climb any supposed ladder of ecclesiastical success. At the age of twenty-two he was called as pastor of the Praed Street Baptist Church in London. The congregation later moved to Porchester Road and changed its name to Westbourne Park Baptist

---

[5]Marchant, *Dr. John Clifford,* 15.

[6]Byrt, *Fighting Free Churchman,* 36.

Church, but for fifty-seven years Clifford ministered in the Paddington area of London as the leader of one congregation.

His ministry extended far beyond the neighborhood where he served. The Westbourne Park Church, under Clifford's leadership, became one of the earliest institutional churches, pioneering the development of diverse programs aimed at improving the conditions of all people: adult education and recreational facilities, a building society, thrift clubs, a home for stranded women, three mission centers, a free meal service in one of London's worst slum areas—the list is almost endless.

Yet Clifford led a church that was not primarily a social agency. The many social programs were a natural outgrowth of a kindled evangelistic spirit. In an address delivered at the dedication of the Westbourne Park Chapel in 1877, Clifford reminded his friends that their very reason for existence as a church was to preach the living and exalted Christ as Savior and victor over all evil.[7] In the heart of the thickly populated borough of Paddington John Clifford preached Christ, and the tiny chapel soon grew into a church that weekly served thousands of people.

His Passion for Evangelism

Clifford's warm evangelistic spirit never diminished, even during the dark days of war and throughout various political controversies in which he was frequently the mouthpiece for the struggling poor and disenfranchised. (He was one of the early leaders in the battle for women's suffrage.) Undergirding his entire ministry was the conviction that "love is older than sin," and from the foundation of the world God "had his love-formed image of each one of us."[8] In a challenge to the leaders of the London Baptist Association in 1879, Clifford held up the record of the Methodists as an inspiration to the Baptists.

> Methodism was born in a baptism of fire, and spent its best years in the white heat of a divinely glowing zeal to save men; and its proved successes are at once its justification and our instruction. It has . . . surpassed all other forms of denominationalized Christianity in the energy

---

[7]John Clifford, "The Church of Christ" (London: E. Marlborough and Co., 1877) 14.

[8]See "John Clifford Will Speak" (published by the Westbourne Park Baptist Church, Porchester Road, London, W2), 24.

and range of its aggressiveness, in steadfastness of its zeal, and in its additions to the number of the "saved."[9]

Clifford's "divinely glowing zeal" can only be imagined as his printed sermons are read, yet his force and earnestness, his scorn of half-truth, his denunciation of sin and hope in Christ, his humility and burning seriousness can all be seen in every line of his sermons. Although his discourses cover a wide range of topics, his central focus in them all is "that Person who has been to me the centre of intellectual repose, as well as the guide and inspiration of my life, my Saviour and Master, Leader and Companion, Brother and Lord."[10] One person who frequently heard him preach stood amazed at the huge variety of themes Clifford brought to his pulpit over a year's time, yet his sermons were always "brought to the touchstone of Divine truth and discussed in the light of the teaching of the Son of God."[11]

As a leader in evangelistic outreach, Clifford was among the first to urge his fellow Baptists toward cooperation. "As leaders of a church," he said, "we should be prepared to lead *together,* all going in the same direction, and towards the same goal."[12] And what was that goal? "By our own example in unselfish service, let us lead our churches to greater zeal and devotedness, to more unflagging effort to win souls to Christ."[13]

Soon after World War I, Clifford was asked to address the annual meeting of the Baptist Union on "The Problems after the War." At the end of his speech, he laid aside his manuscript and said to a hushed audience,

> If an old man may speak to his brethren in the ministry, it shall be the word my mother gave me when I went to college: "John, find out the teaching of Jesus. Make yourself sure of that, and then stick to it, no matter what may come." Our first business is to make men see Christ. Get away anywhere, hide yourselves anywhere, if only to make men see Him in the brightness of the glory of the Father.[14]

---

[9]John Clifford, "The Work of Church Leaders" (London: E. Marlborough and Co., 1879) 13.

[10]Quoted in Marchant, *Dr. John Clifford,* 105.

[11]Denis Crane, *God's Soldier,* 251.

[12]Clifford, "The Work of Church Leaders," 6.

[13]Ibid., 12.

[14]Quoted in Marchant, *Dr. John Clifford,* 93.

At the age of eighty-five, when his eyesight was almost gone and he had filled virtually every leadership position available in his denomination, he still had a passion for evangelism. He challenged the National Free Church Council to a concerted effort toward awakening a renewed sense of responsibility for personal evangelism. White-haired and stooped, he campaigned before scores of religious gatherings for the cause of evangelism. On one occasion Clifford happened to attend a minister's recognition service. Although he was not scheduled to speak, he was recognized and asked to say a few words. With arms outstretched he said to the gathering the one thing that was uppermost in his mind: "I want to address a word to you young people. I cannot see you, but I assume you are there, and I do implore you to accept my Saviour."[15]

His model for evangelism was not the big business approach that sways the masses by overpowering emotional surges. Clifford urged every Christian in the land to realize afresh a personal responsibility for evangelism. This method, he believed, not only worked but followed the steps of the Master.

John Clifford was active in evangelism until the day he died. While attending a meeting of the Baptist Union Council in London on 20 November 1923, a meeting he especially wanted to attend because of plans being discussed to further the cause of personal evangelism, Clifford quietly bowed his head and died. Charles Brown, a fellow minister who was with Clifford when he died, later wrote that it was the chief passion of Clifford's life to preach the gospel and to inspire younger ministers with his own fine enthusiasm to bring people to the Saviour in whom he steadfastly believed.[16]

His Passion for Education

To think of John Clifford is to think of genuine evangelism wedded happily to a rigorous intellect. Clifford came from a poor family that could hardly afford a fine education for their eldest son. But to make matters doubly difficult, he came from a poor *Nonconformist* family, which made it impossible, in Clifford's day, to attend Oxford or Cambridge even if his family could afford it. He received his theological training at Leicester

---

[15]Byrt, *Fighting Free Churchman*, 119.

[16]Charles Brown, "The Passing of Dr. John Clifford," *The Baptist Times and Freeman*, 23 November 1923, 812.

Academy which, like many other Nonconformist schools, was led by some of the most vibrant minds in the country. John Clifford came to believe that there was no area of knowledge that was foreign to the gospel and that could not be put to good use in behalf of the gospel. Rather than running in fear from the great ferment in biblical scholarship occasioned by the advent of the critical study of the Bible, John Clifford labored to understand the most recent findings of biblical scholars. He early concluded that the critical study of the Bible was not wholly negative or destructive; rather, it could be used to great advantage in deepening faith and throwing new light on the Scriptures.

When Clifford accepted the pastorate of the Praed Street Baptist Church in London, one of his college tutors wrote him a letter that said, in part, "It will not, I trust, tend to make you vain when I say that, in my opinion, God has endowed you with considerable ability for the acquisition of knowledge, and has bestowed on you powers which, with a large and liberal culture, may enable you one day to render good service in . . . the cause of Christ."[17] Clifford took seriously that advice to obtain a "large and liberal culture," and during his early years in the pastorate he earned both the Master of Arts and the Bachelor of Science degrees at the University of London.

Clifford's education was not private in the sense of earning degrees merely for his own advancement. He wanted to raise the level of education for as many of the working people in London as possible. Westbourne Park Baptist Church was surrounded by thousands of young men and women employed by businesses in the district. There was no place for the young people to gather for social or educational purposes. The need was there, and John Clifford saw it. "The business of a Christian Church," he claimed, "is to find out the real needs of the people in the neighborhood in which it is placed and, as far as it can, supply all that will make for brightness and joy, for strength and service."[18] With a breezy optimism and unflinching courage John Clifford led the church to organize

---

[17]The complete letter from his tutor, Mr. W. R. Stevenson, may be found in Bateman, *John Clifford, Free Church Leader and Preacher,* 44-46.

[18]H. Edgar Bonsall and Edwin H. Robertson, *The Dream of an Ideal City, Westbourne Park 1877-1977* (York, England: William Sessions Ltd., 1978) 31. This book may be obtained through the Westbourne Park Baptist Church, Porchester Road London, W2 5DX.

the Westbourne Park Institute, which eventually became one of the most remarkable local church organizations in any denomination.

During the six months of winter each year, up to seventy classes a week were provided for instruction in an incredibly wide range of subjects. Within a few years well over a thousand students had enrolled in classes on subjects such as mathematics, chemistry, geometry, physics, English grammar, literature, bookkeeping, violin, shorthand, and many others, including courses in various foreign languages. Associated with the course work were social activities and clubs that drew hundreds of young people into the church. In 1879 Clifford organized a Literary and Debating Society, at which some of the finest intellects in the world spoke and debated. Persons such as Arthur Conan Doyle, Hermann Adler, George Bernard Shaw, Winston Churchill, and G. K. Chesterton were among those who appeared, not primarily because of their Christian witness (indeed, some speakers had little to do with the Christian faith), but because these people possessed the greatest minds of the time and John Clifford encouraged his people not to allow differences of opinion or religious faith to cause Christians to turn a deaf ear to the world's leading thinkers. Associated with the Institute was a library, which filled a vacuum caused by the absence of a public library. For eleven years the church sponsored a weekly concert series, and each year in September the church organized an Annual Industrial Exhibition, in which members of the Institute exhibited works of art and handicrafts.[19]

In addition to all the general education classes provided at Westbourne Park, John Clifford threw himself wholeheartedly into the task of training Christian leaders for the ministry. He therefore in 1879 established The Preacher's Institute where he taught prospective ministers theology, logic, New Testament Greek, and the basis of sermon preparation. In later years the school was expanded to bring in other well-known biblical scholars, such as G. P. Gould, who came from Oxford to teach a course on Hosea. Among the many "boys" trained under Clifford's leadership was J. H. Rushbrooke, who in 1925 became the first Baptist Commissioner for Europe and later President of the Baptist World Alliance. Rushbrooke later wrote of Clifford's influence, "He led me through the dangerous years when all kinds of questionings were arising.

---

[19] Ibid., 34.

He helped me because his preaching was always positive. Mere negation had no place in his discourses. He dealt with error by preaching the truth which would crowd it out of the mind."[20]

Clifford held a special attraction for the young intellectuals of London who were struggling with their newly discovered scientific or philosophical knowledge and how they should relate to the Christian faith. At a normal Sunday service the Westbourne Park Chapel was filled with alert young people, eager to grapple with the difficult questions of faith. They were not disappointed. John Clifford was anything but an obscurantist. He concluded at an early age that "the so-called conflict between Religion and Science is really a conflict between science and . . . a little veneer of Christian teaching."[21] He was equally at home with scientists and theologians, and he was the first to admit that "consistency is the last virtue of the human race,"[22] and that all thinkers—scientific or theological—had every reason to be humble. On no account, he claimed, should opposition to current forms of stating the faith be confused with opposition to the faith itself. Opposition to Christian faith, no matter how authoritarian, does not make it less true. "Christians cannot raise Christ if He be not already risen; nor can scepticism bury Him if indeed He has ascended on high."[23] Intellectuals, at long last, knew they had found a preacher who could meet them on their own ground.

Clifford, in fact, took great delight in challenging the thinking of intellectuals. Modern thinking, he claimed, was one-dimensional and too often unrealistic. "Give to your thinking," he challenged, "the courage of the heart, the force of resolute energy, the patience of an inflexible will, and as sure as you are true to your whole self, God will be found by you in Christ Jesus, and become the sunshine of your life, and the joy of your heart."[24] Inquiry, he believed, is always better than indifference, and he therefore led many an inquiring mind away from blind credulity to the fuller

---

[20] Quoted in Marchant, *Dr. John Clifford,* 61.

[21] John Clifford, "The Attitude of Men of Science to Christianity" (London: Hodder and Stoughton, n.d.) 15n.

[22] Ibid., 18.

[23] Ibid., 30.

[24] John Clifford, "Manly Thinking," in *The Dawn of Manhood* (London: The Christian Commonwealth Publishing Co., 1887) 75.

light of a reasoned faith. "True science," he claimed, "may begin with a menace; it is sure to end with a Gospel."[25]

Clifford wrote one of his finest books on the question of biblical criticism, *The Inspiration and Authority of the Bible*.[26] He prepared the book in the hope that it would help those who "shrink from heartily accepting the 'treasures' of Divine Revelation, because of the 'earthen' character of the 'vessel' in which they are offered."[27] Yet Clifford did not flinch from the fact that current biblical manuscripts, both Old and New Testaments, are *not* absolutely inerrant. He was careful to distinguish between the revelation itself and the vehicle of the revelation. "The grass withers, theories of Inspiration change, views of the composition of the books of the Testaments alter, mistakes as to chronology, history, numbers and morals are undeniable, but the Word of the Lord is there, and it endures for ever."[28]

As to the inerrancy of supposed "autographs" of the Bible, Clifford denounced such a theory as "unwarranted as it is useless, and as mischievous as it is unwarranted."[29] Why? For the simple reason that autographs do not exist, not even a page of one. To make absolute conjectures about the inerrancy of biblical autographs is to move out of the realm of facts and into "the insecure and airy world of theory."[30] The victories of the Word of God have come with the *present* Bible, and Clifford welcomed every competent guide in explaining the sense of its contents.

CONCLUSION

John Clifford carefully outlined the problems posed by serious biblical criticism, and he concluded that words of argument and shouts of denunciation were the least effective ways to defend the Bible. "The best de-

---

[25]John Clifford, "Comparative Religion and Missions to Non-Christian Peoples" (London: The Baptist Missionary Society, 1912) 11.

[26]John Clifford, *The Inspiration and Authority of the Bible* (London: James Clarke and Co., 1895).

[27]Ibid., preface.

[28]Ibid., 89.

[29]Ibid., 64.

[30]Ibid., 60.

fence of the Bible," he concluded, "is a biblically inspired life."[31] With all his insights into the world of scholarship, John Clifford provided a consistent model of a biblically inspired life. He never gained knowledge at the expense of reverence. To him knowledge for its own sake was something, but to use that knowledge for Christ's sake was everything.

Descending the stairs from the balcony at the close of an evening service at Westbourne Park Chapel, a young student remarked to a man standing beside him, "That's what I call preaching; and I heard Parker this morning and Liddon this afternoon."[32] The Parker to whom he referred was the famous Congregationalist preacher, Joseph Parker, minister of the City Temple. Liddon was the scholarly, thoughtful Canon H. P. Liddon, of St. Paul's Cathedral. One student's judgment of a single sermon, of course, is not the final word, but it is significant that during a long pastorate of fifty-seven years, in the London of C. H. Spurgeon and Joseph Parker, John Clifford consistently filled the sanctuary of Westbourne Park Church to overflowing and was recognized in his day as one of the greatest among the great preachers in the land.

John Clifford's long ministry flies in the face of the belief that genuine evangelism and genuine scholarship are antithetical. Never did Clifford arrogantly claim to have the final word in understanding Scripture. He was one with another John—John Robinson, the Pilgrim Father—who said, "God has yet more light and truth to break forth from His Holy Word." He hailed every contribution to knowledge with delight. For John Clifford, God's word "thinks in the scholar, sings in the poet, paints in the artist, preaches in the evangelist, fights in the hero, rebukes in the reformer."[33] Yet John Clifford's heart and soul were committed to personal evangelism, not just a shallow evangelism that buttonholes a person and asks, "Are you saved?" His evangelism was an authentic and determined attempt to lead all kinds of people to Jesus Himself, "to His mind, with its illuminating discoveries; to His heart, with its boundless love; to His will, with its quickening and uplifting strength; to His character, with its deathless charm and infinite beauty; to His story, with its

---

[31]Ibid., 172.

[32]Byrt, *Fighting Free Churchman*, 78.

[33]John Clifford, in "Westbourne Park Record for 1891," unpublished material in the archives of Westbourne Park Baptist Church, London, 37.

inexhaustible suggestiveness; to His Cross, with its message of pardon and grace; to His throne, from which He rules the ages; to His indwelling Spirit, by which He is with us to the end of the world."[34]

In an address delivered to the annual assembly of General Baptists in 1872, Clifford revealed his deepest desire for all churches: "not a barren intellectual eminence, not social dignity and respectability, but a Christ-like spirit that lives, loves, and suffers."[35] If the life of John Clifford could inspire later generations to possess that same Christ-like spirit, that would indeed be a fitting legacy.

---

[34]Quoted in Bonsall and Robertson, *The Dream of an Ideal City*, 92-93.

[35]John Clifford, "Jesus Christ and Modern Social Life" (London: E. Marlborough and Co., 1872) 42.

Chapter 5

ALEXANDER MACLAREN
This One Thing I Do

At the beginning of the twentieth century Alexander Maclaren told a group of ministers the story of a shrewd old Scottish lady who was asked what she thought about the power of the pulpit. She answered, "The power o' the pulpit! That depends on wha's in it."[1] As for the pulpit of Union Chapel in Manchester, "wha's in it" for forty-five years was Alexander Maclaren, aptly described by one of his deacons as "a cask of wine wanting vent."[2] During the last half of the nineteenth century, he produced a steady stream of brilliant expository sermons, which, in printed form, reached the whole English-speaking world and still influence preaching today. That he was a Baptist by conviction is almost incidental, for Alexander Maclaren was "the preacher's preacher" for all denominations.

THE SCOTLAND CONNECTION

Maclaren's love for expository preaching can be traced back to his father, David Maclaren, who was a lay preacher for a newly formed Baptist church in Glasgow. Although he worked for an export firm during the week, David Maclaren gave his fullest concentration on Sundays to his sermons, so that his son Alexander later described them as "richly scriptural, expository, and instructive, and withal earnestly evangelistic."[3]

Greatly influenced by the steadfast faith of his parents Alexander Maclaren entered theological college in London in 1842. He was only sixteen, and he looked so young that the college authorities refused to let him preach in any of the local churches until he looked more "elderly." Yet young Maclaren proved to be quite a serious scholar, and his thor-

---

[1] Alexander Maclaren, "An Old Preacher on Preaching" (London: Baptist Tract and Book Society, 1901) 12.

[2] Quoted in David Williamson, *The Life of Alexander Maclaren* (London: James Clarke and Co., n.d.) 34.

[3] Ibid., 9.

oughness of preparation is shown by the fact that while he worked on his theological degree at Stepney College, he was also enrolled as a B.A. student at the University of London. By the time he was twenty he had completed his theological training, and his tutors were anticipating a brilliant ministry for the student who had taken his work so seriously.

Later in life, at a breakfast attended by many ministers, Maclaren made the comment that what often spoils young ministers is that they get "pitchforked into prominent positions at once," where they fritter themselves away at tea parties instead of staying at home and studying. "I thank God," he said, "for the early days of struggle and obscurity."[4]

Maclaren was definitely not "pitchforked" into a prominent position early in his ministry. Instead, he was called to Portland Chapel, Southampton, a struggling church that was doing well to gather a congregation of twenty people in their chapel, which was built to seat eight hundred. Two things happened during his twelve years' ministry in Southampton that helped set the course for the rest of his life. In the first place, he established a systematic method of study and sermon preparation to which he clung tenaciously throughout his ministry and which enabled him consistently to produce sermons of depth and clarity. He became a skilled craftsman, rising at dawn and working steadily for nine or ten hours with only a short break for lunch. In the middle of the afternoon he visited the sick, but in the evening he was in his old-fashioned rocker with a clay pipe in one hand and either a Greek Testament or a Hebrew Bible in the other. He had learned the biblical languages so well that he had no need for dictionaries, and he committed himself to understand and proclaim the Scriptures from the original languages.

The other influential event during his Southampton ministry was his marriage to his cousin, Marion Maclaren, of Edinburgh. She had a profound influence on her husband, which prompted him to write as an old man, "But I would fain that, in any notices of what I am, or have been able to do, it should be told that the best part of it all came and comes from her."[5] Thus in his marriage he kept his Scottish connection, and even

---

[4]Ibid., 200.

[5]E. T. McLaren, *Dr. McLaren of Manchester, a Sketch* (New York: Hodder and Stoughton, 1911) 271. Maclaren's name is spelled in more than one way. He signed his name "McLaren," but in his many volumes of sermons his name is spelled "Maclaren" because he thought it looked better that way in print.

though he spent his entire ministry in England, he always placed a high value on his Scottish heritage and never lost his Scottish accent.

In Southampton the empty pews began to fill. Within a few years the chapel was full on Sundays, and more than two hundred people came to the weekday service. In addition, he taught a Preparation Class for Sunday school teachers, instructed a group of young men in New Testament Greek, and led a class in reading Carlyle and the poets.[6] Soon his reputation as a great expository preacher reached northern England, and he was invited to become the pastor of Union Chapel, Manchester.

MACLAREN OF MANCHESTER

Union Chapel was by no means a small congregation when Alexander Maclaren became its pastor in 1858. His predecessor had established and retained a large and intelligent group of people who were at first a bit threatening to their shy new pastor. Maclaren's first sermon was based on Matthew 23:8: "One is your Master, even Christ; and all ye are brethren." Soon he discovered that he was welcomed and appreciated, and he made Manchester his home for the rest of his life.

Biographers love action and drama; thus they find Alexander Maclaren's life difficult to describe. His action and drama took place in his study and pulpit. For forty-five years he remained faithful to Union Chapel, even with numerous invitations to leave for more prominent pulpits. Once he was invited to become preacher to the University of Chicago, but he remained at his post.[7]

When Maclaren moved to Manchester at age thirty-two, he found himself in the center of an influential city and surrounded by thoughtful, committed men and women. Within a few years after his arrival, the church membership had more than doubled, and the need for a new building became obvious. In 1869 a new chapel that could seat 1,500 people was completed, and when extra seats were brought in, it could accommodate 1,800. Soon, however, 2,000 people would pack themselves into

---

[6]James Stuart, "Dr. Alexander Maclaren, the Prince of Biblical Expositors," *Review and Expositor* 8 (January 1911): 36.

[7]William C. Wilkinson, *Modern Masters of Pulpit Discourse* (New York: Funk and Wagnalls Co., 1905) 116-17.

Union Chapel, some seated behind and around the pulpit, to hear Maclaren preach.[8]

The congregations were as varied as they were large. People of all classes and creeds sat side by side under the uniting influence of the gospel. Groups of theological students came to learn Maclaren's art, distinguished professionals came early to get a good seat, and young people who worked in the many local warehouses squeezed in beside visiting clergymen from other denominations and countries who came to hear Maclaren preach.[9]

Other signs of success followed. Union Chapel established missions, several of which became active churches on their own and in turn gave birth to other churches. A "People's Institute" was founded to meet the needs of the working class. This established Union Chapel as an institutional church, for it provided a perpetual round of useful activities for young people and adults.[10] Maclaren became a natural leader of the Lancashire and Cheshire Association of Baptist Churches and was frequently called upon to preach the annual associational sermon or to write the circular letter. He became a trusted friend and counselor to his fellow ministers.

It was a surprise to no one but Maclaren himself when he was asked to become president of the Baptist Union in 1875. He was forty-nine years old, the youngest man ever elected to lead his denomination. He was called a second time to head the Baptist Union in 1901. Four years later he was elected to the presidency of the Baptist World Congress, meeting in London. His presidential address expressed his gratitude.

> My first words cannot but be the expression of my deepest gratitude for the great honour done me in placing me in this chair. I thank my fellow-countrymen, the Baptists of England amongst whom it has been my pride and pleasure to work all my life. There is no honour to be compared with the honour of being in the hearts and confidences of the people who know you best and have known you longest. I have had drops of that benediction all my life, but it has descended upon me in a full flood in the end of my days. I thank my brethren beyond the seas who, with less knowl-

---

[8]Harold L. Calkins, *Master Preachers* (Washington DC: Review and Herald Publishing Association, 1960) 37.

[9]James Stuart, "Dr. Alexander Maclaren," 38.

[10]See Williamson, *The Life of Alexander Maclaren*, 40-41.

edge, have shown greater faith and confidence in the choice of the brethren who knew me best.[11]

In 1896 Maclaren completed his fiftieth year in the Christian ministry, and his friends in Manchester would not allow that date to pass without a celebration. Letters and addresses from different theological bodies both in England and America were read, all expressing appreciation for his preaching ministry. The city of Manchester commissioned a well-known artist to paint Maclaren's portrait, and it was hung in the city's art gallery. When the portrait was formally presented to the city, one of Maclaren's closest friends commented that "all are deeply indebted to him not only for his high scholarship, but for the marvelous power he has of getting round men's hearts, elevating their desires and making them think more and more about spiritual things."[12]

In 1903 Maclaren announced his retirement. Immediately the press responded: "It is not too much to say that Dr. Maclaren has altered the whole manner of British preaching. It may be doubted whether any preacher of the last fifty years . . . has had a more profound and penetrating and transforming power."[13] He became pastor emeritus upon his retirement and died seven years later.

"THIS ONE THING I DO"

Alexander Maclaren received many honors in his lifetime, but no recognition equaled his pleasure in being a preacher of the gospel. J. E. Roberts, who was Maclaren's successor in Manchester, said that "Dr. Maclaren's devotion to preaching was so complete that a fitting motto for his life would be, 'This one thing I do.' . . . Dr. Maclaren might have reaped a rich harvest had he desired to use his gifts for personal aggrandisement. But he focused his many-coloured beams upon the pulpit, until that pulpit shone with a brilliant white light."[14]

To read volume after volume of Maclaren's printed sermons today is to be reminded of the timeless quality of Scripture. His expositions all share the quality of aliveness. Even with an occasional antiquated phrase

---

[11]Ibid., 223.

[12]E. T. McLaren, *Dr. McLaren of Manchester,* 153-54.

[13]From the *British Weekly.* Quoted in Williamson, *The Life of Alexander Maclaren,* 189.

[14]Ibid., 255-56.

or overused alliteration, such as "in the wild weltering wastes of solitary space,"[15] his sermons still penetrate the deep fundamental needs of ordinary people. He determined early in his ministry that he would allow nothing to hinder him from his primary task of preaching expository sermons. He did not write his sermons in manuscript form; rather, he wrote sketchy notes from which he preached extemporaneously. His well over forty volumes of published sermons are transcripts of his spoken sermons taken down in shorthand by members of Union Chapel. Unlike Spurgeon's published sermons, Maclaren's printed sermons were rarely revised for publication.

Knowing that he spoke essentially what is printed, a modern reader cannot fail to be astounded by Maclaren's amazing ability to compose beautiful English as he spoke it. It is not difficult to understand how a professor of English at the University of Manchester could say that Maclaren was "one of the chief, if not the chief, literary influences in Manchester."[16] Yet with the arresting beauty and polish of his sentences, there is also an obvious simplicity about his sermons, which allowed the least educated to understand clearly what he was saying. Said an old friend about Maclaren,

> Once, in speaking about simplicity of style, he asked me whether I knew So-and-so, a member of his congregation who was not endowed with specially brilliant gifts. "Well, now," he said, "often when I am preparing my sermons I keep that man before me and say, What I have to do is to get this thought behind his skull."[17]

Alexander Maclaren did not write a great deal about his methods of sermon preparation and delivery—he was too busy with the task of preaching. Rarely did he speak publicly about the one work that consumed most of his energy (he was asked—but refused—to give the Lyman Beecher Lectures on preaching at Yale University). In 1901, as president of the Baptist Union, he gave an address to a combined audience of Baptist and Congregationalist ministers at the City Temple in London. He was seventy-five years old, an esteemed father in the faith

---

[15] Alexander Maclaren, *Sermons Preached in Manchester,* 1st ser. (London: Macmillan and Co., 1874) 22.

[16] E. T. McLaren, *Dr. McLaren of Manchester,* 157.

[17] Williamson, *The Life of Alexander Maclaren,* 259-60.

to most of those present. He chose as his topic "An Old Preacher on Preaching," and although it was never published within the covers of a book, it had wide circulation in the form of a pamphlet.

Maclaren's purpose in the address was simply "to offer some considerations as to the preacher's office, its themes, its demands, its possibilities."[18] As usual, he used a very simple outline in considering the preaching task: the preacher as evangelist, teacher, and prophet. He, of course, was speaking of preaching in the ideal, but one cannot help but apply his ideals to his own ministry. Thus, Maclaren's own outline will be used to describe his preaching.

The Preacher as Evangelist

The secret of Maclaren's power in the pulpit was that his preaching was totally Christ-centered. He was not interested primarily in convincing people to believe certain doctrines about Christ; rather, he wanted them to meet the living Christ. "The essence of the whole," he said in one sermon, "is not the intellectual process of assent to a proposition, but the intensely personal act of yielding up a heart to a living person."[19] Regardless of where he started, he eventually focused on the living Christ, for as he said in another sermon, "Take it as a piece of the simplest prose, with no rhetorical exaggeration about it, that Christ is *everything.*"[20]

More than anyone else of his generation, Maclaren freed himself from the abstract and technical theology of the study and made his words "throb with the miracle of that loving, human heart, and with the pathos and power of that death for a world's sins."[21] Over and over again his sermons returned to the simple, elementary truth of Christ as the Savior of those who place their full trust in him. Yet Maclaren was careful to emphasize that it is not the faith that saves, but the power of God in Christ. He spoke of a person running into the arms of God: "it is not the running that makes him safe, but it is the arms to which he runs."[22]

Maclaren regretted that he no longer heard the old ring of urgency in preaching, the earnest appeal to the unconverted, and the old, simple

---

[18] Maclaren, "An Old Preacher," 5-6.
[19] Alexander Maclaren, *The Holy of Holies* (London: Hodder and Stoughton, 1905) 3.
[20] Alexander Maclaren, *Psalms for Sighs* (Grand Rapids MI: Eerdmans, 1945) 83.
[21] Maclaren, "An Old Preacher," 8.
[22] Maclaren, *Psalms for Sighs,* 13.

preaching of salvation, repentance, and faith. In a striking illustration he said that if a person wished to build a house in Rome or Jerusalem, he must go fifty or sixty feet down, through potsherds and broken tiles, and the dust of ancient palaces and temples. "We have to drive a shaft," he concluded, "clear down through all the superficial strata, and to lay the first stones on the Rock of Ages."[23] Evangelism, for Maclaren, was the foundation of everything he did, and he was not afraid of emotionalism: "We have much more need to dread and be ashamed of an unloving handling of the message of love."[24]

So Alexander Maclaren fulfilled in his own ministry precisely what he advocated as an elder statesman: the preacher must first be a herald of the Good News—not an arguer, not a performer, but a preacher.

The Preacher as Teacher

"The educational is never to be separated from the evangelistic office," said Maclaren.[25] His own life provided ample evidence for that conviction. From his early years at Stepney College, he stretched his mind and formed habits of study that never left him. Of primary importance to Maclaren was the study of the Bible in its original languages. Every day he read from both the Hebrew Old Testament and the Greek Testament, and he frequently found a nuance of meaning or an alternative translation to be the doorway to truth. To the students at Rawdon College in 1864, he urged diligence in studying the biblical languages: "Unless you are competent students of the original . . . you will be living to expound a book which you cannot read."[26] Yet there was more to teaching than knowing Greek and Hebrew. Maclaren was not blind to the higher criticism of the Bible, and although he did not accept much of what the higher critics claimed, he made himself a master of their thought and called genuine biblical scholarship a blessing not to be neglected.[27]

Maclaren was aware of the problem of studying the Bible only as an academic exercise, a trap into which preachers can easily fall. Yet the

---

[23]Williamson, *The Life of Alexander Maclaren*, 130.

[24]Ibid., 81.

[25]Maclaren, "An Old Preacher," 12.

[26]Alexander Maclaren, "Counsels for the Study and Life," *Review and Expositor* 22 (April 1925): 166.

[27]Ibid.

preacher, he believed, had to take the risk, for to be fully understood, the Bible must be studied both academically and devotionally. He compared the study of a preacher to that of an astronomer. One studies the lights of God's Word, and the other in an observatory studies the lights of God's universe. An outside observer would imagine that the astronomer spends most of his time delighting in the majesty and beauty of the universe, but in reality, the competent astronomer spends long hours working out dry mathematical problems that are nonetheless abstract and difficult because the planets have given the data.

The preacher's work, claimed Maclaren, is analogous to the astronomer's: "Dry toils with lexicon and grammar and concordance, laborious discrimination of finely-shaded meanings, and the slow elaboration of results into a coherent system, are not in themselves favourable to devout emotion."[28] He was ready to admit the difficulty of the toil, but he also underlined its necessity. Only with painstaking intellectual labor could the worthiest Christian emotions be tapped, for then the emotions would rest upon clear knowledge.

Primary for Maclaren was not academic study, but communion with Christ: "see to it that you rectify the threatening preponderance of merely critical study by communion with your Saviour," he advised his students.[29] Whatever his own heights of academic discipline and achievement, he always returned to the heart of the Christian faith: "simple personal trust in Jesus Christ."[30] He was an inevitable enemy of what he termed "cold-blooded intellectualism"[31] and insisted that the ideal of the Christian preacher is always to use the full powers of both the mind and the emotions. He believed that the evangelistic and teaching functions of the preacher must always be blended.

The Preacher as Prophet

John Brown, in the Beecher Lectures at Yale University in 1899, referred to Alexander Maclaren when he said, "If ever a prophet of God stood in the midst of our modern nineteenth century life with the burden of God upon his heart . . . this preacher of whom I am speaking is that

---

[28]Ibid., 173-74.

[29]Ibid., 176.

[30]Maclaren, *Sermons Preached in Manchester,* 171.

[31]Maclaren, *Holy of Holies,* 126.

prophet."[32] Yet "prophet"—as used both by John Brown and Alexander Maclaren—had little to with one who has certain powers of prediction, as is commonly supposed. Maclaren understood the chief function of the prophet to be "an incarnation of the national conscience."[33] It was the prophet's task to hold aloft the Divine Ideal for the nation, to stand before king and people undismayed, to speak God's truth even when it runs counter to popular currents of thought and practice. The predictive element of a prophet's life comes because the prophet knows the inevitable outcome of personal and national sin. It was in that sense that Alexander Maclaren was a prophet.

Maclaren's prophetic voice did not ring out in tones of political rhetoric. He steadfastly refused to engage in partisan politics. His platform was the gospel, his flag bore the sign of the cross, and his ultimate goal was to proclaim Christ as King over all political positions. He had the unique ability to stand above local political questions and to call for a rugged kind of Christian righteousness that was not blind to the political complexities of his age. "Love without righteousness," he said, "is flaccid, a mere gush of good-natured sentiment, impotent to confer blessing, powerless to evoke reverence."[34]

Maclaren believed that it was the function of the Christian church, and particularly of its preachers, to make clear the ethical principles of the gospel as applied to ordinary living. The preacher must witness against "the cancerous vices which are eating out the life of the nation. He has to bring national acts to the standard of Christ's teaching."[35] He urged the church always to be a standing rebuke to the world until the world accepted the gospel and its implications for personal and social life.

With his emphasis on prophetic preaching, however, he was careful not to allow his ethical emphasis to overshadow his evangelistic and teaching ministries. "Let us have applied Christianity by all means—the

---

[32]John Brown, *Puritan Preaching in England* (New York: Charles Scribner's Sons, 1900) 271.

[33]Maclaren, "An Old Preacher," 19.

[34]Maclaren, *Psalms for Sighs,* 54.

[35]Maclaren, "An Old Preacher," 20.

more the better, but let us make sure first that there is the Christianity to apply."³⁶

CONCLUSION

Wherever there are English-speaking preachers, Alexander Maclaren will live. His sermons are timeless because they proclaim the timeless Word. To conceive of Maclaren as only an evangelist, or only a teacher, or only a prophet is to misunderstand his whole approach to the preaching task. To read his sermons is concurrently to be moved to a greater loyalty to Christ, to be led to a deeper understanding of the Christian faith, and to be challenged to live a life more consistent with the gospel.

Maclaren once commented that "the wonderful new lamps of one age become the dim twinkling candles of the next."³⁷ His light still shines in many a lonely pastor's study, even though he has passed from the stage of history.

---

[36] Ibid., 22
[37] Ibid., 24.

Chapter 6

HENRY WHEELER ROBINSON
In Debt to Life

"The only way to read the psalms is on your knees." A former student of H. Wheeler Robinson was quoting his beloved professor, emphasizing the happy marriage of Robinson's rigorous scholarship and devotional heart.[1] To write of Baptist preachers who combined intellectual rigor and evangelistic warmth is to enter a room full of very diverse personalities unified in their loyalty to Jesus Christ. H. Wheeler Robinson was an Old Testament scholar of world class and the principal of Regent's Park College, Oxford, from 1920 to 1942. He is remembered in most circles primarily for his brilliant scholarship and educational leadership among Baptists in England. His biblical and theological writings fill an entire bookshelf, but there is an important aspect of H. Wheeler Robinson that has been largely ignored: his influence both as a preacher and a teacher of preaching.

EARLY INFLUENCES

As a boy, H. Wheeler Robinson spent just about as much time in the College Street Baptist Church of Northampton as he did in his own home. Thus, it is not surprising that at the age of sixteen he had a profound conversion experience that completely changed his life. While practicing shorthand during his pastor's sermon, his interest in reproducing the preacher's words faded into the background and, without warning, his "mind and heart were taken captive by the . . . grace of Christ."[2] When the preacher reached the end of his sermon, Robinson vowed to make his beginning as a disciple of Christ. That was in 1888, and for the rest of

---

[1] I am here referring to a conversation I had in April 1983 with Edwin H. Robertson, then pastor of the Westbourne Park Baptist Church in London. I was visiting that church to do some research on John Clifford, a famous former pastor there. Robertson was delighted to hear that I was also interested in H. Wheeler Robinson, and he gratefully spoke of Robinson's influence on him.

[2] H. Wheeler Robinson, *The Cross of the Servant* (London: S.C.M., 1926) 40.

his life he understandably honored the preaching of the gospel as the primary vehicle for the grace of God.

Through the constant shepherding of his church and the influence of his pastor and particularly the pastor's assistant, F. W. Pollard, Robinson began to preach in the small country churches near Northampton. For a shy youth, such preaching was not easy. His first sermon was preached at Moulton, where William Carey had ministered before going to India. Robinson's intensity and earnestness impressed his church, and in 1890, when Robinson was only eighteen years old, he left home for London where he was determined to prepare for the Christian ministry at Regent's Park College.

For the next ten years Robinson devoted himself fully to his education. His understanding of ministerial readiness was not limited to a grasp of common theological subjects; he wanted a broader experience. After one year of the theological school in London, he entered the University of Edinburgh for a four-year course of studies in the classics, including Latin, Greek, mathematics, natural philosophy, logic and psychology, moral philosophy, and English literature. Following his work in Scotland Robinson continued his theological studies at Mansfield College, Oxford, for three years, and for two more years he did graduate work on the Continent and at Oxford.[3]

Who can adequately describe what such a decade of studies can do for a young person of serious bent? H. Wheeler Robinson mastered the Old Testament, and particularly the Semitic languages in which it was written. Yet during his intense, technical studies Robinson also devoted himself to evangelical piety, preaching often and listening to other well-known preachers when he could. In a later description of A. M. Fairbairn, the teacher who most influenced him, Robinson unknowingly described himself: "He hated all insincerity, moral or intellectual, with a holy passion of warmth. . . . To this thoroughly moral and religious personality its very thoroughness added those gains of hard study which made him famous."[4]

---

[3]A firsthand account of Robinson's years at Edinburgh has been written by his close friend Benjamin Horlick and is included in the biography of Robinson written by Earnest A. Payne, *Henry Wheeler Robinson* (London: Nisbet and Co., Ltd., 1946) 18-27.

[4]Quoted in ibid., 32.

By the end of that decade (which was also the turn of the century), H. Wheeler Robinson completed his formal academic preparation for the ministry with a mind so keenly prepared that many thought he should at once be appointed to a teaching post in a Baptist college. But there was another call to be heard and heeded—a call into the pastoral ministry that he loved and to which he devoted the next six years.

PASTORAL MINISTRY AND PREACHING

For H. Wheeler Robinson, the move from the spires of Oxford and the intellectual stimulation of European scholarship to rural Scotland and the village of Pitlochry was a tremendous change. The church to which he was called was begun as a mission only nine years earlier, and when Robinson arrived he was greeted by a membership of twenty-nine people. In some ways such a tiny, out-of-the-way congregation may have been just the thing Robinson needed. Because he had moved out of the mainstream of current national and international events, two things were thrust upon him that served him well in years to come.[5] For one thing, he came face to face with the elemental spiritual needs of his people. As never before, he came to realize the truth that faith in Christ is not *primarily* intellectual. Even in later years when he was considered one of the shining intellectual lights of the faith, he repeatedly reminded his students and his readers the world over that the only satisfying faith in Christ is something much deeper and more profound than merely accepting some doctrine. It is, in Robinson's words, a "personal trust and obedience making essentially moral demands."[6] That basic conviction was nourished by his experience in Pitlochry.

The other great advantage of his years in Pitlochry was that he had time to ponder and meditate on the ways of God and how his life might fit into the scheme of things. Away from the noise of the city, he was able to assimilate his ten years of intense academic training and learn to apply that knowledge in ministering to the needs of ordinary people.

---

[5]Robinson later referred to his days in Pitlochry by telling of a Scottish gamekeeper he knew who could remember when the first news of the Battle of Waterloo came up his glen "by word of mouth just a year after the event." See H. Wheeler Robinson, *The Veil of God* (London: Nisbet & Co., Ltd., 1936) 20.

[6]H. Wheeler Robinson, *Redemption and Revelation in the Actuality of History* (New York: Harper and Brothers, 1942) 18.

Thus prepared and experienced in ministry, Robinson accepted the call in 1903 to become pastor of the St. Michael's Baptist Church in Coventry, where he was described by a local newspaper as a preacher who "wears his weight of learning lightly and comes near to the average hearer in a way not generally characteristic of the eminent scholar."[7]

While in Coventry, Robinson continued to develop his careful expository preaching style, which appealed to his people and brought him many invitations to speak outside the confines of his own church. It was soon recognized that in H. Wheeler Robinson the Baptists of England had a young minister of unusual gifts, and inevitably he was sought as a teacher of young ministers. In 1906, Robinson left his very happy pastorate in Coventry for what would become his life's work of teaching, but throughout the years he maintained the spirit of a pastor and had great influence on the preaching of generations of ministers.

THE PREACHING TEACHER
AND THE TEACHER OF PREACHING

Without diminishing Robinson's reputation as a renowned Old Testament scholar, his great contributions to Baptist preaching need also to be recorded. For fourteen years Robinson taught at Rawden Baptist College in Yorkshire, interrupted by the war years when his students were in uniform. During the war he naturally answered a call to serve a church until he could return to his teaching post, and he entered that interim pastorate with all the dedication and enthusiasm called for by his loyalty to Christ and the suffering caused by the First World War. In 1920 he became principal of Regent's Park College, then located in London and later, under Robinson's leadership, transferred to Oxford. There he led the college until his retirement in 1942 at the age of seventy.

The Model for Preachers

As a teacher, Robinson loved the churches and gladly served as a preacher whenever he was able. Sundays frequently found him traveling to various churches in England, where his reputation as a preacher was well established. One of the finest descriptions of Robinson's preaching is found in an article written in 1925 and published in *The Baptist Times and Freeman*. The author, who is identified only by the pseudonym

---

[7]Quoted in Payne, *Henry Wheeler Robinson*, 43.

"Nicholas Notewell," tells of visiting London on a holiday to discover that H. Wheeler Robinson was the guest preacher at the Westbourne Park Baptist Church. He described Robinson's preaching as "singularly impressive."

> Though a scholar of distinction, his diction is mercifully free from technical theological terms, old or new. His language is clear, living, understandable, inescapable. He never creates a mist in which you can evade him by saying, "I don't see what he is driving at." You do see what he is driving at; you see it every time, whether you like it or not; and you know that what he is driving at is God's truth . . . and that, in the dialect of today, it is up to you to say to your soul, "what about it?"[8]

"Nicholas Notewell" went on to warn his readers not to hear H. Wheeler Robinson if they were out for comfort at any price; rather, Robinson's preaching was strenuous and exacting and required the congregation to take the gospel as seriously as did the preacher.[9]

The Teacher of Preaching

Robinson required of his preaching students the same kind of seriousness in learning to preach. He taught preaching to Baptist ministerial students for thirty-four years, and although other elements of the college curriculum varied from generation to generation, the sermon class was constant. Why? Robinson's lofty view of preaching is revealed in a statement written toward the end of his life: "The Word of God as recorded in Scripture or preached by the evangelist is not conceived simply as a word about God; it is a sacramental means by which God the Holy Spirit makes Himself present to faith."[10] That is to say, preaching the gospel, in Robinson's view, was a sacrament—a means of grace—and therefore of the greatest importance. God becomes most real when the Word is proclaimed, which is the only justification for the central place of the sermon in evangelical worship.

Some of Robinson's preaching students compared his preaching class to the dissecting room of a medical school. Robinson was the first to admit that preaching sermons without the conditions of regular worship and

---

[8]Nicholas Notewell (pseud.), "A Sunday in London," *The Baptist Times and Freeman,* 27 August 1925, 611.

[9]Ibid.

[10]Robinson, *Redemption and Revelation,* 189.

before the critical ears of a teacher and fellow students evoked great stress. Yet when the criticism was constructive and sympathetic, Robinson believed the sermon class to be "a most valuable feature in a College course."[11]

What did Robinson teach his students about preaching? After thirty years of teaching the subject, he tried to summarize what he had taught through the years.

Personal Conviction. Robinson had heard enough sermons that spoke the truth, but spoke it in a dull and boring fashion, to be absolutely convinced that personal conviction concerning the truths of the gospel was the first requirement for the preacher. Robinson had learned this truth from a difficult personal experience. Early in his ministry he had experienced a physical breakdown that threatened his life and required months of recuperation. To his surprise, the truths of evangelical Christianity—truths which he believed and preached—did not bring him personal strength at that crucial time. These truths remained intellectually valid to him, but he failed to draw strength from his beliefs. His faith seemed to demand an active effort for which the physical energy was lacking. Through that difficult experience he found a renewed faith in the presence and ministry of the Holy Spirit, which later evolved into a much needed book entitled *The Christian Experience of the Holy Spirit,* published in 1928.[12]

Out of that deeply personal religious experience, Robinson learned that real conviction "is not mere opinion, and it is not simply intellectual assent to an argument."[13] He taught his preaching students the etymological meaning of the word *conviction:* namely, that a person is *conquered* by someone or something greater than himself. A person cannot merely get a conviction; a conviction must get the person. Only then can one become an effective ambassador for Christ.

From the very beginning of his teaching ministry, Robinson raised the flag of Christian conviction as the banner under which he intended to

---

[11]H. Wheeler Robinson, "Thirty Years in the Sermon Class," *The Baptist Quarterly* (January 1938): 1.

[12]Robinson relates his experience of illness in *The Christian Experience of the Holy Spirit* (New York: Harper and Brothers, 1928) 4.

[13]Robinson, "Thirty Years," 2.

march. In his inaugural address as principal of Regent's Park College he said it plainly:

> Tonight, as we gather from a restless and troubled world to inaugurate a new session of ministerial training, the memory of that other night bids me begin by saying again the familiar truth, "our message is Christ the crucified." I do not say it as a tribute to convention, but as a personal conviction that has deepened with the years, and was never stronger than today, when I stand on the threshold of my new task.[14]

Great Truths. Robinson had heard enough arid and trivial sermons exhibiting little more than clerical cleverness to see the need for stressing the great truths of the gospel in preaching. He urged his students to live above the antics and shallowness of those who preached only for show. "Life can be interpreted only from above," he said, "and the preacher's unchanging task is to bring great truths—the great truths of the Christian Gospel—into relation with life, as its only adequate interpretation."[15] Robinson was utterly serious in such an emphasis, as can be seen in his own writings. His three major books, which took a lifetime in writing, form a trilogy on three great truths: the doctrine of man, the doctrine of the Holy Spirit, and the doctrines of redemption and revelation.[16] Thus he prompted his students to "plunge into the depths of man's sin, and rise to the heights of God's grace."[17]

Of the many great truths that exist, the one at the heart of all is the truth of personal faith in Christ as the way of salvation. Robinson did not put a straitjacket on a person's conversion: it "may be sudden or gradual, intellectual or emotional, highly complex or astonishingly simple."[18] Yet the one thing in common is this: salvation comes by "repentence toward God, faith in our Lord Jesus Christ and new birth through the Holy

---

[14]H. Wheeler Robinson, "The Making of a Minister," in Payne *Henry Wheeler Robinson,* 132.

[15]Robinson, "Thirty Years," 4.

[16]See H. Wheeler Robinson, *The Christian Doctrine of Man* (Edinburgh: T. and T. Clark, 1911), *The Christian Experience of the Holy Spirit,* and *Redemption and Revelation.*

[17]Robinson, "Thirty Years," 4.

[18]H. Wheeler Robinson, "The Faith of the Baptists" (Manuscript Collection, Regent's Park College, Oxford) 3.

Spirit."[19] Robinson was an evangelical through and through, holding a faith that deepened through his long years and culminated in his last days of illness when he identified with John Bunyan's statement at the end of his life: "I will leap off the Ladder even blindfold into Eternity, sink or swim, come heaven, come hell; Lord Jesus, if thou wilt catch me, do; if not, I will venture for thy name."[20]

Intelligible Expression. "Simplicity is a work of great art,"[21] he told his students, and by that he meant that the sometimes complex language of theology and serious Bible study must be translated into the language of the people—simple, understandable, to the point. "I am inclined to think," said Robinson, "that when people say of their minister that he is preaching 'over their heads,' what they really mean, or ought to mean, is that he has not learnt to speak their language. It is not that his intellect is too great . . . but that his sympathetic toil has been too small."[22] During the years when Robinson was in the pastorate, he would frequently go into the chapel and sit in the empty seats to allow his hearers to come vividly and personally to mind. Then he would prepare his sermons in language that would clearly appeal to them.[23]

The Unity of Worship. All of preaching, Robinson taught, is couched in the central act of worship. This concept was basic, for it placed the sermon among the offerings brought to God. The hymns, the prayers, the gifts, and the sermon are all presented to God as the congregation's grateful recognition of God's worth. In the sermon, the preacher's humanity is offered to God as an instrument of the Spirit. When that happens, all vanity, all display of knowledge, all self-complacency, all offenses against good taste, are consumed in the white heat of praise and adoration.

---

[19]I am quoting from Robinson's self-written creed, which he gave in an address to the London University Theological Students' Union on 23 February 1921. It was published in *The Baptist Quarterly* 2 (1924-1925): 348-57.

[20]John Bunyan, *Grace Abounding to the Chief of Sinners* (Oxford: Clarendon Press, 1962) 101.

[21]Robinson, "Thirty Years," 7.

[22]Ibid.

[23]Payne, *Henry Wheeler Robinson*, 40.

THE TASK OF THINKING

H. Wheeler Robinson believed that one of his major tasks was to teach preachers to think. He had learned from experience not to be afraid of hard thinking, and he challenged his students to offer their finest power of thought to God. One of the most important methods of right thinking, he believed, was to search for truth at its sources—and that required hard intellectual work, especially in the study of Scripture.

Robinson had such a high view of Scripture that he would not—could not—take refuge in what he called "an impossible theory of verbal inspiration,"[24] even though he was absolutely convinced that God is revealed in and through the Bible. The ultimate ground of authority for the Christian is God made known in Christ. All other forms of authority, he believed, are derivative and subordinate. As a young man preaching his first sermon at his church in Coventry, he made his stance clear from the outset: "Let me express frankly and fully my friendliness toward all sound scholarship, research and inquiry into the Bible. For we have absolutely nothing to fear from such honest and sincere inquiry."[25]

Baptists, in particular, he believed, had much to gain from the discoveries of sound biblical scholarship. In his book *The Life and Faith of the Baptists,* Robinson showed three ways in which critical study of the Bible had undergirded the very contentions Baptists had been claiming for generations. First, critical scholarship had shown clearly that in the very center of Old Testament thought is the idea that every soul can have immediate access to God—what Baptists and others called the universal priesthood of all believers. Critical scholarship cut through the elaborate rituals of biblical worship practices and proved that from the very earliest times human priesthood was not necessary for personal fellowship with God.

Second, critical scholarship had undergirded another Baptist conviction: God calls every believer to be a saint. That basic idea has been traced by reverent scholarship far beyond its obvious New Testament growth to the teaching of the great prophets of the Old Testament. That inward ethical emphasis stands in contrast to Israel's idolatry and later legalism.

---

[24]Robinson, *Redemption and Revelation,* 180.
[25]Quoted in Payne, *Henry Wheeler Robinson,* 43.

The third way in which biblical scholarship supported Baptist principles was to show that the idea of a regenerate church was already found in the Old Testament before it was asserted in the New Testament. Scholarship was able to trace a "little Church within the Church" of the nation on to New Testament times. Such a finding suggests that from the earliest times God's search was for a society of people bound together by ties of faith, not of nationality—a basic Reformation and Baptist concept.[26]

If the Bible was not verbally dictated by God, then what is its authority? Simply this: the Word of God finds us through the words of the ancient writers. The words become the vehicle for the Word, so that through the Scriptures the Spirit of God finds us. A Christian "holds the Bible to be authoritative because of the truth of its teaching; he does not hold the teaching to be true simply because he finds it in the Bible."[27] He urged his students to use all their knowledge of languages, biblical culture, and historical facts to dig beneath the words of Scripture to discover the life-giving source of the Bible.

Such a commitment to rigorous thinking impelled Robinson's students to intellectual honesty. They were taught that "personal conviction not welded to thought is no more than prejudice."[28] Yet with his intense regard for the intellect, Robinson was careful to nurture the devotional spirit of his students. Each morning he conducted a prayer service for the college, and he himself started a weekly communion service on Friday evenings, which soon became the center of the devotional life of the community.[29]

CONCLUSION

To the very end of his life, H. Wheeler Robinson remained true to his evangelical faith as well as his intellectual rigor. "He was a greater Christian than any Christian scholar I had ever known,"[30] said one who had

---

[26]This whole argument is worked out in more detail in Robinson, *The Life and Faith of the Baptists* (London: Methuen and Co., Ltd., 1946) 12-14.

[27]H. Wheeler Robinson, "The Bible and Protestantism," *The Congregational Quarterly* 16, no. 1 (1930):48.

[28]Robinson, "The Making of a Minister," 139.

[29]See Payne, *Henry Wheeler Robinson*, 70-71.

[30]Ibid., 109.

known him for many years. To the last, his trust and hope was in Christ. This giant of an intellect also knew the simple and profound faith that carried him calmly and uncomplainingly through eight weeks of total dependency before death came in 1945.

H. Wheeler Robinson will justly be remembered as one of the dominant Old Testament scholars of the twentieth century. But generations of preachers, and through them multitudes of churches, have been strengthened through his influence in the crucial area of the preaching ministry. One of Robinson's sayings was that "We are born in debt and never become solvent. Every life has had more invested in it than it can possibly repay."[31] He was indeed in debt to life, and we are indeed in debt to him.

---

[31]Ibid., 9.

PART II

BAPTIST PREACHING IN AMERICA

Chapter 7
A "HAZARD TO THE COMMONWEALTH"
Colonial Baptist Preaching

> *. . . it is not because we are against Learning, for we do esteem it, and honor it in its place; and if we had such among us . . . duly qualified for the work of the Ministry, we should readily improve them.*
>
> John Russel, 1680

> *. . . incendiaries of the commonwealths, and the infectors of persons in main matters of religion, and the troublers of churches in all places. . . .*
>
> 1644 Massachusetts law banishing Baptists from the colony

> *Anabaptism we shall find hath ever been lookt at by the Godly Leaders of this people as a Scab to be contended against.*
>
> Urian Oakes, president of Harvard College, 1672

One of the pleasant pastimes of Americans is to luxuriate in the myth that early settlers came to the New World to enjoy religious freedom and that once they arrived on the blessed shores of America they could worship as they pleased with total freedom of conscience in religious matters. There is only a grain of truth in that idea, but that grain has grown into a great harvest of sermons and political speeches that totally ignore the fact that until the American Revolution most of the colonies practiced a certain level of religious intolerance, and sometimes persecution, that made even Old England blush. Rhode Island, the earliest "safe" place for dissenters, was established precisely because Roger Williams was kicked out of Salem, Massachusetts, on the heels of religious intolerance. John Clarke and others were forced from Boston for the same reason. Rhode Island became a refuge from the dominant persecution, but not even Rhode Island was free from all problems, for Roger Williams could hardly abide the presence of the Quakers.[1] During the seventeenth century, America was, for many dissenters, hardly a place of religious freedom.

The Puritans in Massachusetts were particularly oppressive. Those with Baptist sentiments who kept quiet and attended the nearest Congregational church were safe enough, but any who dared express their Baptist beliefs and dissent from the established church were dealt with so severely that a modern person can hardly keep from gawking in disbelief. How could the very ones who left England to escape religious oppression establish a stronghold in New England that persecuted any who disagreed with them? And how could something so simple and personal as a commitment to believer's baptism threaten the establishment to such an extent that in 1644 the Massachusetts General Court passed a law banishing all "Anabaptists," labeling them "the incendiaries of the commonwealths, and the infectors of persons in matters of religion, and the troublers of churches in all places"?[2]

The answer to those questions lies in an understanding of the Puritans themselves. The early settlers of New England were indeed leaving what they believed to be a corrupt Anglican church. Their answer to a corrupt church was to set up a *"New* England" based on a pure church. There was not the slightest thought of a separation of church and state. Civil government and church government were virtually one and the same. The principle on which their new society was founded can be seen in infant baptism, for it was there that their sense of being God's chosen people—the New Israel—was symbolized. Just as Moses and Aaron had symbolized God's covenant by the act of circumcision, so the Puritans baptized infants as a picture of God's new covenant in a new land. Infant baptism was loaded with all kinds of emotional baggage. It was more to them than a religious rite; it was the foundation on which their whole so-

---

[1]Roger Williams wrote a very detailed account of his disputes with the Quakers entitled *George Fox Digg'd out of his Burrowes, Or an Offer of Disputation On fourteen Proposalls made this last summer 1672 (so call'd) unto G. Fox then present on Rode-Island in New-England* (Boston, 1676). Only the most persistent scholars of Williams would venture to read the whole tedious work. Perry Miller has quoted the most pertinent passages in his *Roger Williams, His Contribution to the American Tradition* (New York: The Bobbs-Merrill Company, Inc., 1953) 246-53.

[2]The law is quoted in full in Isaac Backus, *A History of New England With Particular Reference to the Denomination of Christians Called Baptists,* 2d ed. (Newton MA: Published by the Backus Historical Society, 1871) 1:126.

ciety stood. To question the practice was to question their *raison d'être*. To challenge the practice was treason! Thus John Cotton, the leading Puritan minister in Boston, could logically refer to the Baptists in charging that "the mischiefe of a blind Pharisee's blind guidance, is greater than if he acted treasons, murders, etc. And the losse of one soule by his seduction, is a greater mischiefe, than if he blew up Parliaments, or cut the throats of Kings and Emperours."[3]

JOHN CLARKE

Many generations of Baptists have claimed Roger Williams as the chief herald of the Baptist denomination in America, the founder of the first Baptist church in the country, and the first great Baptist preacher in the New World. There is indeed some indication that Williams became a Baptist, but he remained within the Baptist fold for a period of only four months at the most. There is some question as to the role he played in forming the First Baptist Church of Providence. John Callender, writing in 1739, studied all the available sources and talked with many of those who had known Williams. He concluded, "The most ancient inhabitants now alive, some of them above eighty years old, who personally knew Mr. Williams, and were well acquainted with many of the original settlers, never heard that Mr. Williams formed the Baptist church there."[4] There are few accounts of Williams as a preacher after 1640; he seems to have been much more interested in running his trading house than a church. To claim Roger Williams as a great Baptist preacher is a travesty of justice. Even if he had been a committed Baptist, few of the denomination today would claim that his wild allegorical interpretations of Scripture represent the best tradition of Baptist preaching. It is far better for Baptists to put Roger Williams to rest as a self-styled Seeker. Baptists have invested him with an ill-fitting halo.

---

[3]John Cotton, *The Bloudy Tenent Washed and Made White in the Bloud of the Lambe* (London: Matthew Symmons, 1647) 64.

[4]John Callender, "An Historical Discourse on the Civil and Religious Affairs of the Colony of Rhode-Island and Providence Plantations, in New-England, in America, from the First Settlement, 1638, to the End of the First Century" (Boston: S. Kneeland and T. Green, 1739), printed in *Collections of the Rhode Island Historical Society* (Providence: Knowles, Vose and Company, 1838) 4:110 (see footnote). Subsequent citations will refer to this source as Callender's "Century Sermon."

Better to begin with John Clarke, who is far more worthy of praise, both for his leadership as a Baptist preacher and his statesmanship in securing the 1663 charter of Rhode Island from King Charles II. Clarke was twenty-eight years old in November 1637 when his ship arrived in Boston harbor from England. The John Clarke who walked down the gangplank with his newly wed wife Elizabeth was striking both in looks and in education. Over six feet tall, strong and stalwart, enthusiastic, he looked and acted like a leader. He was part of the new breed, fit for the adventure and rigors of a new world. Fresh from the liberal University of Leyden, he was thoroughly inoculated with the democratic spirit of the Baptists who fled to Holland to escape religious persecution. His broad scholarship had prepared him for three professions: law, medicine, and the ministry.

It did not take long for Clarke to realize that Boston's Puritan stronghold was no place for him. Boston was only seven years old, a community of little more than a thousand people, but already they were embroiled in a bitter theological controversy. Anne Hutchinson, who may be considered one of America's great women, had challenged the Puritan clergy on the subject of salvation. She maintained that the Puritans were too legalistic and based salvation more on works than on grace. An intelligent and aggressive woman with a magnetic personality, she soon had a large following. The only way the clergy could maintain their authority was to silence her. In 1638 she was excommunicated from the church and banished from Boston.

The city was at the very height of the controversy when John Clarke arrived. He himself was immediately under suspicion. After all, he had been at that liberal University of Leyden, and in due time he seemed drawn to the theological position of Anne Hutchinson, supporting salvation by grace. Thus when Hutchinson was banished, John Clarke, along with fifty-seven other supporters of Hutchinson, was disarmed. Although not banished, they were left unable to defend themselves or their property.

It comes as no surprise that Hutchinson's supporters were all disgusted with the Puritans of Boston. All they needed was a leader. They naturally turned to John Clarke, who agreed to seek out a new place for them to settle—a place where they could live peacefully with freedom of conscience in religious matters. In the spring of 1638 Clarke and his friends sailed south, "having Long Island and Delaware-Bay in our eie

[eye] for the place of our residence."⁵ But after consulting with Roger Williams in Providence ("by whom we were courteously and lovingly received"), they eventually bought the island of Aquidneck from the Indians and renamed it Rhode Island. There Clarke helped establish both the towns of Portsmouth and Newport, settling himself and his family in Newport and establishing there the First Baptist Church, which he served as pastor until his death on 20 April 1676.

It would be difficult to overestimate the significance of John Clarke to the Baptists in general and Baptist preaching in particular. At the very opening of Baptist history in America, Clarke stands as an ideal: broad in his catholic sympathies, deep in his Baptist conviction, committed to an intelligent and intelligible ministry. His training in law and medicine, as well as theology, uniquely equipped him to play a prominent role in the life of the colony.

Consider his legal training. During the early years of the colony of Rhode Island there were many times when the legal status of the colony was in jeopardy. A charter of incorporation obtained by Roger Williams in 1643 required that a code of laws be drawn up by the people in order for the charter itself to become effective. The code, declaring the inviolability of liberty of conscience, was written primarily by John Clarke. Writing laws may have been simple enough for a man of his training, but diplomatic service was another matter. Yet this Baptist preacher was needed by his colony to represent their interests in England under the Protectorate of Oliver Cromwell and later under the restored monarchy of Charles II. His diplomacy was especially important under Charles II, who looked with disfavor on the whole idea of an English colony based on liberty of conscience. In what some historians have concluded was Clarke's greatest contribution, he not only persuaded the king to grant a new liberal charter to the colony of Rhode Island, but wrote the charter himself. The famous phrase "to hold forth a lively experiment," which is engraved above the main entrance to the present Rhode Island State House, was penned not by Roger Williams (as is commonly supposed), but by John Clarke in the charter of 1663. That charter was written with

---

⁵These and other first person quotations in this story come from Clarke's own account entitled *Ill News from New England: or A Narrative of New Englands Persecution Wherein is Declared That While Old England is Becoming New, New England is Become Old* (London: Printed by Henry Hills, 1652).

such breadth and wisdom that it served as the basis of Rhode Island's government for one hundred and seventy years. It was so universal in its provisions that Thomas Jefferson later used it as one of the sources on which he based the Declaration of Independence.

Consider Clarke's medical training. During a time when his church could hardly support him and the colony was barely able to reimburse him for his diplomatic travels, Clarke was able to support his family as a physician—the only physician in Rhode Island for many years. Throughout his ministry in Newport he always maintained his medical practice. It is not hard to imagine that his lasting popularity lay at least in part in the fact that Clarke ministered both to the physical and spiritual needs of his people.

Consider his theological training. We know little of his life at the University of Leyden, but we do know that Holland was filled with English separatists, many of whom eventually returned to England as Baptists. When Clarke became a Baptist is unknown; what is known is that he remained a faithful Baptist preacher throughout his life, and at times his commitment to believer's baptism was severely tested.

Few episodes of persecution have been more influential in colonial America than the events that centered around John Clarke and two of his deacons, Obediah Holmes and John Crandall.[6] On 19 August 1651, Clarke and his two friends rode quietly into Lynn, Massachusetts, to visit their friend and fellow Baptist William Witter, who was no longer able to attend worship because of old age and blindness. They were well aware of the danger, but the next day, a Sunday, Clarke led a worship service in Witter's home. While Clarke was preaching they were interrupted by two constables, who (in Clarke's words) "made an interruption in my Discourse and more uncivilly disturbed us, than the Persivants of the old English Bishops were wont to doe."[7] Their subsequent arrest and imprisonment in Boston led to a trial in which they were sentenced to pay stiff fines or else be "well whipped." All three refused to pay their fines, but only Holmes was whipped. Crandall was released on his promise to

---

[6]Little is known of John Crandall, but it is worth noting that Obediah Holmes succeeded Clarke as pastor of the Newport church. It is also of interest to note that Holmes's great-granddaughter became a Lincoln by marriage and was the great-great-grandmother of Abraham Lincoln.

[7]Clarke, *Ill News from New England*, 2.

return to a later session of court. Clarke went as far as the whipping post, but when he stood there tied and stripped, ready for the lash, a bystander was so moved by the sight of "a scholar, a gentleman, and reverent [sic] divine in such a situation" that he paid the fine despite Clarke's protest. Thus only Obediah Holmes was finally whipped, and his first-person account of the ordeal is moving.

> And as the man began to lay the strokes upon my back, I said to the people, though my Flesh should fail, and my Spirit should fail, yet God would not fail; so it pleased the Lord to come in, and so to fill my heart and tongue as a vessell full, and with an audible voyce, I broke forth, praying unto the Lord not to lay this Sin to their charge, and telling the people, That now I found he did not fail me, and therefore I should trust him for ever who failed me not; for in truth, as the stroaks fell upon me, I had such a spirituall manifestation of Gods presence, as the like thereto I never had, nor felt, nor can with fleshly tongue express, and the outward pain was so removed from me, that indeed I am not able to declare it to you, it was so easie to me, that I could well bear it, yea and in a manner felt it not, although it was grievous, as the Spectators said, the Man striking with all his strength . . . with a three-corded whip, giving me therewith thirty stroaks; when he had loosed me from the Post, having joyfulness in my countenance, as the Spectators observed, I told the Magistrates, you have struck me as with Roses.[8]

The willingness of John Clarke, Obediah Holmes, and John Crandall to suffer for their Baptist beliefs did not go unnoticed. Their suffering, and particularly the whipping of Holmes, proved again the ancient truism of Tertullian that "the blood of the martyrs is the seed of the Church." Deeply influenced by their suffering was one of the most prominent and highly respected leaders of New England, Henry Dunster.

HENRY DUNSTER

It is easy to forget that the planters of New England were in many cases the country gentlemen of England, wealthy in land holdings and broadly educated. Thus it is no surprise that Harvard College, named after its principle benefactor, was established in 1638, just eight years after the first settlement of Boston. When the college was barely two years old and still without a president, Henry Dunster's ship arrived at Boston harbor. He brought with him a liberal Cambridge University education

---

[8]Holmes's account of the whipping is contained in ibid., 21-22.

during which he had been the friend of fellow students John Milton and Jeremy Taylor. He was a profound scholar, a master of the biblical languages, a popular preacher, and a deeply humble person—the ideal candidate for the first president of Harvard. Almost before he knew it he was elected, as if by acclamation, to the presidency of the first college in America.

One of Dunster's first acts as president was to join the Congregational church in Cambridge, where he submitted his "Confession of Faith and Christian Experience," which is happily still in existence. "I hold no fayth," he declared, "which is not grounded on the revealed Word of God in the worlde."[9] That position, faithfully followed, would eventually cause him great grief. But in the meantime he had a college to develop, and although Massachusetts was still largely a wilderness, Dunster steered the young Harvard College into such a degree of excellence that within the first decade of its existence some wealthy families in Old England began sending their sons to Harvard to receive their education. He developed the college's philosophy of education, and wrote both its rules of admission and its requirements for graduation, modeling the college on his own experience at Cambridge University. He took special interest in providing for the conversion and education of the Indians who lived among them. He preached frequently, not only in his own church, but in the college itself. Dunster was adamant about one of the basic rules of the college—the foundation on which all education stood:

> Let every student be plainly instructed, and earnestly pressed to consider well, the maine end of his life and studies is, to know God and Jesus Christ which is eternall life, John 17.3, and therefore to lay Christ in the bottome, as the only foundation of all sound knowledge and Learning.[10]

Dunster placed stringent academic requirements upon his students, demanding fluency in Latin and some knowledge of Greek just to be admitted. The college course embraced the study of arithmetic, geometry, rhetoric, logic, ethics, physics, metaphysics, and divinity, as well as the biblical languages. Attendance at prayer was required twice a day, and

---

[9] A copy of his confession may be seen in Jeremiah Chaplin, *Life of Henry Dunster* (Boston: James R. Osgood and Company, 1872) 257-65.

[10] *New Englands First Fruits* (London: Printed by R. O. and G. D., 1643) 26.

Dunster maintained a well-deserved reputation for training his students in "Learning and godlinesse also."[11]

It is no wonder that Henry Dunster was greatly loved and appreciated by the leaders of New England. He was bringing to reality their fondest dreams for the college they had founded. He was not only a brilliant leader but also a friendly and humble neighbor. He threw all his energy and much of his wealth into the college. He built the president's home with his own funds and gave it to the college. His many gifts and his obvious devotion to his task helped make Henry Dunster the shining star of New England.

There was one gift, however, that caused Dunster great problems: he was an independent thinker. Add that to his already stated conviction that the Bible was to be his sole standard of faith and practice, and the stage was set for a dramatic clash between Dunster and the Puritan authorities.

Dunster's Baptist sentiments had probably been planted back in England when he was a student at Cambridge. His close friendship with John Milton alone would assure us that he was aware of the Baptist positions, but his presence at Cambridge—the veritable headquarters for radical dissenters during the seventeenth century—guarantees that he was exposed to Baptist principles. Upon his arrival in New England, he was certainly not out of the sphere of Baptist thought. Not only were Baptist churches organized in Rhode Island, but there were Baptists among the first settlers of Massachusetts. William G. McLoughlin picturesquely described the earliest Baptists as "scattered individuals maintaining a furtive hole-in-the-corner existence,"[12] but they were nevertheless present.

Sometime before 1651, when Dunster had led the college for over a decade and stood at the zenith of his popularity and influence, he privately came to the Baptist position on believer's baptism. In every other way he was an orthodox Puritan. What should he do? Should he withhold his children from infant baptism? Preach in favor of believer's baptism? Leave his job, his church, his friends, and move to Rhode Island? Or,

---

[11]Ibid., 25.

[12]William G. McLoughlin, *New England Dissent 1630-1833*, (Cambridge: Harvard University Press, 1971) 1:14.

should he, like most other Baptists in Massachusetts, keep his opinions to himself and quietly go about his business?

While Dunster was considering his options, John Clarke and his two Baptist friends were arrested in Lynn. Their imprisonment and the public whipping of Obediah Holmes brought the matter to a crisis in the mind of Henry Dunster. If Clarke, Holmes, and Crandall were willing to suffer such great persecution for their beliefs, how could he keep silent? "By searching into these matters [their persecution]," said early historian Isaac Backus, "Mr. Dunster, President of Harvard College, was brought openly to renounce infant baptism."[13] He boldly preached in favor of believer's baptism from the pulpit in Cambridge in 1653. His logic was flawless:

> If parents' church membership makes their children members, that John admitted makes his first-born a church-member; excommunicated for 7 yeares makes suppose 4 children non-members; restored in ye 9th yeare makes his 6th child a member. Show me where Christ ever indented [*sic*] such a covenant.[14]

All logic aside, Henry Dunster, in that moment, fell from grace in the eyes of Puritan New England. All he had to do was remain silent, and he could have spent the rest of his life as the revered first president of Harvard. Too honest for silence, he was brought before the General Court in May 1654, where he presented an able defense of his position, but the court nevertheless condemned him and instructed the Overseers of the College "not to admit or suffer any such to be continued in the office or place of teaching, educating, or instructing . . . that have manifested themselves unsound in the faith"—an obvious reference to Dunster.[15] A month later he sent in his resignation from the presidency of the college. For fourteen years Dunster had labored sacrificially. He had earned the esteem of his colleagues and neighbors, and he had led the college to a level of excellence that exceeded the vision of its founders. He had served and preached among them with no suspicion of unorthodoxy. Their trust in him was so great that the only printing press in all of America—a pow-

---

[13]Backus, *A History of New England*, 453.

[14]Quoted in Chaplin, *Life of Henry Dunster*, 114. Original in "Dunster MSS," Library of the Massachusetts Historical Society.

[15]Ibid., 124.

erful instrument indeed—was entrusted to his care and kept in the basement of his home. Yet solely on the basis of his declared support of believer's baptism, he was forced to resign and leave the house he had built with no place to go and a family to support.

For a time he stayed in Charlestown, Massachusetts, with his close friend and fellow Baptist, Thomas Goold. Dunster's suffering influenced Goold and others to go public with their Baptist beliefs and organize what would become the First Baptist Church of Boston in 1665, with Goold as the first pastor. The story of Goold's suffering is a dramatic tale itself and is well told in Nathan Wood's *The History of the First Baptist Church of Boston*.[16] Dunster eventually moved to Scituate where he preached and served the Independent church there until his death in 1659.[17]

It is worth noting the progressive influence of persecution on the early Baptists of New England. The imprisonment of Clarke, Holmes, and Crandall (along with the public whipping of Holmes) prompted Dunster's courage to make a stand for believer's baptism. His suffering, in turn, influenced Thomas Goold and others to form the First Baptist Church of Boston, which appointed one of its members, William Screven, to organize and lead a Baptist church in Kittery, Maine. Because of persecution in Maine, Screven led his congregation to immigrate south, where sometime before 1693 they organized the earliest Baptist church in the south—what would become the First Baptist Church of Charleston, South Carolina. Out of that church, in turn, came leaders like Richard Furman and others, whose widespread influence can hardly be overestimated. All of that can be traced to the courage and conviction of early Baptist leaders such as John Clarke and Henry Dunster, who offered their whole minds and hearts to God and never thought of divorcing learning and faith.

THE CALLENDER CONNECTION

Cotton Mather, the leading Puritan minister in New England at the end of the seventeenth century, illustrates in his diary the low opinion the Puritans had of Baptists in general and Baptist preachers in particular. He tells of a preacher named May who arrived from England in 1699

---

[16]Published in 1899 by the American Baptist Publication Society

[17]This independent church had been founded in 1634 by John Lathrop of the "Jacob-Lathrop-Jessey Church" in London, which played an important role in the origin of the English Particular Baptists. See chapter 1.

and began preaching publicly. Mather called him "a wondrous Lump of Ignorance and Arrogance" and bemoaned the fact that many people were drawn to him.

> Multitudes of the giddy People are as much bewitched with him, as if hee were another Simon Magus. There is evidently a Satanic Energy on the People in this Town; and Satan is attempting, tho' by a very little Tool, a great Shock to our churches.[18]

Whether the man was a Baptist or not is never proven; Mather just assumes as much. The irrational and illogical attempts to defame the Baptists resulted in frequent outbursts from the Puritan establishment. Some of their accusations were proven to be completely fabricated, such as a pamphlet circulated in 1673 that claimed that an orthodox New England minister named Baxter was barbarously skinned alive by angry Baptists. The pseudonymous author concludes, "Dares any man affirm the Anabaptists to be Christians? For how can they be Christians who deny Christianity, deride Christ's Institution of Baptism, and scoffingly call it *Baby sprinkling,* and in place thereof substitute their prophane *Booby dipping?*"[19] Many were ready to believe this incredible story, but it was soon proven that there was no such minister by the name of Baxter in all of New England! Yet the prevalent attitude of the Puritan establishment toward the Baptists can be summed up in a statement made by Urian Oakes, the president of Harvard College in 1672: "Anabaptism we shall find hath ever been lookt at by the Godly Leaders of this people as a Scab to be contended against."[20]

Ignorance and arrogance, as Cotton Mather charged, could very well have characterized some of the uneducated Baptist preachers of colonial days, especially during the emotional excesses of the Great Awakening. But to apply such an epithet to Baptist preaching in general is too hard on the struggling denomination. With all the efforts put forth by the Puritans to suppress the Baptists, one would think that there must have been a threateningly large number of them to contend with the establishment. The best estimates, however, indicate that "not more than one in one

---

[18]Cotton Mather, *Diary of Cotton Mather 1681-1708* (Boston: Published by the Massachusetts Historical Society, 1921) 313-14.

[19]Benjamin Baxter (pseud.), "Mr. Baxter, Baptiz'd in Bloud, or A Sad History of the unparalleled Cruelty of the Anabaptists in New England" (London: n.p., 1673) 1.

[20]Quoted in Chaplin, *Life of Henry Dunster,* 179.

hundred persons in New England (including Rhode Island) was an acknowledged Baptist in the year 1700."[21] The great increase in the number of Baptists came only after the Great Awakening. Most colonial Baptists were not ignorant enthusiasts or fanatics, much less "Scab[s] to be contended against." They were ordinary hard-working citizens who wanted to make a good life in a new world and conscientiously wanted the freedom to interpret Scripture as they honestly believed it was written. They wanted educated pastors, but the fact that the Puritan establishment in Massachusetts would not allow an avowed Baptist to attend Harvard College forced them to call the best and most gifted ministers they could find, educated or not. Some, like John Myles, came over from Great Britain well prepared for the ministry.[22] But others, as an early Baptist described them, had "not bin bred up in Colledges, and taught in other tongues, but have bin bred up to other callings."[23] John Russel, the pastor of the First Baptist Church of Boston in 1680, stated that Baptists both esteemed and honored learning and would gladly call educated men as pastoral leaders. "But," he went on to say, "we do not think that the Spirit of God is locked up within the narrow limits of Colledge-Learning . . . we cannot find that the Lord (by Divine Institution) hath tyed the work of the Ministry unto men of such Learning only, but whom he will, he fits and qualifies for that work."[24]

In spite of the severe limitations imposed upon colonial Baptists in many colonies, there was indeed a company of well-educated and ardent Baptists called out to lead the young denomination. New England was blessed with a number of them during the early eighteenth century.

Elisha Callender

The scribbled and faded handwriting in the "Church Records" of the First Baptist Church of Boston belies the significance of the following entry:

---

[21]McLoughlin, *New England Dissent*, 10.

[22]John Myles came from Wales and established the Swansea Church in Plymouth Colony in 1663.

[23]John Russel, "A Brief Narrative of some Considerable Passages Concerning the First Gathering and further Progress of a Church of Christ, in Gospel Order, in Boston . . . In New . . . England, Commonly (though falsely) called by the name of Anabaptists" (London: Printed by J. D., 1680), as published in Nathan E. Wood, *History of the First Baptist Church of Boston* (Philadelphia: American Baptist Publication Society, 1899) 170.

[24]Ibid.

> On Wednesday the 21st of May 1718—Elisha Callender was ordained pastor of this Church of Christ by the Reverend Doctor Mathers & Mr. Webb of the new north Church.[25]

It was a remarkable notation because it signified the first time in the entire history of Baptists in New England that the Puritan leaders recognized them as legitimate. For both the Mathers, Increase and his son Cotton, not only to attend the ordination but for Cotton to preach the ordination sermon, was to come full circle from the early days when the Mathers were among the most persistent persecutors of the Baptists. Yet it would have been difficult for the Mathers to refuse the invitation. They had both known Elisha Callender for many years. They had witnessed his excellent record as a student at Harvard College. They knew and respected Elisha's father, Ellis, who, though uneducated, was serving as pastor of the First Baptist Church.

It is difficult to continue the persecution of people with whom one lives and whom one sees daily. Perhaps Cotton Mather had the Baptists in mind when at the beginning of the year 1718 he wrote in his diary, "One of the best Things that can be done for my poor Country is, to extinguish as far as tis possible, that cursed, and senseless Party-Spirit, which is now among us, in a most abominable Operation."[26] He did not have long to wait before his resolution was tested. The invitation to preach Elisha Callender's ordination sermon came, and on Wednesday, 21 May 1718, Mather made this entry in his diary:

> This day, I do a very uncommon Action, and what will occasion various Discourse in the world. I visit the Church of the Baptists in my Neighborhood, and ordain a Pastor to them.[27]

Ordain him he did, and Elisha Callender became the first Baptist minister in America to have received a college education in his own land. What was he like? We are not favored with a great deal of material on Elisha Callender, but college records offer a revealing glimpse into the personality of this precocious youth when we learn that in his early college days

---

[25]"Record Book of the First Baptist Church, Boston." The original is located in the vault of the Franklin Trask Library, Andover-Newton Theological School, Newton Centre, Massachusetts.

[26]Mather, *Diary of Cotton Mather,* 515.

[27]Ibid., 535-36.

he made "persistent assaults on the college laws" and that he was not averse to breaking a few college windows.[28] Perhaps he had some rebelling to do as a result of his strict upbringing in the Baptist church. Yet by the time he graduated from Harvard in 1711, Elisha Callender had come through his rebellion to a deeper faith. Nine days after graduation he was baptized by his father, Ellis Callender, in the quiet mill pond before the church. Elisha taught school until the church called him to become its pastor in 1718. He served the church faithfully until his death in 1738.

During his twenty-year pastorate, the Baptists were raised to a new level of influence in New England. No longer could they be considered only as ignorant fanatics when a man of the stature of Elisha Callender was their leader. The leaders of New England all knew him either personally, from college days, or by reputation. It was a far cry from the days of Henry Dunster, when solely because of his openly expressed Baptist views, he was driven from his office. Elisha Callender led the church with a depth and genuine friendliness that prompted a local newspaper to print that he was "universally beloved by People of all Perswasions, for his charitable and catholic Way of Thinking. His Life was unspotted, and his Conversation always affable, religious, and truly manly."[29]

The church records portray an active, growing church during Callender's ministry. New members, many of them people of great material and intellectual substance, began to join the church. Expanded membership required the ordination of new deacons, some of whom were notable people in Boston. Shem Drowne, for example, was chosen for the office of deacon on 5 May 1721 and faithfully served in that capacity for fifty-three years. Drowne was a widely regarded and highly respected leader as the general supervisor of all the fortifications of the city, and he lived to the age of ninety-one.[30]

Callender insisted on carefully prepared sermons, unwilling to offer anything to God that was less than his best. To his friend John Comer, who was about to become pastor of the Baptist church in Newport, he offered this advice: "To study well all your public discourses and look upon

---

[28]See Clifford K. Shipton, *Sibley's Harvard Graduates* (Boston: Massachusetts Historical Society, 1937) 5:512-13.

[29]*Boston News-Letter,* 6 August 1738, 2.

[30]See further description of Drowne in Wood, *History,* 205.

it your business to compose sermons in a handsome style and good method."³¹

A "handsome style and good method," for Elisha Callender, obviously did not mean dry intellectual discourses. The increasing number of baptisms during his ministry indicates a warm evangelistic spirit that filled the soul of this Baptist leader. Even to the chagrin of some of his Congregationalist friends, he never refused a request from small rural Baptist churches to hear him preach. He had a message of Good News for all people, Boston upper crust as well as rural farmer.

Elisha Callender died in 1738, leaving the church with one piece of advice, which was faithfully entered in the church records:

> away with all Lukewarmness, away with it. Live in love that the God of Love and peace may be with you. Improve your Standing for your time in the Church will be short and that is the way to prepare for the inheritance of the Saints in Light.³²

Then we are told that at 5:00 A.M. on 31 March 1738, Callender said, "I shall now sleep in Jesus," and at that moment he died.

Elisha Callender stands as an extremely important person in the history of Baptist preaching in America, not because he was the first Baptist preacher with an education—he was not—but because with him came the earliest recognition of Baptists as a legitimate Christian body in Puritan New England. This was a tremendous breakthrough and must have been a stirring event for some of the older members who had lived through the early days of persecution. Callender helped set a standard for great Baptist preaching, which, although interrupted by the Great Awakening, has maintained its strength until the present day.

John Callender, Jr.

The nephew of Elisha Callender, John Callender, Jr., was baptized by his uncle in Boston in 1727. John had recently graduated from Harvard and was still not certain about the ministry. He practiced medicine for a while, preached occasionally at the Baptist church in Swansea (where he met and married one of the belles of the town, Elizabeth Hardin), but finally gave up medicine for his life work as pastor of the First Baptist

---

³¹John Comer, *The Diary of John Comer,* ed. C. Edwin Barrows (Philadelphia: American Baptist Publication Society, n.d.) 36.

³²"Church Records," no pagination.

Church of Newport. His qualifications for the task were described by a friend:

> The purity and evangelistic simplicity of his doctrine, confirmed and embellished by the virtuous and devout tenor of his own life, endeared him to his flock, and justly conciliated the esteem, love and reverence of all the wise, worthy and good.[33]

That "purity and evangelistic simplicity" is clearly seen in his sermons that have survived. In simple language that hid the depth of his preparation, Callender urged his hearers to call Christ "Master and Lord." He especially counseled young people to devote themselves early to Christ, so that "by leading quiet and peaceable Lives in all Godliness and Honesty, we may effectively serve our Generation."[34]

In a sermon he preached at the ordination of his friend Jeremiah Condy in 1739, Callender spoke of the hard labor required for the ministry. "Competent knowledge," he insisted, is a reasonable expectation for Christian ministers to fulfill. But such knowledge is not enough: "it requires that they be *faithful* and *diligent* in their Labour, that they do the Work of an Evangelist *faithfully* to God."[35] His coupling of "competent knowledge" with the "work of an evangelist" was as characteristic of his preaching as it was of his Uncle Elisha's before him.

One of John Callender's sermons was not only highly regarded in his own day, but it has dramatically increased in importance during the nearly two and a half centuries since it was preached. In 1738, to celebrate the centennial of the founding of the colony of Rhode Island, John Callender preached what has become known as his "Century Sermon." In it he related the history of Rhode Island, drawn from his careful study of the earliest records as well as from conversations with the "most ancient inhabitants" who had personally known Roger Williams, John Clarke, and others. The grateful citizens of Newport enthusiastically demanded that the sermon be expanded and published. Thus a year later Callender pub-

---

[33]*Rhode Island Historical Magazine* 4:180. Quoted in Shipton, *Sibley's Harvard Graduates,* 7:152.

[34]John Callender, "The Advantages of Early Religion" (Newport: Printed by the Widow Franklin, 1741-1742) 23.

[35]John Callender, "A Sermon Preach'd at the Ordination of Mr. Jeremiah Condy, To the pastoral Care of the Baptist Church in Boston" (Boston: Printed by S. Kneeland and T. Green, 1739) 4.

lished what has become the earliest history of Rhode Island and an accurate account of the origin of the Baptists in that colony. His work was so good that an entire century elapsed before anyone produced another book in that field.[36]

By the 1740s John Callender had become one of the most highly respected and honored citizens in Rhode Island. He was called upon to help revise and print the laws of the colony and was elected schoolmaster of the city of Newport. When he died on 26 January 1748, even leaders in neighboring Massachusetts joined in the mourning.

> A Gentleman of superior good Sense, and very Extensive Knowledge. . . . He was an entire Stranger to Cunning and Artifice, to Flattery and Temporizing: as honest as he was learned. . . . His Religion was genuine, manly, and remote from all Affectation. . . . He did often serve the Public with his Advice . . . sought for by Gentlemen of a public Character, who knew him to be a zealous Friend to the Interests of that Colony.[37]

He was loved because he was a sincere and intelligent preacher who embraced fellow Christians of all denominations as rightful members of the family of faith, while maintaining his own Baptist distinctions. There appears to have been not a single bigoted or narrow bone in his body, and his kind catholic spirit spilled over to the whole community.

There were other educated Baptist preachers in New England during the Colonial era, but none of them attained the stature and influence of the two Callenders—Elisha and John. Jeremiah Condy, for example, was a graduate of Harvard and served the First Baptist Church of Boston for twenty-six years.[38] Edward Upham, of the same generation as Condy and a fellow Harvard graduate, succeeded John Callender at the First Baptist Church of Newport.[39] A generation earlier there was John Comer, who attended Yale and served as pastor both at Newport and Rehoboth. His name is most distinguished today through the survival of his remarkable diary, which provides invaluable insights into colonial Baptist life.[40]

---

[36]See footnote 4 above.
[37]*Boston Evening-Post*, 15 February 1748, 2.
[38]See Wood, *History*, 233-44.
[39]The best treatment of Upham is in Shipton, *Sibley's Harvard Graduates*, 9:44ff.
[40]Comer, *The Diary of John Comer*, n.32.

Clarke, Dunster, and the two Callenders, along with Condy, Upham, and Comer, may appear to be a very small number of educated Baptist preachers in colonial New England during the seventeenth and early eighteenth centuries. Yet it is worthwhile to remember that seven ministers make up a formidable percentage of the total number of Baptist preachers in that era of struggle. Henry C. Vedder, the Baptist historian, estimated that in the year 1700 there were only ten Baptist churches in all of New England with a total of about three hundred members.[41] Given the fact that a large number of those Baptists were members of the city churches under the leadership of well-prepared ministers, one soon begins to see the reasoning behind William G. McLoughlin's statement that "among the pre-Awakening generation of New England Baptists, there was a much higher proportion of educated ministers than has been recognized, and they carried considerable weight."[42]

CONCLUSION

This chapter on colonial Baptist preaching has concentrated on New England for several reasons. One is that Baptists first settled in New England, and although they were generally more welcomed in the middle colonies, it was in the northeast that the earliest Baptist influence was felt. The Great Awakening, which spread throughout the colonies during the second quarter of the eighteenth century, was a prelude to the era of the American Revolution. In some ways, indeed, it was a religious revolution born first as the twin of political revolution. Baptist preaching played a prominent role in both and will be examined in the next chapter.

New England Baptist leaders also deserve priority because it is easy to allow the caricature of the fanatical, uneducated Baptist preacher of the frontier—with arms waving to the rhythm of his "holy tone"—to overshadow the earliest Baptist heritage of preaching that illuminates the thesis of this entire study. Baptists are, without doubt, deeply indebted to the farmer-preacher who ministered at great sacrifice to the spreading population far away from the centers of education. Some of them, had their sermons been written and survived, would undoubtedly have deserved a place among the finest preachers of the Baptist heritage. But

---

[41]Henry C. Vedder, *A Short History of the Baptists* (Philadelphia: American Baptist Publication Society, 1907) 302.

[42]McLoughlin, *New England Dissent*, 282.

there is another type of preaching, equally evangelistic and in many cases more biblical in its nature, than that of frontier revivalism. The emotional preaching of the Great Awakening was far more exhortation than biblical exposition. When the preacher on the frontier had no theological training, he could do little more than exhort his hearers toward conversion, which they did in large numbers. It was, rather, the educated Baptist preacher who emphasized biblical interpretation in his sermons and gave to Baptists the foundation for a distinctive biblical theology.

New England Baptists did not remain the most prominent in the colonies. It was the freer atmosphere of the middle colonies that attracted the most Baptists and enabled Philadelphia, in particular, to become the strong center of Baptist life in America for many years. That, however, developed in the eighteenth century and played a decisive role in the revolutionary era.

Chapter 8

THE REVOLUTIONARY PULPIT
Baptist Preaching in the Eighteenth Century

How shall Persons addict themselves to the work of the Ministry, whose Powers of mind, at their highest Pitch, are but shallow and contracted?
Isaac Eaton

Learning is an excellent Handmaid to Grace, and when apply'd to the Service of the Sanctuary may answer great and good Purposes.
Oliver Hart

Hearts under the impressive sense of vital piety, and minds well stored with knowledge, will qualify you to be both acceptable and useful preachers.
Samuel Stillman

The earliest outcry leading to the American Revolution was not the voice crying from the steps of the courthouse, "No taxation without representation!" Rather it was the voice crying from the pulpit, "No religion without conversion!" The political revolution (Revolutionary War) and the religious revolution (Great Awakening) resist being shoved into neat little compartments separated by a wall on which is written, "Never the twain shall meet." The step from the pulpits of "New Light" churches to Independence Hall in Philadelphia was barely a shuffle, for in volatile eighteenth century America the twain *did* meet—and Baptists were in the middle of the embrace.

BAPTIST PREACHING AND THE GREAT AWAKENING

Baptist preaching did not sound reveille, nor did it shake the sleeping churches, but when Americans finally opened their sleepy religious eyes, it was the Baptists who had invited them to breakfast. And what a hungry crowd showed up at their doorstep! In New England alone, Baptists grew from perhaps 1,500 baptized members in 1740 to 21,000 in one generation. This multiplied increase in membership continued uninhibited as the revolutionary century wore on, so that the middle and southern colonies, as well as the western frontier, became so filled with Baptists that they could hardly organize themselves fast enough.

Such a huge influx of people into the Baptist ranks was like an unexpected gift. It had not been the Baptist preachers who had led the Great Awakening. Leading preachers came rather from the more formal, traditional denominations: Theodore Frelinghuysen, the Dutch Reformed evangelist; Gilbert Tennent, the young Presbyterian from New Jersey; Jonathan Edwards, the Congregationalist theologian; and preeminently, George Whitefield, the Anglican open-air preacher, who has been called "America's first really national figure."[1] It was not that Baptist preachers were opposed to the revivals or unable to provide the leadership required. The obvious fact is that for many a year most Baptist preachers had already been proclaiming the kind of experiential faith that ignited the Great Awakening. Such preaching from a Baptist pulpit was expected, but little more than a yawn could be noticed from the established church. However, when one of their own—Whitefield, for example—left the conservative Anglican pulpit for the open air and called for conscious conversions with an emotional fervor that drew thousands to hear him, that was news!

The result was a sweeping revival movement that has had a profound and lasting impact upon America. It is worth noting that the Awakening came about, not primarily from theological reflection, but from powerful preaching. After the event the theological reflections came and helped interpret what had already happened.[2] Yet it was not just emotional preaching that ushered in the Awakening; rather, it was emotional preaching set against the background of what Jonathan Edwards called "an extraordinary dullness in religion." After George Whitefield had preached for only a few weeks in New England, he wrote in his journal, "For I am easily persuaded, the Generality of Preachers talk of an unknown, unfelt Christ. And the Reason why Congregations have been so dead, is because dead men preach to them."[3]

---

[1] C. C. Goen, *Revivalism and Separatism in New England, 1740-1800* (New Haven: Yale University Press, 1962) 28.

[2] Jonathan Edwards, the most influential theologian of the Great Awakening, published his *Narrative of Surprising Conversions* in 1737 after he preached a series of sermons on justification by faith alone. Within six months more than three hundred people in Northampton claimed to be converted.

[3] Quoted in Edwin Scott Gaustad, *The Great Awakening in New England* (New York: Harper and Brothers, 1957) 27.

No wonder over 5,000 people gathered on the Boston Common in early October 1740 to hear George Whitefield. With each service the crowd grew, until on Sunday evening, 12 October, he preached a farewell sermon before 30,000 eager hearers. They had, for the most part, never heard the like. He preached the orthodox Calvinistic doctrines of judgment and mercy, but unlike most of the settled ministers, he did it with an emotional flair that appealed to the masses who had had enough of dry and drab manuscript reading from the pulpit. However correct preaching was in doctrine, the people wanted the pulse of genuine feeling to flow through the pulpit. They found just that in George Whitefield. Even Benjamin Franklin, trying in vain to stand above emotions and to judge Whitefield objectively, wrote in his memoirs, "every accent, every emphasis, every modulation of the voice, was so perfectly well tuned and well placed, that, without being interested in the subject, one could not help being pleased with the discourse; a pleasure of much the same kind with that receiv'd from an excellent piece of musick."[4]

The results of such preaching were not only numerous conversions, but also a large number of preachers who began to model their own preaching on that of George Whitefield or one of his followers. Such modeling did not always produce the happiest results. The Presbyterian James Davenport is a case in point. The natural emotional outlets produced by the preaching of Whitefield became fanatical and crude extravagance under the harangues of Davenport. Whitefield saw the dangers of unbounded emotionalism and guarded against it; Davenport seemed to revel in an unchecked torrent of emotions. It was the often rude and crude voice of Davenport that did much to give Great Awakening preaching a bad name. Not only did he play on the emotions of his hearers until at times the result was akin to hysteria, but he also felt obliged to accuse local ministers of being completely unconverted and to call them by name. He urged the crowds to separate from their reprobate preachers and to start their own churches in the purity of the gospel.

It is not hard to imagine what such preaching did to the revival movement. Christian turned against Christian; churches split down the middle; faithful pastors were often wrongly condemned. Ultimately, many of those who had from the outset favored the revivals had to express their

---

[4]Benjamin Franklin, *Autobiography,* in Charles W. Eliot, ed., *The Harvard Classics* (New York: P. F. Collier, 1909) 1:108.

concern over the judgmental and fanatical preaching of those who followed the likes of James Davenport.

The traditional understanding is that the Awakening divided the churches into two factions based upon support or non-support of the revivals: "Old Lights" opposed revivals while "New Lights" supported them. Yet it is clearly the case that, as C. C. Goen has concluded, the Great Awakening elicited not two, but three divisions.[5] First, there were the Old Lights, such as Charles Chauncy of Boston, who were totally against the revivals. Second, there were the Extreme New Lights, represented by James Davenport, who fanatically supported emotional extravagance as the genuine sign of conversion. But there was a third party, perhaps the largest, that supported the revivals but tried to restrain the emotional excesses. They might be called the Conservative New Lights.

Although Baptists could be found in each of these categories, the most influential Baptist preachers were Conservative New Lights. Such Baptist leaders could be found in every colony. They channeled the emotions of the Great Awakening into a denominational identity that organized new churches, formed associations, and eventually moved toward a national convention of Baptists based on foreign missions. Throughout the eighteenth century growth and expansion, Baptist leaders remained true to evangelistic preaching coupled with intellectual depth. While the sermons of the Extreme New Lights tended to ignore biblical exposition in favor of emotional exhortation, Baptist leaders opened the Scriptures and preached expository sermons. The happy result was a denominational leadership whose preaching matched the description of one Baptist preacher: "he fed, not glutted, his flock with the sincere milk of the word."[6]

THE MIDDLE COLONIES:
TAKING THE LEAD

The eighteenth century saw a shift in the center of Baptist influence from New England, notably Rhode Island, to the middle colonies, notably Philadelphia. The Philadelphia Association, organized in 1707, became

---

[5]Goen, *Revivalism and Separatism*, 34.

[6]From a letter quoted by Reuben A. Guild, *Chaplain Smith and the Baptists* (Philadelphia: American Baptist Publication Society, 1885) 377.

the mother of all Baptist associations, and like a good parent, gave sound advice and encouragement to its many offspring.

The middle colonies offered a much more congenial reception to Baptists than either their Northern or Southern neighbors. A colony like Pennsylvania, founded by the Quaker William Penn, would think nothing of receiving Baptists. The "Great Law" of 1682 recognized God as the only Lord of conscience and provided that no one would be "molested or prejudiced for his or her Conscientious persuasion or practice."[7] Thus Baptists from Great Britain as well as other colonies converged in the middle colonies to form an early and outstanding witness to the faith.

Great Baptist preaching in Philadelphia really began with Elias Keach. In 1687 he was on a ship between England and America. Having been raised in the home of the great English Baptist preacher Benjamin Keach,[8] young Elias thought it would be amusing to dress in clerical black on his arrival in Philadelphia, and then proceed to impersonate a Baptist preacher. After all, it should have come as second nature, having watched his father for all those years. But alas, when he was invited to preach in Philadelphia, his conscience weighed too heavy, and he confessed his charade with great remorse. Seeking out Thomas Dungan, the nearest Baptist preacher, he was eventually baptized and later became the pastor of the Pennepek Church, which became the mother and grandmother of many Baptist churches, including the venerable First Baptist Church of Philadelphia.[9]

If anything, New Jersey was even more open to Baptists than Pennsylvania. Although it was squeezed like a cork between the cities of New York and Philadelphia and lacked an early major metropolis of its own, New Jersey probably produced more great Baptist preachers than any colony in America. Of the five churches that constituted the Philadelphia Association in 1707, three were from New Jersey (Middletown, Piscataway, and Cohansey). The Baptist school founded at Hopewell in 1756 ultimately affected the level of Baptist preaching up and down the Amer-

---

[7] Quoted in Henry C. Vedder, *A History of the Baptists in the Middle States* (Philadelphia: American Baptist Publication Society, 1898) 57.

[8] See the section on Benjamin Keach in ch. 1.

[9] See the account of Elias Keach in Morgan Edwards, *Materials Towards a History of the Baptists in Pennsylvania* (Philadelphia: Printed by Joseph Crukshank and Isaac Collins, 1770) 9-11.

ican seaboard. The Hopewell Church could even boast the membership of John Hart, the only Baptist signer of the Declaration of Independence.

Thus with the addition of New York and Delaware, the middle colonies formed a home for Baptist leadership during the eighteenth century. The Philadelphia Association, whose membership at one time extended as far south as South Carolina and as far north as Massachusetts, gave both unity and theological direction to the struggling Baptists. That kind of direction was accompanied by outstanding preaching. To meet some of the greatest of these preachers is to feel the vibrancy and early depth of the Baptist movement in America.

Isaac Eaton:
Preparing the Way

If Baptists living in America in the early eighteenth century could have looked ahead and known what a momentous century that would be both for their denomination and the country as a whole, they could not have turned to a better person to help prepare the way for those years than Isaac Eaton. Baptists were vigorous, numerous, and enthusiastic, but their leaders needed more training. Isaac Eaton, whose name has been all but lost among those more famous in Baptist history, may have had more to do with the later strength of his denomination than anyone else of his generation.

We know little of his early life other than the fact that he was the son of Joseph Eaton, the Baptist minister in Montgomery, Pennsylvania. The early influences that led to his conversion and call to preach, as well as the method of his own education, are all unknown. What we do know is that in 1748, when he was twenty-four years old, Isaac Eaton was called to be the pastor of the Baptist church in Hopewell, New Jersey, located just forty miles northeast of Philadelphia and one of the leading churches in the Philadelphia Association. He served that church faithfully for twenty-four years, until he died at the early age of forty-six.

If Eaton had done nothing more in Hopewell than preach the gospel and faithfully minister to the people, he would deserve ample space in Baptist history. But he did more, much more. At the request of the Philadelphia Baptist Association, he opened a school to train Baptist ministers. Tucked quietly into the Association minutes for the year 1756 is the following resolution:

> Concluded, to raise a sum of money towards the encouragement of a Latin Grammar School for the promotion of learning amongst us, under the care of Brother Isaac Eaton.[10]

That resolution was anything but business as usual. There were still strong feelings against education among many Baptists To raise "a sum of money"—whatever amount that may be—would be a major undertaking. Yet with a faith that was willing to attempt the impossible, Eaton began the school. He was only thirty-two years old.

Because money was scarce, students boarded in Eaton's home. With a financially uncertain future, the Baptists, under Eaton's leadership, commenced the first Baptist-sponsored school in America. At the outset, he taught all his students both Latin and Greek, essential requirements for entrance into any university. Beyond that, the curriculum depended upon the vocational aspirations of the student, for not all his pupils were training for the ministry. As Eaton himself was a physician as well as a minister, a remarkable number of men were trained under his care to become eminent physicians. Others became attorneys and members of Congress.[11] But the majority of his students came to train under his care for the Christian ministry. They found in Isaac Eaton both a teacher and a practitioner. He did what he taught, and he earned the devotion of his students. One of those students, who had lived with the Eatons for three years and had maintained a lifelong friendship with his tutor, had this to say at Eaton's death:

> The natural endowments of his mind; the improvement of these by the accomplishments of literature; his early, genuine and unaffected piety; his abilities as a divine, and a preacher; his extensive knowledge of men and books; his catholicism, prudence and able counsels; together with a view of him in different relations, both public and private, that he sustained through life . . . : These would afford ample scope had I but abilities, room, and inclination to flourish in a funeral oration.[12]

---

[10]A. D. Gillette, ed., *Minutes of the Philadelphia Baptist Association from A.D. 1707, to A.D. 1807* (Philadelphia: American Baptist Publication Society, 1851) 74.

[11]See a representative list of nonministerial graduates in Morgan Edwards, *Materials Towards a History of the Baptists in Jersey* (Philadelphia: Printed by Thomas Dobson, 1792) 49n.

[12]Samuel Jones, "Resignation; a Funeral Sermon, Occasioned by the Death of the Revd. Isaac Eaton, A. M." (Philadelphia: Printed by James Humphreys, 1772) 24-25.

Eaton's success is best measured by the ministry of his students. His first pupil was James Manning, who became the first president of Rhode Island College, now Brown University, and one of the most highly respected Baptist leaders in the eighteenth century. In addition to Manning, early historian Morgan Edwards listed sixteen other Baptist ministers who trained under Eaton. Their names amount to a "Who's Who" among Baptists in the revolutionary century.[13]

Specifically, what did Eaton teach about preaching? As little remains of Eaton's writings, we are fortunate to have a sermon by Eaton preached in 1755 at the ordination of John Gano, for in it Eaton spelled out clearly the most urgent requirements of a gospel preacher.[14] He stressed in the sermon a marvelous balance between fervor and learning. They were, he believed, mutually dependent for a gospel preacher. First and foremost, Eaton believed that "a true saving and experimental Knowledge of the Work of Grace" was a requirement for the preacher. Nothing was a greater plague to the Church, he claimed, than a "false, ungodly, and extravagant Ministry." No one who was ignorant of the "Preciousness of Christ" could preach Christ to the world.

But there was something more required of a competent preacher than an experience of grace, and that is where Eaton was a leader among Baptists. He called for the gifts of knowledge, prudence, and faithfulness. Preaching, he claimed, requires something more than an emotional experience. It is "a Work which demands the Exercise of all the rational improved Powers of the human Soul." He called for preachers to be familiar with Hebrew and Greek, and to have a good knowledge of logic, rhetoric, and philosophy. He readily admitted that God could use preachers who were not so fully equipped, but an educated ministry, he claimed, would more adequately set forth the doctrines of the gospel "in their unbeclouded Lustre."

---

[13]Edwards lists: Samuel Jones, Hezekiah Smith, David Thomas, Isaac Skillman, John Davis, William Williams, Robert Keith, Charles Thompson, David Jones, John Sutton, David Sutton, James Talbot, John Blackwell, Joseph Powell, William Worth, and Levi Bonnell. See Edwards, *History of the Baptists in Jersey,* 50.

[14]Isaac Eaton, "Sermon Preached at the Ordination of the Rev. Mr. John Gano" (Philadelphia: n.p., 1755). The original is located in the archives of the American Baptist Historical Society, Rochester, New York.

Would such an education diminish the zeal of the ministry? Not in the least. The very content of the gospel, more fully grasped by the well educated, is enough to "enkindle the Zeal of the Ministers into a holy Flame, and make them cry aloud, and spare not, to lift up their voices like Trumpets." The preacher's task, as Eaton understood and taught it, was to be spiritually and intellectually equipped to be a herald for Christ. To move the Baptist denomination closer to that goal, Isaac Eaton devoted his life and labors.

The influence of Eaton and Hopewell Academy may go far in explaining the eventual union of Separate and Regular Baptists. Perhaps they were not as far apart as some may have believed. The Philadelphia Association, Regular Baptists through and through, sent Benjamin Miller of Scotch Plains, New Jersey, to investigate the reputedly unrestrained and emotional preaching of Separate Baptists Daniel Marshall and Shubel Stearns in Virginia. Miller returned to report to the Association that Marshall and Stearns were not so different from them after all! Miller was so taken with Marshall's preaching that "he was highly delighted with the exercises, joined in them cordially, and said if he had such warm hearted Christians in his church he would not take gold for them."[15] Marshall and Stearns later moved to Sandy Creek, North Carolina, where they laid the foundations for Baptist growth in the South.

The very fact that the official representative from the Philadelphia Association was impressed with the preaching of Marshall and Stearns and brought back a glowing report to Philadelphia shows that the evangelistic emphasis of the Regular Baptists in the Middle Colonies was not lacking. Their emphasis on the combination of fervor as well as intellectual preparation for the preaching task added a dimension of depth to their sermons that the Separates frequently did not have. Much of the credit for that approach to preaching should be laid at the feet of the unheralded Isaac Eaton.

Abel Morgan:
The "Bible-divine"

When Morgan Edwards was compiling a history of the Baptists in New Jersey, which was published in 1792, he said of Abel Morgan that "he

---

[15]Robert B. Semple, *A History of the Rise and Progress of the Baptists in Virginia* (Richmond: Published by the author, 1810) 289.

was not a *custom-divine,* nor a *leading string-divine,* but a *bible-divine.*"[16] Edwards's picturesque language left no doubt that the Scriptures stood in the center of the life and ministry of Abel Morgan.

Morgan was known more by reputation than by his own writings until Professor Norman Maring, church historian at Eastern Baptist Theological Seminary, began research on a history of New Jersey Baptists.[17] It was already known that Morgan had been a man of advanced learning and that he had left a substantial library at his death. Maring, however, uncovered about forty volumes of Morgan's library, mostly in poor condition, but very revealing as to the man himself. What Maring discovered was an amazing array of theological books, most of them well annotated and underlined. Morgan's margin notes revealed that he was fluent in a number of languages, including Greek, Hebrew, and Latin. His sermon notes revealed that he was a thoughtful and diligent preacher who was strictly expository in his sermons.

Abel Morgan was called to lead the Baptist church at Middletown, New Jersey, in 1739. He remained there as a revered pastor until his death in 1785—a forty-six year pastorate which spanned a momentous period in the life of the nation. He remained faithful to his church even when British troops moved through Middletown after the Battle of Monmouth. The next Sunday he had to preach in his own barn because "the enemy had taken out all the seats in the meetinghouse."[18] He was a highly respected leader in the Philadelphia Association and was often called upon to preach and preside. His astuteness and his blameless life prompted his friend Samuel Jones to describe him as "the incomparable Abel Morgan."[19]

The annals of Baptist preaching contain a surprisingly large number of preachers who were capable and educated. Many, like Morgan, were faithful to one church for their entire ministry and had a profound influ-

---

[16]Edwards, *History of the Baptists in Jersey,* 19.

[17]See Norman H. Maring, *Baptists in New Jersey* (Valley Forge: The Judson Press, 1964) 69-70.

[18]Quoted in William Cathcart, ed., *The Baptist Encyclopedia* (Philadelphia: Louis H. Everts, 1881) 815.

[19]Samuel Jones, "A Century Sermon" (Philadelphia: Published at the request of the Association, 1807), published in Gillette, *Minutes of the Philadelphia Baptist Association,* 453-68. The quotation referred to is on page 455.

ence on their age. But their writings have largely been lost, or perhaps they are waiting to be discovered, and their names, like that of Abel Morgan, remain virtually unknown by the very denomination they helped shape.

John Gano:
"He believed, and therefore spake."

Paucity of sources is not a difficulty in learning of John Gano, one of the most fascinating Baptist preachers in the Revolutionary era. Small and athletic as a young man, tending to corpulency in old age, he spoke his mind at every age. When asked by a worldly ferryman in South Carolina what was the "best and shortest way to heaven," Gano replied that "Christ was the best way," but the shortest way that he knew would be to "place himself in the front of some army, in an engagement."[20] On another occasion, while serving as chaplain in the American army in the Revolutionary War, Gano said to a soldier who was cursing and swearing, "Sir, you pray early this morning." The soldier, struck with remorse, replied, "I beg your pardon, Sir," to which Gano responded, "Oh, I cannot pardon you, carry your case to God."[21]

Gano came by his outspokenness honestly. It seemed to be a family trait. His great grandfather, Francis Gerneaux, was such an outspoken French Huguenot that he barely escaped martyrdom and sailed to America, where he lived to the age of 103.[22] Gano himself described his mother as a "pious Baptist" and his father as a "steady Presbyterian,"[23] both of whom took care to train their son in the Westminster Confession of Faith and catechism. At the age of nineteen he was converted and faced the dilemma of choosing which denomination he would join. With pressure from both parents, he sought counsel from the celebrated Presbyterian Gilbert Tennent, who convinced Gano that infant baptism was proper. But on the road to his home he had further doubts over Tennent's ad-

---

[20]John Gano, *Biographical Memoirs* (New York: Printed by Southwick and Hardcastle, 1806) 69.

[21]Quoted in L. C. Barnes, "The John Gano Evidence of George Washington's Religion," *Bulletin of William Jewell College,* 15 September 1926, 23.

[22]See the story of Francis Gerneaux in William B. Sprague, *Annals of the American Pulpit,* (New York: Robert Carter and Brothers, 1860) 6:62.

[23]Gano, *Biographical Memoirs,* 12.

vice, and finally concluded that he could find no ground for infant baptism in the New Testament. "I really thought," wrote Gano of the decision, "that if any person was ever induced to take the word of God in hand with a fervent desire to be free from all prepossessions, to see the truth as it really was, and to let the Bible be their guide, I was."[24]

Independent thinking became characteristic of Gano for the rest of his life. He joined the Baptist church at Hopewell, New Jersey, where Isaac Eaton directed his theological education and later preached his ordination sermon in 1755. Before he was thirty years old he had made two evangelistic preaching tours through the South, where he preached as far south as Charleston, South Carolina, in whose First Baptist Church he spoke before a distinguished audience.

> When I arose to speak, the sight of so brilliant an audience, among whom were twelve ministers, and one of whom was Mr. [George] Whitefield, for a moment brought the fear of man upon me; but, blessed be the Lord, I was soon relieved from this embarrassment; the thought passed my mind, I had none to fear and obey but the Lord.[25]

Whitefield later invited the young Baptist to preach in his orphanage.

Gano's preaching grew in reputation until he was called to be the pastor of the newly formed First Baptist Church of New York City. In 1762, he began twenty-six eventful years of ministry in New York, interrupted only by his terms of service as a chaplain in the Revolutionary War. His church soon grew from only thirty-seven to over two hundred members. His ministry was flourishing and his influence growing, but war with England interrupted the regularity of his days.

John Gano was not one to watch the struggle from a distance. He became an army chaplain and earned a reputation for courage during the war, which endeared him to the officers and to Washington himself, who personally chose Gano to lead the prayer of thanksgiving at the close of the war.[26]

---

[24]Ibid., 23.

[25]Quoted in Sprague, *Annals of the American Pulpit*, 63.

[26]There is inconclusive but interesting evidence that Gano may have secretly baptized George Washington during the war, although Washington always remained in the Anglican church. The available evidence is described by Barnes, "The John Gano Evidence."

Upon his return to New York City, Gano found his congregation scattered: "Some were dead, and others scattered into almost every part of the union," he wrote.[27] But his leadership soon reunited those who were left, and a revival ensued that brought many into the church, including forty young people who professed their faith in Christ. Just when the church was flourishing again, Gano, at the age of sixty-one, determined to leave the city and set out to the frontier of Kentucky to preach the gospel. His congregation in New York begged him to stay, but Gano was determined, and in the spring of 1787 he left for a rigorous new life.

The rest of his days were spent as pastor of the Town Fork Church, near Lexington, Kentucky, where he remained active until his death in 1804. His life spanned from the end of the First Great Awakening until the beginning of the Second Great Awakening, with the Revolutionary War in the middle. He was an active participant in all three. Henry Clay said of Gano's preaching, "He was a remarkably fervent preacher and distinguished for a simple and effective manner. And of all the preachers I ever listened to, he made me feel the most that religion was a divine reality."[28] The eminent Baptist leader Richard Furman said of Gano that "he *believed,* and therefore *spake*"[29]—a fitting tribute to an outspoken Baptist preacher.

Samuel Jones

In 1807, when the Philadelphia Association was celebrating one hundred years of existence, Samuel Jones was asked to preach the centennial sermon. It was natural that they would look to him, for, at the age of seventy-two, he had served among them the longest. He was to live seven more years, at which time he had been pastor of the Lower Dublin Baptist Church for fifty-one years. He had known most of the great Baptist leaders during the Revolutionary War era. Isaac Eaton had delivered the charge at his ordination back in 1763. "Let your preaching be distinct, plain, and pungent," said Eaton, "that you may approve yourself in the sight of God."[30] Jones had followed that advice, and over nearly half a

---

[27]Gano, *Biographical Memoirs,* 117.

[28]See Barnes, "The John Gano Evidence," 2.

[29]Sprague, *Annals of the American Pulpit,* 66.

[30]Isaac Eaton, "A Charge, Deliver'd at the Ordination of the Rev. Samuel Jones, A. B." (Philadelphia: Printed by Andrew Stewart, 1763) 45.

century had served his church and denomination with distinction, earning the reputation as "the most influential Baptist minister in the middle colonies, and probably in the whole country."[31]

Samuel Jones was an imposing man to meet in his day. Physically, he was six feet or more in height, large but not fat, and firmly built. His well-to-do Welsh parents had brought him at the age of two to America and had provided him the best advantages of education. He graduated from the College of Philadelphia with a Master of Arts degree in 1762, and a year later was ordained as pastor of the Pennepek Baptist Church, later called the Lower Dublin Baptist Church. His sound ministry quickly earned him the esteem of every class of people. Honorary degrees were awarded to him by Rhode Island College in 1769 and by his alma mater in 1788. The Philadelphia Association honored him with virtually every position of responsibility available throughout his ministry. His name pervades the Association minutes to such an extent that it is obvious that he was the leading spirit for many years. Whenever there was a dispute, Jones seemed able to unravel any perplexity.[32]

In spite of his physical size, he had a calm and graceful manner as a pastor. With all his educational attainments, he identified with the common people. They loved him. He was not pompous, but simple; not arrogant, but humble; not sarcastic, but good-natured. "I do not remember," said a longtime friend, "ever to have witnessed in him the least sign of anger, or to have seen him even thrown off his guard."[33] They loved him, too, because he shared their sorrows, and they willingly shared his. In 1778, at the height of his success as a preacher, three of his children died within two weeks. Two of them, Thomas and Samuel, aged thirteen and ten, were buried in the same grave. He observed to a friend after the funeral that he was astonished to find himself able to speak over their grave.[34]

---

[31]See Cathcart, *The Baptist Encyclopedia*, 619.

[32]See William Staughton, "The Servant of God Concluding His Labours; a Sermon on the Death of the Rev. Samuel Jones, D. D." (Philadelphia: Published by R. P. and W. Anderson, 1814) 28. Staughton said of Jones, "The Philadelphia Association, will long remember how often, as by a touch, he has dissipated darkness, and unravelled perplexity."

[33]Letter from William Duncan, in Sprague, *Annals of the American Pulpit*, 106.

[34]Staughton, "The Servant of God," 29.

There is little wonder, then, that people of every class heard him gladly. His bearing in the pulpit reflected the same kindness he bore in his daily relations. "Grace ever seemed to pour from his lips," remembered one friend, "while, with flowing tears, he lamented the miseries of the fall, or pointed the awakened transgressor to the Lamb of God."[35] His command of language enabled him to choose just the right word for every occasion, yet the words he chose were always plain and easily understood. His voice, until old age made it husky, was particularly well-adapted to public speaking. His sermons, preached from an outline printed neatly on two or three small pieces of paper (about 3 by 5 inches), reveal a studied and logical mind, but also a heart that kindled at the truths he proclaimed. The back page of one such outline lists fifteen places where he had preached that sermon.[36]

As an old man, Jones identified what to him made a preacher great:

> namely, true piety, ardent zeal, ministerial gifts, and indefatigable diligence, and faithfulness in saving the souls of men and promoting the kingdom of our Redeemer.[37]

Few if any were more devoted to the preaching task in his era. The foundation of his sermons was enlightened evangelical truth, spoken with freedom and sincerity. He devoted himself to the work of his denomination; at the same time he had a broad liberal spirit about him that embraced other denominations as "part of the Lord's vineyard."[38] There is no wonder that at his death at the age of eighty-two, many wondered how leaders in Philadelphia could rise up to fill his place. They felt as Theodore Beza did at the death of John Calvin: "Since he is gone, life has become less sweet, and death less bitter."[39]

What they did not know at Jones's funeral was that the Baptists were on the verge of a great movement to organize in behalf of foreign missions—a movement that would produce an even greater number of out-

---

[35]Ibid., 28.

[36]Samuel Jones, "Outline of a Sermon, Nov. 26, 1765" (Archives, John Hay Library, Brown University, Providence, Rhode Island).

[37]Samuel Jones, "Century Sermon," 464.

[38]Ibid., 462.

[39]William Staughton in the funeral sermon at Jones's death quoted Beza in reference to their own feelings about the loss of Samuel Jones. See page 30.

standing preachers than the eighteenth century had witnessed. But before we consider the next century, we must glance at the preaching in the South as well as in New England during the Revolutionary War era.

THE SOUTHERN COLONIES: THE EMERGENCE OF OLIVER HART

If you were living in the North in 1750 and needed to move to a warmer climate, and you wanted to move to a place where you would find an active Baptist church, you would likely have chosen Charleston, South Carolina, as your destination. Virginia had some well-settled towns, but the established Anglican church was busy persecuting the Baptists and other dissenters. North Carolina had no flourishing seaport, and Baptist churches were weak. Georgia was still too much of a frontier to hold much interest. It had to be South Carolina. It would be easy enough to find passage on a ship to Charleston, for it had one of the busiest ports in all the colonies. The Baptist church you would find in Charleston would be struggling to find new life after a period of decline and controversy. But when you met the pastor, you would soon predict that brighter days were in store for the Baptists of Charleston. He was the twenty-seven-year-old Oliver Hart, who had preceded your arrival by only one year.

The young Baptist pastor at Charleston was "tall, well-proportioned and of a graceful appearance"; such was the description of Hart by his friend Richard Furman.[40] He must have seemed like an angel sent from God to the church in Charleston. Ministers were scarce in those days, and for several years the church's only preaching had been supplied no more than once a month by Isaac Chanler, pastor of the Ashley River church. The church had written letters both to England and other parts of America seeking ministerial help, but no one had arrived until the very day the Baptists buried the body of Isaac Chanler. On that mournful day, young Oliver Hart stepped off the ship in Charleston. Two months later he accepted the call of the church to become their pastor and began what would become thirty eventful and productive years in the South.[41]

---

[40]Richard Furman, in Sprague, *Annals of the American Pulpit,* 49.

[41]The best biographical treatment of Oliver Hart has come from Loulie Latimer Owens, *Oliver Hart* (Greenville SC: The South Carolina Baptist Historical Society, 1966) and from Robert A. Baker, *Adventure in Faith: The First 300 Years of First Baptist Church, Charleston, South Carolina* (Nashville: Broadman Press, 1982) ch. 5 and 6.

Spiritually, Hart had indeed come from God, but physically he had come from the Philadelphia Association, bringing with him the enlightened approach to preaching and pastoral leadership so characteristic of the leaders of the middle colonies. Hart was of the generation of Isaac Eaton. The two had indeed grown up together in the same church. They both surrendered to the ministry and were licensed at the same time by the Southampton, Pennsylvania, church. Eaton, as has been discussed above, made his great contribution as pastor of the Hopewell church and died at an early age. Ironically, Hart became a successor of his old friend Eaton at the Hopewell church in 1780. Thus Hart came full circle, beginning his ministry in the Philadelphia Association, making his greatest contribution in the South, and concluding his ministry where he had begun.

Hart brought to Charleston the best characteristics of the Philadelphia Association. So convinced was he of the benefits of an associational organization that he welded the South Carolina churches into the Charleston Association in 1751, the second such organization in America. So convinced was he of the need for an educated ministry that he established the Baptist Religious Society at Charleston in 1755, and even though the work was not fully supported by the association, Hart assisted in the education of a number of young ministers, some of whom became prominent national leaders.[42] Under Hart's leadership, the Charleston church became strong and active. "A remarkable revival in our church began in August 1754," wrote Hart in his diary.[43] That revival may have ended, but the sustained growth of the church under Hart's leadership continued until the ravages of the Revolutionary War scattered the members and profaned the meetinghouse. Hart's patriotism during the war and his active involvement in convincing skeptical pioneers in the South Carolina backcountry to support the cause of independence made him a prime target for British soldiers, who invaded

---

[42]Particularly Samuel Stillman, who became the renowned pastor of the First Baptist Church of Boston, and possibly Hezekiah Smith, who served the Baptist church in Haverhill, Massachusetts. Others who were trained by Hart are listed in Baker, *Adventure in Faith,* 162.

[43]Oliver Hart, "Diary," 3. The page numbers are from the mimeographed typed copy by Loulie Latimer Owens.

Charleston early in 1780. Eventually he had to leave South Carolina for his own safety. His diary tells the story:

> having left Mr. Screven's on Lord's Day April 16th when we received certain intelligence that a strong detachment from the British army had that morning crossed Bouncan's Ferry, and were actually within a few miles of us. I then packed up a few clothes in haste, and about 12 o'clock took my leave of my dear wife and the family (the most affecting parting I ever experienced) and mounting my horse, set off but whither I was going or when I should return I knew not, but endeavored to leave my connections and place myself in the hands of the great and wise Disposer of all Events.[44]

He never returned to Charleston. Instead, he traveled back north to friends who knew him. On Christmas Day 1780, Hart accepted the unanimous call from the Hopewell church to settle there as pastor. He was fifty-seven years old, a veteran in the ministry, and a denominational leader. His wife joined him the following summer, and he ended his days at Hopewell in 1795 without ever being able to visit his beloved Charleston again. The epitaph carved on his tombstone characterized his life:

> *His walk so steady, and his hope so high*
> *He neither blush'd to live, nor fear'd to die.*

Oliver Hart unknowingly described his own preaching when he said of a friend that "he did not content himself with delivering a little dry morality, but unfolded and applied the great and glorious doctrine of the Gospel."[45] Hart was an animated preacher who aimed at the hearts and wills of those before him. His good reputation spread quickly, even among nonbelievers. Edmund Botsford, a young immigrant from England who sought religious counsel, was told by a "scoffer" that Hart was the only minister in town who could help him. Botsford later described his reaction to Hart's preaching.

> To describe the exercise of my mind under his sermon would be impossible. However, upon the whole, I concluded it was possible there might be salvation for me, even for me. I then determined, that, in future, I would attend worship in this place. I do not remember, that, when able

---

[44]Ibid., 13.

[45]Ibid., 8. He was referring to his friend Francis Pelot, a wealthy planter and pastor of the Euhaw Baptist Church in South Carolina.

to go, I ever once omitted attending, while I lived in Charleston. Indeed, I would not have omitted one sermon for all the riches in the world.[46]

Botsford was not only converted, but was also called to the ministry under the influence of Oliver Hart. Botsford became an eminent pastor among the Baptists in the Charleston Association.

Among others influenced by Hart to enter the ministry were Nicholas Bedgegood and Samuel Stillman. The former became Hart's assistant at the First Baptist Church of Charleston and in 1760 became pastor of the Welsh Neck Baptist Church in South Carolina. The latter became the esteemed pastor of the First Baptist Church of Boston, Massachusetts. Among the sermon manuscripts and notes left by Hart are extensive notes from an ordination sermon addressed to "my dear young friends, just entering upon the most important Work in ye World."[47] From the context of the sermon it appears that it was preached at the joint ordination service of Bedgegood and Stillman.[48] A good account of Hart's approach to the preaching task can be found in these notes.

At the outset of the sermon, Hart made it crystal clear that "Nothing can be more awful than to preach an unknown Ch.^t" A preacher must first of all have what Hart called "an actual Closure" with Christ. That is to say, a true conversion and a consistent Christian life stand as the two great pillars that support effective preaching. On another occasion Hart said that the position of a minister is enough to cause anyone of sensibility to tremble: "he stands between the living and the dead—the living God and dead sinners."[49] The greatest wisdom and training cannot adequately prepare one for that task, but Hart was convinced that preaching the gospel was the most effective means of eliciting the salvation of individuals and society.

---

[46]Charles D. Mallary, *Memoirs of Elder Edmund Botsford* (Charleston SC: W. Riley, 1832) 30. Quoted by Baker, *Adventure in Faith,* 132.

[47]I am indebted to J. Glen Clayton, Curator of the Baptist Historical Collection, Furman University Library, Greenville, South Carolina, for supplying me with typescript copies of these sermon notes. Subsequent quotations come from these notes.

[48]See Hart, "Diary," 3: "On Monday, Feb. ye 26th 1759 assisted Rev. Mr. Francis Pelot and John Stevens in the ordination of Nicholas Bridgegood [Bedgegood] and Samuel Stillman to the work of the ministry."

[49]Oliver Hart, "A Gospel Church Portrayed, and Her Orderly Service Pointed Out" (Trenton: Printed by Isaac Collins, 1791) 23.

With such a great challenge, it was only sensible that every effort should be made to have a liberally educated ministry. Hart himself, although not blessed with a formal college education, read widely and became so respected in the academic community that he was awarded an honorary Master of Arts degree by Rhode Island College at its first commencement in 1769. He urged the two young ordinands to "make your knowledge of the learned Languages, and liberal arts, and Sciences, as copious, and extensive as you can." Hart was an early leader in overcoming opposition to a liberal education for the ministry. "In ancient times," he claimed, "there were schools of the prophets; and they are not less needed now."[50]

He advised the young ministers before him to study diligently, but to be very practical and simple in their sermons.

> A plain and simple stile, seems best to compart with ye Simplicity of the Gospel, but let it not be low, or groveling. However plain, it ought to be manly, & striking.[51]

In this respect Hart's own preaching lived up to his advice. His published sermons, as well as his extant sermon notes, reveal a polished and eloquent style. His use of language was deliberate—not to impress his hearers, but to communicate clearly. Richard Furman would later describe Hart's eloquence as the kind that "afforded pleasure to persons of true taste, and edification to the serious hearer."[52]

Oliver Hart was the first of an amazing succession of great preachers who led the First Baptist Church of Charleston to become one of the most prominent and influential Baptist churches in the nation. Preachers and denominational leaders such as Richard Furman, Basil Manly, Sr., and W. T. Brantly, Sr., followed in succession, but it was Oliver Hart who set the preaching standard. If his successors made greater contributions, it was largely because they stood on the solid foundation laid by Oliver Hart.

---

[50]Ibid., 16.
[51]Hart, "Sermon Notes," 6.
[52]Furman, in Sprague, *Annals of the American Pulpit*, 49.

THE NEW ENGLAND COLONIES: REAPING A RICH HARVEST

In New England during the eighteenth century there was a group of Baptist ministers who were extraordinary not only in preaching the gospel, but also in their capacity for personal friendship and support. Baptists were still the minority. Those in Massachusetts still carried the burden of an established church, but the days of active persecution had ended. Instead, Baptists in some areas became highly respected leaders, and Baptist preachers drew some of the most prominent citizens into their congregations.

The Great Awakening split some churches. The First Baptist Church of Boston suffered a breaking away by a group of its members in 1743 to form the Second Baptist Church. But by the end of the century the two churches shared a mutual respect and a cordial relationship. In the rural areas, the Separate Baptists were represented by some preachers who were characteristically jealous and even hostile toward the more educated city preachers. One illiterate Baptist preacher grumbled about scholarly ministers: "it has got so far already as scarcely to do for a common Illiterate Minister to preach in the baptist meeting at providence [Rhode Island]."[53] Noah Worcester, a non-Baptist, wrote a scathing description of some Baptist preaching:

> Many people are so ignorant, as to be more charmed with sound than with sense. And to them, the want of knowledge in a teacher . . . may easily be made up, and over-balanced, by great zeal, an affecting tone of voice, and perpetual motion of the tongue. If a speaker can keep his tongue running, in an unrelenting manner, during the time of exercise; and can quote memoriter, a large number of texts from within the covers of the Bible, it matters not, to many of his hearers, whether he speaks *sense* or *nonsense;* or whether his quoting of scripture be *pertinent* or *impertinent.* And when such persons hear a speaker, who has had but little advantage for education, preach in such a manner, and this too without forethought or study, as he may profess, and we may believe, they think he is most certainly called of God, that he is wonderfully assisted, and speaks as the Spirit gives him utterance. Ergo, he must be a good man and his sentiments are doubtless right.[54]

---

[53]Quoted in C. C. Goen, *Revivalism and Separatism,* 276.

[54]Noah Worcester, *Impartial Inquiries, Respecting the Progress of the Baptist Denomination* (Worcester MA: Leonard Worcester, 1794) 19-20.

Worcester wrote that description on the heels of a debate with Thomas Baldwin, pastor of the Second Baptist Church of Boston. Baldwin himself was an able debater, a former lawyer, and onetime member of the New Hampshire legislature. Worcester's description was surely a caricature of the worst of preachers and not representative of the most influential Baptists of the day.

Samuel Stillman:
The "Little Man Eloquent"

Among the most influential of the New England Baptists was a man who stood barely over five feet tall and never weighed over one hundred pounds. His name was Samuel Stillman, and he served as pastor of Boston's First Baptist Church from 1764 until his death in 1807. During those forty-three years Stillman both observed and played a part in the momentous national events that occurred in Boston. This was quite a difficult time to take the reins of the First Baptist Church. Attendance and enthusiasm were low, the church building was in need of repair, and money was difficult to get. Boston was the center of great national unrest. During Stillman's first years as pastor, the Stamp Act was passed and repealed and two regiments of unpopular British soldiers were quartered in the town, events which culminated in the famous "Boston Massacre." The conflict between the British soldiers and the people of Boston foreshadowed the Revolution. Patriots such as Samuel Adams and Paul Revere were active in resisting the British. There was a vague uneasiness and disquiet among the people that could have made Stillman's ministry even more difficult.

Those difficult days, however, seemed to match the gifts of the young Stillman. From the December day in 1764 when he was installed and found the church too small to accommodate the throngs, until his death, his eloquence never failed to attract large crowds. The church immediately gained significant numbers of new members and continued its growth until a new building had to be constructed only six years after Stillman came. Twice the new building had to be expanded during his ministry.[55] His reputation was so widespread that to visit Boston and miss hearing Stillman was considered a major disappointment. President John Adams reg-

---

[55]See Nathan E. Wood, *The History of the First Baptist Church of Boston* (Philadelphia: American Baptist Publication Society, 1899) 261-86 passim.

ularly attended Stillman's church whenever he was in Boston, as did other leaders of the era.[56] He was the first Baptist preacher ever to be invited to preach the annual election sermon before the Massachusetts legislature. He did so on 26 May 1779 and made an eloquent plea for the separation of church and state.[57] During the siege of Boston leading to the Battle of Bunker Hill, the First Baptist Church was used as barracks for British troops and later turned into a hospital. Stillman and his family settled temporarily in Philadelphia until he could reopen the church building in the summer of 1776. The city of Boston did not forget his patriotism and in 1789 asked him to deliver an anniversary oration on independence to the entire city.[58] The list of his honors and public involvement could go on and on, but enough has been written to emphasize his unusual gifts and success as a preacher.

Of more importance for Baptist preaching is to ask what qualities made his preaching great. Was it simply his unusual gifts? Or did he practice some basic principles of preaching that, combined with his natural ability, made him such an extraordinary preacher? The large number of his sermons that were published and are still extant makes it possible to answer these questions with confidence.[59]

Stillman was endowed with exceptional gifts for the ministry. These gifts were recognized and nurtured by none other than Oliver Hart of Charleston, South Carolina, who baptized, ordained, and trained Stillman in the ministry. Hart referred to young Stillman as one of the "Seals of

---

[56]Sprague, *Annals of the American Pulpit*, 75.

[57]See Samuel Stillman, "A Sermon Preached Before the Honorable Council, and the Honorable House of Representatives of the State of Massachusetts-Bay, in New England, at Boston, May 26, 1779" (Boston: Printed by T. and J. Fleet, 1779). Stillman was well received in spite of objections by several of the staunch Congregationalists in the legislature. He told them in no uncertain terms that "ignorance in politicks as well as in religion, is fatal in its tendency." Three times in the sermon he emphasized that "the care of souls is not committed to the civil magistrate."

[58]See Samuel Stillman, "An Oration, Delivered July 4th, 1789, at the Request of the Inhabitants of the Town of Boston, in Celebration of the Anniversary of American Independence" (Boston: Printed by B. Edes and Son, 1789).

[59]After Stillman's death, the deacons of his church published twenty of his sermons in one volume, prefaced by a memoir of his life. See *Select Sermons on Doctrinal and Practical Subjects, by the late Samuel Stillman, D. D.* (Boston: Manning and Loring, 1808). A large number of other sermons by Stillman have been preserved in pamphlet form in the archives of the Andover-Harvard Library, Harvard Divinity School.

My Ministry, my Joy and Crown."[60] Stillman always called his mentor "Father Hart," and they remained affectionate friends throughout life.

Stillman's voice was naturally fit for preaching. Contemporaries described it as "pleasant and most commanding,"[61] an especially important gift when one considers his small physical size. In addition, he possessed the gift of relating cordially to the highest and lowest ranks of society. The wealthy and the poor all felt they had a friend in the pulpit.

But what about those aspects of his preaching that were not natural gifts? What did he do to help improve his natural abilities? The answer lies foremost in the fact that throughout his ministry he preached Christ as the beginning and end of the gospel. "I have no time to trifle with men's souls by directing them to depend on their own exertions," he said, "but I will point them to Jesus."[62] That was not just insincere, pious talk for him. He lived in Boston during the days when Unitarianism (the belief that God exists only in one person, that is, the rejection of the Trinity) became extremely popular among almost all of the orthodox churches. Toward the end of his ministry all the Congregational churches in Boston except the Old South had adopted Unitarianism, and Stillman and Thomas Baldwin (of Second Baptist) were virtually the only traditionally orthodox preachers in town. A great revival broke out under Stillman's preaching in 1803 and 1804, which was credited with influencing the pastor of the Old South Church and thus preserving orthodox Congregationalism in Boston.[63]

Not only was Unitarianism popular, but a more subtle threat to orthodoxy came in the wave of American patriotism during and after the Revolutionary War. Stillman, an ardent patriot himself, nevertheless was, I believe, the first Baptist preacher to warn against what is known today as "civil religion." Stillman called it "political religion" and described it as nothing more than "natural religion, sanctified by the name of Christianity." God was frequently invoked in such religion, but the uniqueness and demands of Christ were conveniently left out. All that was necessary for political religion, he claimed, was the necessity of a good life and the

---

[60] See Hart, "Sermon Notes."
[61] "Biographical Sketch," in *Select Sermons*, xii.
[62] Ibid., xvi.
[63] See Wood, *First Baptist Church of Boston*, 296.

maintaining of a good appearance by attending public worship.[64] Instead, Stillman preached the sovereignty of God *in Christ*—a sovereignty that superseded that of any sovereign state. Christ, to him, constituted the center of Christianity and to preach a mere program of public morals was to forget the preacher's calling. In a sermon on apostolic preaching he made his position clear.

> Had a sermon been delivered in the apostolic age, to a Christian assembly, that had but little of Christ in it, they would at once have concluded, the preacher had forgot his errand; and with the disappointed woman at the sepulchre, have cried out, "They have taken away my Lord out of his place, and I know not where they have laid him." Where would Jesus Christ be as the object of affection, if not in the hearts and conversation of his disciples?—Where indeed, if not in the preaching of his ministers?[65]

In addition to preaching an orthodox gospel, Stillman had the ability to combine simplicity of presentation with an obvious depth of learning and study. As a result, he was heard gladly by both the learned and the illiterate. Honored with degrees from both Harvard and Rhode Island College, he promoted an educated ministry throughout his life. He was among the leaders in Baptist life who helped break down the many prejudices against learning. He was successful primarily because his life and preaching demonstrated that intellectual rigor and evangelistic warmth need not be mutually exclusive. "A lazy minister," he declared, "is an odious character; and a trifling minister no less so."[66]

Samuel Stillman helped break down the walls of resentment between Regular and Separate Baptists. Like his mentor Oliver Hart, Stillman encouraged Regular Baptists not to dismiss the Separates because their revivals were "sometimes attended with irregularities," an obvious reference to the emotional excesses that offended many of the more cul-

---

[64]Samuel Stillman, "A Sermon, Preached at Boston, April 25, 1799; the Day Recommended by the President of the United States for a National Fast" (Boston: Manning and Loring, 1799) 11-12.

[65]Samuel Stillman, "Apostolic Preaching Considered in Three Discourses" (Boston: B. Edes and Son, 1791) 21.

[66]Samuel Stillman, "A Sermon Preached at Charleston, October 7, 1802; at the Installment of the Rev. Thomas Waterman, to the Pastoral Care of the Baptist Church and Society in That Town" (Boston: Manning and Loring, 1802) 16.

tured and educated among his congregation.[67] He urged them to support what was right in the revivals: people were changed for the better. For the first time since the formation of the Second Baptist Church in 1741, the two Baptist churches in Boston, whose meetinghouses were less than a block away, became cordial in their relations. Stillman and Thomas Baldwin presented a united front to their congregations, and the two churches turned their attention away from resentment of each other toward the common cause of promoting Christian missions. The Massachusetts Baptist Missionary Society was formed in 1802 under Stillman's leadership, and that society later became the basis for the organization of the Triennial Convention in 1814.

Stillman died in March 1807, leaving a legacy of great preaching, pastoral fidelity, and a liberal spirit. More than fifty years after his death, one who had known him remembered Stillman as combining "a happy union of the gentleman, the scholar, and the devoted Christian Minister."[68] Over two hundred years after his death, perhaps the denomination he served, and particularly, its leaders, will benefit from the revival of his memory.

Hezekiah Smith:
The Educated Evangelist

Samuel Stillman was not the sole representative of great preaching among the Regular Baptists of New England in his day. His two closest friends in the ministry were equally influential and deserving of honor. One was Hezekiah Smith, the pastor of the Baptist church of Haverhill, Massachusetts, from 1766 until his death in 1805. Smith and Stillman were the same age, and their effective ministries ran parallel to each other. During the Revolutionary War, Smith became famous as a chaplain, frequently exposing himself to danger in battle in order to minister to the soldiers. Unlike Stillman, Smith was tall and sturdily built and made an imposing figure of inspiration as he stood on the heights of Bunker Hill during the famous battle with the British. But his most lasting influence came not in battle, but in his daily routines as pastor and evangelist.

A graduate of Hopewell Academy, under Isaac Eaton, and Princeton University, Smith was clear and scholarly in his thinking. At the same

---

[67]See Samuel Stillman, "A Discourse Preached in Boston Before the Massachusetts Baptist Missionary Society" (Boston: Manning and Loring, 1803) 18.

[68]Sprague, *Annals of the American Pulpit,* 77.

time, he was an inveterate evangelist. His preaching reminded people of George Whitefield's, and, like Whitefield, Smith made occasional evangelistic tours, which increased his renown and proved very successful. In his own town of Haverhill he once attracted 3,000 people to one of his services at a time when there were only 5,800 people living in the town. Unfortunately, his surviving sermons are scarce, largely due to his own humility. He would not even allow his portrait to be painted.[69]

James Manning:
The "Elegant Scholar"

Stillman's other dear friend was James Manning, pastor of the First Baptist Church of Providence, Rhode Island, and the first president of Rhode Island College. He was the "elegant scholar" among eighteenth century Baptists. He was Isaac Eaton's first student at Hopewell Academy, and he graduated with highest honors from Princeton in 1762. Eight years later he found himself carrying one of the heaviest loads of responsibility of all Baptists in America. He was "President, and Professor of Languages, and other branches of learning" at Rhode Island College, as well as pastor of the oldest Baptist church in America. How he succeeded in carrying that load can be seen in the subsequent history of Brown University. In the center of the campus today is a beautiful chapel standing between the two original buildings erected under Manning's leadership before the Revolutionary War. The chapel is appropriately named after Manning, for he indeed provided the spiritual heartbeat of the campus while also serving as the intellectual mentor of the students.

Likewise, the church grew under his powerful preaching and experienced several revivals during his ministry, one of which resulted in 104 conversions. The large number of additions to the church during Manning's ministry required the building of a new meetinghouse to be used both for worship and for the college commencements. The result was the erection of the beautiful building that is still used by the First Baptist Church of Providence. Largely because of his dual responsibilities with

---

[69]See Reuben A. Guild, *Chaplain Smith and the Baptists; or, Life, Journals, Letters, and Addresses of the Rev. Hezekiah Smith, D. D., of Haverhill, Massachusetts* (Philadelphia: American Baptist Publication Society, 1885). Most of his extant correspondence and papers are located in the archives of the John Hay Library, Brown University, Providence, Rhode Island. The few surviving sermons are in such poor condition, and his handwriting so difficult to read, that I was unable to analyze them.

the college and the church, Manning preached extemporaneously for the most part, and seemed to have been gifted in that respect.

To the people of Rhode Island, Manning was revered as a spiritual and educational leader. In civic life he was elected in 1786 to a term in the United States Congress, even though he did not seek the post and gladly gave it up a year later. His early death at the age of fifty-three removed one of the great Baptists of the day. A biography of Manning, published in 1864, was written by Reuben A. Guild.[70]

Isaac Backus:
The Reconciler

The tall, dark-haired man in the pulpit looked like a farmer and was one. His voice was sharp, almost to the point of irritation. His language was direct and simple, hinting that he had no college education and knew little of literature. His habit of looking up and closing his eyes during important parts of his sermon seemed unusual to those used to preachers who read a manuscript. Backus, in some ways, stood alone among Baptist preachers. He was not the cultured and educated Regular Baptist of New England. Nor was he like some of his fellow Separate Baptist preachers: his sermons were not emotional harangues, but well prepared, deeply earnest messages springing from his intense study of God's Word. He stood out from nearly every Baptist leader and became, in T. B. Maston's judgment, "the outstanding Baptist of his day."[71] Judging Backus as a denominational leader and by his efforts to disestablish religion in Massachusetts and in the Constitution of the United States, he doubtlessly fit Maston's assessment. Backus was also a tireless historian of the Baptists and produced a history of the denomination, which has left all its adherents in debt to him.[72] His extensive diaries and tracts offer a

---

[70]Reuben A. Guild, *Life, Times, and Correspondence of James Manning* (Boston: Gould and Lincoln, 1864).

[71]T. B. Maston, *Isaac Backus: Pioneer of Religious Liberty* (Rochester NY: American Baptist Historical Society, 1962) 102.

[72]See *A History of New England With Particular Reference to the Denomination of Christians Called Baptists,* 3 vols., 1777, 1784, and 1796. The second edition, in two volumes, was edited by David Weston and published by the Backus Historical Society, Newton, Massachusetts, in 1871. Also, see *An Abridgment of the Church History of New England from 1602 to 1804 Containing a View of Their Principles and Practices, Declensions and Revivals, Oppression and Liberty, with a Concise Account of the Baptists in the Southern Parts of America and a Chronological Table of the Whole* (Boston: E. Lincoln, 1804).

wealth of primary material to the scholar and a firsthand description of eighteenth century life in New England.[73] Backus has been the subject of much study among Baptists, but his other significant contributions have overshadowed his ministry as a preacher.

How does Backus rank among Baptist preachers in the eighteenth century? Like many Separate Baptists, he was raised as a Congregationalist. Under the influence of the Great Awakening, he moved through the familiar stage of becoming a "New Light" Congregationalist on the way to becoming a Baptist. His conversion came in the wake of the Whitefield revivals, but he did not exhibit the kind of emotional excess so common among some Separates. He was simply "mowing in the field alone" when he was struck with the futility of his way of life. He sat down under a tree and prayed. The result was immediate: "I felt a calm in my mind—them tossings And tumults that I felt before seemed to be gone."[74] His call to preach was similar in that he was "alone in the woods." While praying, Backus felt a distinct call from God to face possible persecution and certain loss of prestige by becoming a Separate preacher. He offered many objections to God: his "own ignorance and weakness" seemed a major obstacle. "I was slow of speech and very bashful," he added. But God's voice to him was clear: "Cannot he who formed man's mouth make him to speak?"[75] So Backus gave up all objections and plunged into a life that would lead him from many an humble home to the floor of the Continental Congress in Philadelphia, and eventually to a revered position among Baptists of every subsequent age. By 1762, only six years after the Separate Baptist church of Middleborough was organized under his leadership, Backus was pastor of the largest concentration of Separate Baptists in New England. His preaching was at the center of his great appeal.

Backus was one of those rare people who had the gift of drawing both the ignorant and the educated to his preaching. Some of his church members in Middleborough were among the most highly respected citizens of

---

[73]The momentous work of William G. McLoughlin has made it possible for all to read *The Diary of Isaac Backus,* 3 vols. (Providence: Brown University Press, 1979).

[74]Isaac Backus, "Some Particular Account of My Conversion," in McLoughlin, *The Diary of Isaac Backus,* 3:1525.

[75]McLoughlin, *The Diary of Isaac Backus,* 1:4.

the community.[76] Others were among the very emotional type who could be easily swayed by any speaker. His appeal to such a diverse congregation can be found in his preaching. Unlike many of his contemporary Separates, Backus did not condemn education for the ministry. His own lack of education did not prevent him from throwing the full weight of his influence behind the attempts of Regular Baptists to organize and support Rhode Island College. Backus was among the few Separate Baptists who saw that the Regular Baptists were not opposed to evangelism just because they would not condone some of the emotional excesses of the revival movement. When he first met that "elegant scholar" James Manning, Backus was impressed.

> The more I get acquainted with Mr. Manning the more I esteem him for his own temper and for his gift in opening the clear doctrine of the gospel.[77]

From that day in 1764 the two men remained close friends. Backus served as a trustee for Rhode Island College for the rest of his life. Nothing could have done more to promote harmonious relations between the Regular and Separate Baptists than for Isaac Backus to support an educated ministry. In the face of much prejudice and hostility toward education, Backus stated publicly as early as 1754, "Let none think me an Enemy to Learning . . . for true Learning is what I highly prize."[78]

On the other hand, Backus pleased the revivalists by his unmistakable love for evangelism. He constantly urged the learned to beware of losing their zeal. A true minister's qualifications, he insisted, rest more upon an internal call to preach than in human learning.[79] He preached an average of three hundred sermons a year during most of his ministry, and the evangelical call for conversion was the common thread. His theology was basically evangelical Calvinism similar to that of George

---

[76]See William G. McLoughlin, *Isaac Backus and the American Pietistic Tradition* (Boston: Little, Brown, and Co., 1967) 27-28.

[77]Quoted in ibid., 103.

[78]Backus, "Discourse Shewing the Nature and Necessity of an Internal Call to Preach the Everlasting Gospel" (Boston: Printed by Fowle, 1754) xii. The largest collection of Backus papers and publications may be found in the library of Andover-Newton Theological School, Newton Centre, Massachusetts.

[79]Ibid., 16ff.

Whitefield. He preached that a sinner was guilty and worthy of death until he received the free pardon of God.

> If a man that is under sentence of death should slip from his confinement, and do ever so much in hopes of being again received as a good subject, don't all men know that his doings can never be true *obedience* to the authority that condemned him, till that authority either reverses the sentence, or grants him a pardon?[80]

Yet unlike many of the revivalists, he did not stop with exhortations to be saved. He studied the Bible constantly, and his sermons demonstrated his attempts to lead his new converts into a deeper understanding of the Christian faith. He believed that the promises of God's Word were "firmer than a rock."[81] He emphasized in his preaching the call of God not only to trust, but also to obey the Word.

> tho' rulers, fathers, mothers, wife or children say the contrary; and tho' we loose house, lands, or life, in the cause: And he that will turn from truth for any or all of these, CANNOT *be* Christ's *disciple*.[82]

To obey the Word, however, was to follow the spirit, not the letter of the Scriptures. He advised one young preacher, "But where the letter only is preached, it killeth, as it takes life and courage from men."[83]

This is precisely the place where Isaac Backus made his most important contribution to Baptist preaching: his Christian spirit. He was a strong and courageous bridge between the Regular and Separate Baptists. His preaching reminded the Regulars of their need for zeal; it reminded the Separates of their need for learning; and it reminded all of their need for Christ. Thus Backus may be the most important of all the eighteenth century New England Baptist preachers—not because he was the best preacher—but because he paved the way for that dramatic next step in the Baptist story: the unifying of all Baptists in America under the banner of missions.

---

[80]Backus, "Evangelical Ministers Described, and Distinguished from Legalists" (Boston: Philip Freeman, 1772), 25.

[81]Backus, "Some Particular Account of My Conversion," 3:1525.

[82]Backus, "True Faith Will Produce Good Works" (Boston: D. Kneeland, 1767) 91-92.

[83]Backus, "Evangelical Ministers Described," 16.

CONCLUSION

Baptist preaching during the Revolutionary War era resulted in changes in the climate of Baptist life. Compared to the previous century, it is obvious that Baptists were far more readily accepted and even esteemed in some quarters. That new status is not to be explained simply by their great increase in numbers. It is found rather in the fact that Baptists were tested during the eighteenth century, and they were not found wanting. Some had suspected that Baptists would support the British during the struggle for independence. Instead, Baptists fought bravely and proved to be loyal patriots.

The new nation, having defeated Great Britain, was injected with a fervor for independence and freedom of conscience that seemed to fit like a glove around Baptist polity and church life. Just as the nation was freed from British control, the climate was right for churches to be separated from state and even ecclesiastical control. Frontier individualism was in harmony with the democratic church polity of the Baptists. Requirements for ordination among Baptists stressed an internal call from God rather than an external college diploma. Although that fact may have decreased the *quality* of Baptist preaching on the frontier, it increased the *quantity* of preaching.

Baptists also shared in the amazing optimism of the era. Whereas Thomas Jefferson was convinced that by 1830 the whole nation would become Unitarian, Isaac Backus and many others believed that by 1830 the whole nation would become immersed evangelical Baptists![84] Unlike Jefferson, the Baptists did not wait confidently for their prediction to come true. Baptist preachers like John Gano followed the footsteps of Baptist pioneers like Daniel Boone into the western frontier.

By the turn of the century the quality of Baptist preaching was as diverse as the population of the growing nation. With all the advantages of Baptist independence, many felt the need for something larger than a cooperative associational structure to unite the widely separated denomination. The call of Christian missions was the only thing that could weld them into a national structure. Once again, preaching played a dominant role.

---

[84]See McLoughlin, *American Pietistic Tradition*, 186.

Chapter 9

TOGETHER WE PREACH:
Baptist Preaching from 1800 to 1845

All the vigor of his noble intellect was consecrated to God.
William T. Brantly
in reference to Richard Furman

In your preparations for the pulpit, never be satisfied with the offspring of a moment. Such productions, like the ephemerae of the natural world, may be expected to be short-lived and useless.
William Staughton

When America won the Revolutionary War and gained independence from Great Britain, the thirteen colonies were faced with the task of forming a new country. It was one thing to fight and win a war; it was another thing to organize a new government from scratch. To make matters more difficult, the original colonies never had been very unified. Each had developed an intense individualism more closely connected with the mother country than with one another. The common danger of war had temporarily unified them, but when the war was over, the natural tendency was to return to the old rivalries and antagonisms of earlier days. Of course, money spoke eloquently as a motive for uniting, since financial dealings with other countries as well as within America could be facilitated more easily by some sort of union. But what or who could form thirteen hardheaded, separate states into a well-organized group of *united* states?

When General-turned-Gentleman-Farmer George Washington was summoned in 1789 to give up his retirement at Mount Vernon and return to public life as President of the United States, he was likely the only person in America who could engender the degree of trust required to forge some semblance of unity in the nation. Whatever he did as President, it was his very presence that inspired confidence. There were indeed many great leaders in America, but only Washington could unite them.

Baptists, at the end of the eighteenth century, were like America in that they needed some great unifying force. Like the states where they lived, Baptists tended to be very individualistic, and their church polity encouraged it. While Baptist independence enabled the massive spread of Baptist churches on the frontier, it also hindered attempts to coordinate the efforts of many churches so widely separated in a vast country. The only official organizations of Baptist churches were a few associations. What or who could unite the Baptists into a unified denomination?

The answer came in the form of foreign missions. The work of William Carey in India, as well as the writings of Andrew Fuller, had not failed to strike enthusiasm in the hearts of Baptists in America. Several prominent Baptist preachers, such as William Staughton of Philadelphia and Thomas Baldwin of Boston, carried on extensive correspondence with Carey and even formed societies to raise money for the mission cause in India. But none of that brought the Baptists together into a national movement to combine their energies under the banner of missions.

Baptists received an unexpected boost when two Congregational missionaries, Adoniram Judson and Luther Rice, became Baptists on their way to India. As a result, they both sent in their resignations to the Congregational Board, and Rice returned to America to try to gain support from the Baptists for Judson's work in Burma. The year was 1813, and Rice could not have arrived among the Baptists at a more opportune time. He spent the rest of his life traveling among Baptists from Maine to Georgia promoting missions and education. But it was not Rice who unified the Baptists. The answer to the question of who would achieve that goal came in the form of an imposing Southern preacher: Richard Furman.

RICHARD FURMAN: THE REIGNING BAPTIST

Richard Furman once passed through Washington, D.C., on a journey and happened to meet an old friend in the company of James Monroe, then a member of the Cabinet. His friend introduced Furman as "Mr. Furman of Charleston." While shaking Furman's hand, Monroe had a quizzical look on his face, as if trying to recall something. "Furman, Furman . . . ," he repeated. "May I inquire if you were once of the High Hills of Santee?" asked Monroe. Furman answered affirmatively. "And were you the young preacher who fled for protection to the American camp, on account of the reward which Lord Cornwallis had offered for his head?"

"I am the same," said Furman. Monroe was deeply moved and insisted on telling Furman's friend of the great influence the preacher had exerted in the interior of South Carolina on behalf of the American cause. Furman's eloquent appeals became widely known; indeed, Cornwallis made the remark that he "feared the prayers of that godly youth more than the armies of Sumter and Marion."

Soon the news spread that Furman was in the capital city, and an appointment was made for him to preach before Congress, which was then in session. When he arrived, the room was crowded not only with legislators, but also with the president, members of the Cabinet, foreign ambassadors, and other dignitaries who had heard of his eloquence. In the midst of that dignified assembly, Furman's voice rang out as it had done years before during the American Revolution, but now he was at the height of his maturity. His text was characteristic: "And now why tarriest thou? Arise and be baptized." His eloquence riveted their attention, and toward the close of the sermon, he paused and stared at the dignitaries, who sat in utter silence. Then he repeated the words of his text in a clear, stentorian voice: "AND NOW WHY TARRIEST THOU? ARISE AND BE BAPTIZED." As Furman said "Arise," not a few of his electrified hearers actually did rise from their seats! James Monroe soon became president and always retained the highest regard for Richard Furman.[1]

This was the same Richard Furman who could very well be called the father of united Baptist work. He was not the first to suggest some kind of organization to bring together all the Baptists in America. Nor was he in the forefront of organizing the first meeting of the Triennial Convention in 1814. In fact, he was not even sure he could attend that first historic meeting in Philadelphia. His responsibilities in Charleston were so heavy, and the time and expense required to go to Philadelphia were so great that he had reservations about attending at all. But his church in Charleston somehow sensed the importance of that gathering and voted to give Furman a six-month leave of absence in order for him to be in Philadelphia. America was at war with England again, so the seas were not safe. He traveled by land and arrived in Philadelphia one day before

---

[1]This story is told in *A Biography of Richard Furman,* ed. Harvey T. Cook (Greenville SC: Baptist Courier Job Rooms, 1913) 72-73.

the meeting began. Furman's very presence inspired the gathering. He was unanimously elected the first president of the Triennial Convention, and he was asked to preach the first sermon to Baptists united from all over the new nation. He preached from Matthew 28:20—the promise of the Great Commission, which has undergirded Baptist preaching from that day forward.

In Richard Furman Baptists had found their unifier—one who elicited respect and trust among the churches the way Washington had done among the states. What was it about this man that made him one of the greatest Baptist preachers?

His Broad Experience

Furman was not just multitalented; he was multiexperienced. Born in New York State in 1755, he was still a baby when his family moved to South Carolina. Growing up in the High Hills of Santee, young Furman learned frontier life from experience. As a youth he became an expert hunter, often providing his family with venison from the ample forests around their home. He maintained that love for hunting and the outdoor life throughout his life. People who knew him were amazed that he seemed to have matured in every way by the time he was sixteen. Physically, he was broad-shouldered and strong, able to do a grown man's work long before his peers. From his father he learned surveying, which not only helped him as a young man on the frontier, but also years later in Charleston when he probably helped his church survey its property after the Revolutionary War.

From his father he also received his only formal education. Particularly in the sciences and mathematics, Wood Furman taught his son by experience. While surveying, the subject was mathematics, including practical trigonometry. While working on the farm, the subject was science in its various branches. At the fireside, young Furman expressed a voracious appetite for reading. He begged his parents to teach him how to read the Bible, and the prophet Elijah soon became one of his favorite heroes. "His flight was lofty from the first," said William T. Brantly years later when referring to Furman.[2] His home was well-stocked with good books, and he read with delight the works of Milton, Pope, and Swift.

---

[2]William T. Brantly, "The Saint's Repose in Death; a Sermon Delivered on the Death of the Rev. Richard Furman, D.D." (Charleston SC: W. Riley, 1825) 27.

For sheer pleasure he memorized long passages of poetry that pleased him. Even in later life he could still quote most of the first book of the *Iliad* and select parts of others. When he picked up his knowledge of Greek and Hebrew is not known, but it is certain that he constantly used the ancient languages in his study. In short, he had the kind of unfettered, inquisitive mind that only needed room to soar.

His parents, however, were not his only teachers. At an early age Furman became friends with Joseph Howard, the local physician, who taught him the rudiments of medicine. On the frontier, when the doctor was frequently called away to some remote place, young Furman was often summoned as the best available substitute. In this way he learned to use not only the common medical instruments, but also gained a wide knowledge of herbal medicines used in the backcountry. Years later, as a revered city pastor, he was constantly called upon to aid people physically as well as spiritually. In those days such a practice was not the least bit unethical, especially during the frequent yellow fever epidemics in Charleston, when his help was eagerly sought out by all. His method of treating patients with yellow fever was so successful that some of the local physicians claimed that he was unfairly aided by his power of prayer![3]

His religious experiences were also varied, which may have helped enable him to relate to all kinds of Baptists in years ahead. Historian Robert A. Baker, in writing of Furman's ordination, insightfully commented that the two men who conducted the service were symbolic of the broad religious experience of Furman.[4] Evan Pugh was a Regular Baptist, while Joseph Reese was a Separate Baptist. The preaching of Reese first turned Furman's serious attention to the Christian faith, and once he made a commitment to Christ, he could not be silent. The Baptist church at the High Hills of Santee licensed Furman to preach at the early age of seventeen. Two years later he was set apart as the pastor of the church. His preaching immediately attracted large crowds and secured for him many urgent invitations to preach in the sparsely populated outposts of South Carolina, parts of North Carolina, and even Georgia. During his evan-

---

[3]See the description of Furman's medical treatment of yellow fever in *A Biography of Richard Furman*, 123-25.

[4]Robert A. Baker and Paul J. Craven, Jr., *Adventure in Faith: The First Three Hundred Years of First Baptist Church, Charleston, South Carolina* (Nashville: Broadman Press, 1982) 188-89.

gelistic journeys, young Furman gained the confidence of Baptists all over the South, both Regular and Separate.

Soon his reputation began to spread to other parts of the country. In 1774, John Gano visited the High Hills as a representative of the Philadelphia Association. Furman and Gano were mutually impressed. About the same time young Furman began a lifelong friendship with Oliver Hart of Charleston. So Furman, at an early age, gained the respect and esteem of both Regular and Separate Baptists, and as Baker emphasized, he became the finest example of the union of the best qualities of both groups. It would take such a man to lead Baptists into unified efforts later in life.

His Gift of Persuasion

Furman's persuasion was not that of sublime eloquence or pure logic, although he exhibited both at times. Neither did he persuade from brute authoritarianism, far from it. From the very first time he stood before a congregation to speak, his power of persuasion came from a humble dependence on a greater power. At the age of sixteen, Furman stood for the first time before the church at the High Hills of Santee. He had just made his public profession of faith in Christ and was asking for baptism. The custom was for such a person to relate his experience of conversion to those present, but Furman had little to relate in words. All he knew was that he was a sinner willing to accept the free grace of the gospel. He had come to that decision not through a traumatic emotional upheaval, but quietly and thoughtfully as he had prayed in the woods.

Joseph Reese, the Separate Baptist preacher who had greatly influenced young Furman, gently asked him some questions about his experience. Others from the congregation added their questions, and soon Furman found himself speaking rather freely about his personal religious faith. To his surprise, he found that many present were deeply affected by his simple and humble testimony, among whom was his own mother, who then and there presented herself for baptism along with her son.[5]

From that day forward Furman's preaching could be identified as great, but not in the sense of causing people to be awed by some magnificent pulpit performance. Rather, Furman's preaching was great be-

---

[5]H. A. Tupper, ed., *Two Centuries of the First Baptist Church of South Carolina* (Baltimore: R. H. Woodward and Company, 1889) 131.

cause people could identify with what he said. They trusted him, even as a very young preacher. When he rose to speak, they knew that he would not smash them with overwhelming rantings and ravings, but would proclaim the truths of the gospel with transparent humility.

Such was Furman's gift of persuasion both in and out of the pulpit. One of the most profound commitments of his ministry was the movement to provide adequate education for young ministers. To raise funds for ministerial training was far from easy in those days. It took extraordinary gifts just to persuade some people that ministers should have any education past the rudiments of reading and writing. Yet at the age of thirty-six Furman convinced the Charleston Association to begin a fund for the gratuitous education of "pious young men" for the ministry. That was an achievement in itself, but an even greater achievement was his ability to use his powers of persuasion on another member of the committee that drafted the proposal, Silas Mercer, one of the staunchest opponents of ministerial education in the association. Furman met with Mercer at his home in the High Hills, and when the meeting was over, Mercer was wholeheartedly in favor of the fund. We do not know what young Furman said to the older man, but we do know that only one year after the fund was established, Mercer's son Jesse was among the first recipients of aid.[6] Furman's gift of persuasion in that case carried greater influence than he could have known, for Jesse Mercer's great ministry in the state of Georgia, as well as the influence of the university that bears his name, continues as a tribute to Richard Furman's extraordinary gift of persuasion.

Furman's powers of persuasion reached their height while he was pastor of the First Baptist Church of Charleston (1787-1825). He preached three times on Sunday to his own congregation and was frequently called away to churches outside of Charleston to preach during the week. When he arrived in Charleston in 1787, he was already known and loved by the people, for he had frequently supplied their pulpit after Oliver Hart had left. Thus he entered Charleston with a great reservoir of good will and soon became the most prominent Baptist minister in the South.

---

[6]Wood Furman, *A History of the Charleston Association of Churches in the State of South Carolina* (Charleston: J. Hoff, 1811) 49.

In civic life, as well as in the church, his voice of persuasion was heard gladly. In 1790 he was asked to be a member of South Carolina's constitutional convention. He took an active part in the deliberations, but he soon returned to his pulpit with renewed commitment to the preaching task.

His greatest moment, however, the moment he seemed especially prepared to meet, was his call to lead Baptists in America as the first president of the Triennial Convention. Unanimously elected on the first day of the Convention in May 1817, he was asked to preach the convention sermon on the first night. Without enough time to write the sermon before preaching it, he depended upon some sketchy notes, which he evidently prepared the afternoon before. He preached a powerful sermon on the text "Lo, I am with you alway, even to the end of the world." His notes indicate a careful analysis of the text and its relation to their historic meeting. He closed with a resounding challenge.

> Let therefore all the considerations we have urged from the word of God on this sublime subject be duly regarded, that they may concentrate their whole force upon the heart, and give an impulse to action, which through the grace of the Redeemer no difficulties can retard, no oppositions withstand. Let the wise and good employ their counsels; the minister of Christ, who is qualified for the sacred service, offer himself for the work; the man of wealth and generosity, who values the glory of Immanuel and the salvation of souls more than gold, bring of his treasure in proportion as God has bestowed on him; yea, let all, even the pious widow bring the mite that can be spared; and let all who fear and love God, unite in the prayer of faith before the throne of Grace; and unceasingly say, "Thy Kingdom come." And O! let it never be forgotten, that the Son of God hath said: "Lo, I am with you alway, even to the end of the world." Amen and Amen.[7]

His Pulpit Presence

Although it is impossible to recover it from Furman's writings, all who heard him testified that he had a certain aura when he preached that virtually demanded the listener's utmost attention. William B. Johnson, president of both the Triennial Convention and the Southern Baptist Convention, said that Furman "seemed to reign over them with irresist-

---

[7]His sermon notes may be found in Albert L. Vail, *The Morning Hour of American Baptist Missions* (Philadelphia: American Baptist Publication Society, 1907) 389-93.

ible influence."[8] Like his predecessor Oliver Hart, Richard Furman wore a pulpit gown on Sunday. His manner was never light or humorous, but at the same time he did not impress people as gruff or judgmental. Always his kindness and humility combined with the utmost seriousness of demeanor.

His presence added luster to the gospel. The very fact that it was Furman who preached it made it more convincing. According to Johnson, whenever Richard Furman presided over any ecclesiastical body, "his very appearance preserved order." Johnson went on to describe his pulpit presence:

> As a *Minister of Jesus Christ,* the *tout ensemble* of Dr. Furman was more solemn and imposing than that of any other man whom I have ever beheld. When *he* arose to speak in Church-meeting, Association, Convention, or any other assembly, all eyes were turned upon him, with profound attention, and reverential awe. In the services of the sacred desk, such was the appropriate solemnity of his manner, that the audience *felt* themselves to be in the presence of a man of God, who had "studied to show himself approved unto God, a workman that needed not to be ashamed, rightly dividing the word of truth."[9]

Such descriptions were evidently not just reverent exaggerations. Those who knew him actually had a hard time putting into words that special pulpit presence he always seemed to possess. When he died in 1825, Baptists all over the country, but especially those in South Carolina, wondered who could fill so large a scope and catch the falling mantle from one who had served them for so long. William T. Brantly, in trying to describe Furman's preaching, said that "his lips appeared to be touched with hallowed fire whilst he unfolded the privileges of that communion with God."[10]

Of course, no one could wear the mantle just as Furman did. The Baptist denomination has seen very few leaders of the stature of Richard Furman. He was uniquely gifted and devoted, and he was at his height of maturity when Baptists needed him most. But the story of Baptist preaching does not end with Richard Furman. In his own day, there were

---

[8]In William B. Sprague, ed., *Annals of the American Pulpit* (New York: Robert Carter and Brothers, 1860) 6:164.

[9]Ibid.

[10]Brantly, "The Saint's Repose in Death," 40.

others who carried on the great tradition of preaching with both intellectual rigor and evangelistic warmth.

LISTEN TO THE RHYTHM

The preaching of Richard Furman did indeed stand out above all others during the first quarter of the nineteenth century, and the echoes of his voice could still be heard for many years after his death in 1825. But to listen to Baptist preaching during that era is to hear a great harmony of well-trained voices which, for a period of about thirty years, rang true with hardly a discordant note. Together they preached. Their voices were heard from all parts of the country, as if directed by the Master under the impulse of missions. The formation of the General Convention of the Baptist Denomination in the United States for Foreign Missions (the official title for the Triennial Convention) was merely the tangible by-product of a general spirit that pervaded Baptist leaders. The gospel had to be preached to every creature, they believed, and nothing could hinder that great task.

John Mason Peck established a home mission station in St. Louis, Missouri, that became the prototype for Baptist home missions. The work of Adoniram Judson in Burma, made more visible by the ubiquitous presence of Luther Rice in every Baptist stronghold in America, inspired Baptists to believe that world conversion to Christianity really could take place if only they preached, prayed, gave, and worked hard enough. Thus the preaching of the era was optimistic, evangelistic, and above all, missions oriented. Theological and organizational differences, for a time, receded into the background. All eyes were on the Master, and all were caught up in the rhythm of mission preaching.

Along with the tidal wave of support for missions came a strong undercurrent of support for a better educated ministry. The obvious fact was that the greatest preaching undergirding missions was not primarily the emotional exhortations of many Separate Baptists on the frontier. Indeed, they seemed so bent upon maintaining total independence that they rarely cooperated in any joint venture with other Baptist churches. The impulse for Baptist missions came from the expository sermons of Regular Baptists who were better educated and less afraid of cooperation with others. They knew from experience that some things were done better together, and missions was one of them. They also proved from the outset that evangelistic and strongly biblical preaching grew concurrently with an educated ministry. Inspired by Richard Furman's sermon at the second meeting of the Triennial Convention in 1817, Baptists began an unprecedented expansion of church-supported schools and colleges.

One of the most loved and respected Baptist preachers to lead the march under the banner of missions and education was William Staughton.

William Staughton:
Carey's Visible Link in America

Among that handful of daring Baptists who met in Kettering to form the Foreign Mission Society in England in 1792 was a young student from Bristol Academy. Already he had shone as the leading preacher in the college, and English Baptists were expecting great leadership from him in the future. He met that night with Carey, Fuller, Ryland, Pearce, and the others in what would become one of the most significant meetings in the history of the Baptist denomination. When at the end of the meeting the small group pledged themselves to form the Foreign Mission Society, young William Staughton emptied his pockets of all the money he had—half a guinea. Yet in later years Staughton observed that the giving of that mite was the greatest achievement of his life.[11]

English Baptists were not to keep the promising young preacher. His eyes were set on America. Even the offer of the prestigious Northampton Church could not keep him from fulfilling his dream. When English Baptists received an urgent request from Richard Furman to send a young minister to serve the newly formed church at Georgetown, South Carolina, Staughton knew his time had come. His ship arrived in the Charleston harbor in the fall of 1793.

Staughton's preaching was an immediate success. Furman became his staunch ally and introduced him to his many friends within South Carolina. Staughton's stay in the South was only seventeen months long, but his contact with Furman and their later correspondence proved to be a source of great strength to the work of the Baptists for missions. Staughton moved to New York to seek a cooler climate, but no sooner had he arrived than he contracted the dreaded yellow fever. After a slow recovery he resumed his search for a new home. He preached for a short

---

[11]S. W. Lynd, *Memoir of the Rev. William Staughton, D.D.* (Boston: Lincoln, Edmands, and Company, 1834) 173.

time in New Jersey, and his reputation soon caught the attention of the First Baptist Church of Philadelphia. He accepted the pastoral charge of the church in Philadelphia in 1805, and there he began a long and influential ministry in one of the great centers of Baptist life. His ministry took him from the First Baptist Church to the Sansom Street Baptist Church in the same city, and late in life he accepted the presidency of the newly formed Columbian College in Washington (now George Washington University).

When Staughton moved to Philadelphia, the First Baptist Church had dwindled to a handful of faithful members trying to keep the church doors open. The venerable church had seen better days, and the members were looking for someone to lead them to the level of vibrancy that some could remember from long days before. Soon after Staughton arrived, a great change began to take place in the old church. Crowds came to hear the new preacher, and they kept coming. Soon the very aisles of the building were crowded. Sometimes he preached four sermons on a Sunday, beginning at daybreak when he preached for the sailors near the wharf in an outdoor service that at times attracted a thousand persons.

Staughton's preaching brought Philadelphia to attention. He was learned, evangelistic, enthusiastic, and eminently biblical. He attracted people of every class of society and every level of learning. While his preaching ministry was proving to be superlative, his teaching ministry undergirded all he did. He taught in two girls' schools and conducted an informal seminary in his own home through the years for scores of young preachers who reflected the comment made by one of his students: "To say that his pupils respected him, is cold—they loved him as a father." The same former student reminisced on his days under Staughton's tutelage.

> The writer of this sketch can never forget the earnestness and solemnity with which he urged two points upon the attention of the class. . . . The first was, to pursue a condescending course to those brethren in the ministry who had not received the advantages of education. . . . The second was, to make Christ and him crucified the substance of all our preaching. It pained his heart, to hear a discourse, however excellent as to style and delivery, which was not sanctified with the blood of the Saviour. Christ was his theme, the burden of all his pulpit exhibitions.[12]

---

[12]Ibid., 161.

That same student could very well have added a third point to his memory, for Staughton also placed great stress on meticulous preparation for preaching. He did not practice himself or require of his students the writing of a manuscript for each sermon. But they were nevertheless prepared. "Never be satisfied with the offspring of a moment," he told them. Such slipshod sermons, he declared, were "like the ephemerae of the natural world" and could be expected to be "short-lived and useless."[13]

An ample supply of Staughton's published sermons catches the spirit of great preaching and shows beyond a doubt that he practiced what he taught. He thought in pictures, and more than any Baptist preacher of his age he used illustrations masterfully. His metaphors and similes took flight and rarely failed to hit the intended target. In his address at the opening of Columbia College, he said that "Learning, without virtue, is a torch in the hand of a lunatic."[14] He was devoted to the education of Baptist ministers. He had little good to say for those who gloried in their ignorance, calling such nonsense "a sleeping and pestilential morass."[15] He nevertheless paid tribute to the hundreds of humble and uneducated preachers who had been called and found faithful. Those, he believed, were the very ones who enthusiastically encouraged the establishment of theological schools.

In speaking of Jesus, Staughton once said that from his lips, "nothing frivolous ever fell."[16] Without knowing it, Staughton was surely describing his own preaching. His sermons were a combination of doctrine, experience, practical advice, and pastoral encouragement. Underlying all his preaching was an evangelistic message that sometimes overpowered all other considerations. Even then his words were well chosen and thoughtful.

Without a translation from the kingdom of darkness, into the kingdom of

---

[13]Ibid., 160.

[14]Staughton, "Address Delivered at the Opening of the Columbia College . . . January 9, 1822," *The Latter Day Luminary* 3 (March 1822): 79.

[15]Ibid., 3 (April 1822):105.

[16]Staughton, "The Importance of an Early and Habitual Preparedness for Death" (Philadelphia: John Bioren, 1813) 5.

God's dear son; you have no reason to expect a translation from this earth, to the temple of Jehovah, in heaven.[17]

As a leader in the movement to organize societies to support missionaries abroad and at home, Staughton was the Andrew Fuller of America. His sermons in support of missions can only be described as eloquent. He thought in world terms and acted on his dreams. At the formation of the Triennial Convention, Staughton stood with Furman as one of the most respected leaders present, and accordingly was elected corresponding secretary of the infant organization. He was a frequent correspondent with Carey and his associates in India. In his own country, he constantly preached in support of the mission movement. For Staughton, any congregation had potential missionaries, and his urgent message was that "the world is your theatre of action."[18]

Staughton was an esteemed leader in the Baptist denomination, but he was equally respected within the larger sphere of all Christian churches. His catholicism illuminated his understanding of the faith and made him appeal to a much larger audience than his own church. While helping a friend dedicate a new Baptist meetinghouse in New Jersey, he emphasized that the new building was built by and for the Baptists, but he immediately added this qualification:

> I know I am but adding a voice to the thoughts of my brother, through whose ministrations this house has been raised, and of the members of the church in general; when I give a cordial welcome to every preacher of Jesus to assist in his holy services.[19]

He was secure enough in his own Baptist beliefs to be gracious to those of different persuasions. Toleration of others was not his purpose; rather, he determined to love those who differed from him. He was convinced that the points on which Christians disagreed compared with those on which all agreed "bear no greater proportion to each other, than does the trembling lustre of a star to the meridian blaze of the summer sun."[20]

---

[17]Ibid., 21.

[18]Staughton, "Missionary Encouragement" (Philadelphia: Stephen C. Ustick, 1798) 12.

[19]Staughton, "Divine Condescension, and the Pleasures of Religious Worship" (Burlington NJ: Stephen C. Ustick, 1804) 10.

[20]Ibid.

As a result, Staughton earned universal respect. When Thomas Jefferson and John Adams died on the Fourth of July 1826—the very day on which America celebrated the fiftieth anniversary of her independence—a number of the citizens of Washington requested that William Staughton preach a memorial sermon in the Capitol building. His eloquent discourse on that day can hardly be surpassed by any Baptist sermon preached in the nineteenth century. It was the culmination of genuine patriotism and an even deeper Christian faith. The whole country was almost visibly shaken. Staughton took his text from 2 Samuel 1:23: ' Lovely and pleasant were they in their lives—in their death they were not divided; they were swifter than eagles, they were stronger than lions." With a simplicity that belied his brilliance, Staughton honored the lives of Jefferson and Adams and gently led his hearers to remember that, as he so picturesquely said it, "the rock is unshaken, though the aspen tremble on its side."[21] Although leaders, no matter how great, must fall and die, "the Lord God omnipotent reigneth." He concluded his sermon with a reminder that life can be compared to walking on a bridge that is full of trap doors that lie concealed. "Each step," he said, "is the step of jeopardy." Thus it is wise for every person to be "well prepared for the final plunge."[22]

Staughton's "final plunge" took place on a December day in 1829. He was on his way to Kentucky to become the first president of Georgetown College, but death interrupted his journey. The events of Staughton's life are well established in the annals of Baptist denominational life. But what about the spirit of the man? His commitment to preaching an understandable gospel, true to the Scriptures and profound; his catholicity of spirit coupled with a worldwide view of the faith; his living imagination that elicited stunning word pictures—these qualities play a central part in the Baptist preaching heritage and endure.

Thomas Baldwin:
Just a Country Preacher

The city of Boston never could manage to get the country out of Thomas Baldwin. Raised in what was then the wilds of New Hampshire,

---

[21]Staughton, "Sermon, Delivered in the Capitol of the United States; on Lord's Day, July 16, 1826; at the Request of the Citizens of Washington, on the Death of Mr. Jefferson and Mr. Adams" (Washington: Published at the Columbian Office, 1826) 11.

[22]Ibid., 32.

he was straightforward, unadorned, direct, and powerful until the day he died. But evidently Boston liked that kind of preaching. When the Second Baptist Church of Boston heard of this country evangelist in 1790, he was promptly asked to visit the city church for a series of several Sundays. Immediately a revival commenced in the church, which was well in progress when he accepted the unanimous invitation to settle as its pastor. After his first year he could look out at his congregation and see seventy new members who had joined the church since he had come, as well as many hundreds of people who regularly came to hear his preaching.

At the end of seven years of his ministry, so many thronged to hear him that the sanctuary had to be enlarged. Yet hardly had the renovation been completed than it too was full, with "every aisle crowded like a solid column."[23] Fourteen years later, when Baldwin was preaching the first sermon in an entirely new meetinghouse, which was built in 1810, he was astonished at the changes that had taken place. Nearly twice the number of members who had greeted his arrival in Boston had left to form other churches or had died, and yet he was leading a church of over four times its original size. He was to remain the pastor of the church for another fifteen years, and the growth would continue unabated until his death.

Baldwin became one of the three most prominent leaders of the Baptist denomination, the others being Furman and Staughton. He was as naturally elected secretary of the Triennial Convention as Furman was chosen president and Staughton was chosen corresponding secretary. Baldwin's election made the Convention leadership geographically balanced.

But there was more to his election than merely an attempt to maintain a geographical balance. Baldwin was a powerful preacher. The Baptists respected him, not because his sermons were smooth and eloquent with all the imagination and education of a Staughton. No, Baldwin's preaching never lost the aroma of the northern forests. He published more sermons than any other Baptist in the first half of the nineteenth century, and they all reveal a clear and forcible style that reflects a logical mind and a deep piety.

---

[23]Thomas Baldwin, "A Discourse, Delivered January 1, 1811, at the Opening of the New Meeting-House Belonging to the Second Baptist Church and Society in Boston" (Boston: Lincoln and Edmands, 1811) 30.

That logical mind may have stemmed from his original intention to become an attorney. At an early age he was elected to the New Hampshire legislature. He had married in 1775 and was studying law while he became one of the bright young leaders of the state. The whole world seemed to be in his pocket. Everything was going his way, until the autumn of 1777, when his firstborn child suddenly died at the age of six months. For the first time in his life he stood face-to-face with an event beyond his control. Neither his powerful intellect nor his magnetic personality could change the fact of death. His mind began to move beyond the horizon of this present life, and for the first time he began to pray. It was not, however, until three years later that he made public his new faith and was baptized by Elisha Ransom, the pastor of the Baptist church in Woodstock, Vermont.

Baldwin's preaching followed immediately on the heels of his baptism. He became a traveling evangelist throughout the New England states, and his reputation as a preacher excelled his reputation as a politician. Three churches issued unanimous calls for him to settle as pastor, but he chose the Second Baptist Church of Boston.

His legal training, along with the death of his child and subsequent rural preaching experiences, influenced his preaching in the city. He entered Boston at a time when Christology—the nature of Jesus—was the main issue of debate. Samuel Stillman was ending his brilliant ministry at the First Baptist Church, and Baldwin became his staunch friend and ally. The god of Reason was fast becoming the object of worship for those who considered themselves sophisticated. Baldwin, although lacking the extensive formal education of some, was mentally equipped to join the debate.

The very foundation of his approach to the Christian faith can be found in a statement from one of his sermons.

> Reason's feeble lamp can light us no farther than the tomb. Here it expires, and leaves us to pursue our wayward voyage on the vast ocean of eternity, without either chart or compass, and totally ignorant of our future destination. . . . All inquiry proves ineffectual, until we repair to divine revelation.[24]

He met the worship of reason with the outright rejection of reason's suf-

---

[24]Baldwin, "The Supreme Deity of Christ Illustrated" (Boston: Lincoln and Edmands, 1812) 3.

ficiency. He knew from early experience that reason could not travel past the tomb. Thus, he preached sermons drawn directly from the Scriptures and applied to personal experiences. Every sermon was built around the atonement of Christ. His counsel to one young minister was that "nothing can satisfy their souls, but the uncorrupted doctrine of the Cross."[25]

Baldwin's rural experiences also made him sensitive to the need for home missions. It was Baldwin who, more than anyone else, urged the Baptist denomination to include home missions as part of the task of the Triennial Convention. In the second meeting of the Convention in 1817, Baldwin preached to the delegates:

> Lift up your eyes and look along the fertile banks of the majestic Mississippi. . . . What immense fields, now white already to the harvest, meet the eye. May the Lord send faithful labourers unto them all.[26]

The Convention heeded his call and added home missions to its formal agenda. John Mason Peck and James F. Welch were appointed as the first home missionaries.

Thomas Baldwin may be considered the Northern counterpart to Richard Furman in the South. In many ways they were similar. Both began to preach in rural areas, becoming widely known for their ability. Both accepted a major city pastorate in the chief city of their region. Both turned away from the practice of law to preach the gospel. Both sat as delegates to the constitutional conventions of their states. Both were eminent in their ministry and elected to high office by their denomination. Both died in the month of August, only one year apart.

Francis Wayland, president of Brown University and a close friend of Baldwin, summed up Baldwin's ministry by saying that "he had read little; he had seen little; but God had given him the ability to think."[27] Baldwin, Staughton, and Furman were the leading preachers during the only time in American history when the Baptists were genuinely united. When

---

[25]Baldwin, "A Sermon, Delivered . . . at the Installation of the Rev. John Peak" (Boston: E. Lincoln, 1802) 20.

[26]Baldwin, "Missionary Exertions Encouraged" (Boston: Lincoln and Edmands, 1817) 8.

[27]Francis Wayland, in William B. Sprague, *Annals of the American Pulpit,* 213.

their voices were silenced, it was as if the gates were thrown open for the controversies that eventually divided the denomination North and South.

LISTEN TO THE DISCORD

Furman, Baldwin, and Staughton—the leading Baptist preachers in the early part of the nineteenth century—died in the years 1825, 1826, and 1829, respectively. While they led the denomination, there was a pleasing rhythm to Baptist preaching. An overriding harmony kept any discordant notes from becoming dominant. What influence they could have exerted in calming the tensions that developed after their deaths is hard to say. But the fact remains that their deaths almost precisely corresponded with the outbreak of several severe controversies among the Baptists.

Alexander Campbell, for example, had been promoting his views of baptismal regeneration among the Baptists since the 1820s, but it was not until 1832 that he, along with Barton W. Stone and others, founded the Disciples of Christ and wreaked havoc among hundreds of Baptist churches west of the Alleghenies. Other preachers among the Baptists brought up the old hyper-Calvinist arguments against any organized mission work. They considered it blasphemy to try to convert those whom God had not chosen. One of these was Daniel Parker of Illinois, the leader of the Two-Seed-in-the-Spirit Predestinarian Baptists. In Kentucky were Wilson Thompson and John Taylor, who preached against the entire missionary enterprise as threatening to Baptist democracy. In North Carolina it was Joshua Lawrence, who gathered followers from several Southern states. All of these were preaching against missions before 1825, but their greatest influence came only after the deaths of Furman, Staughton, and Baldwin. The result was severe in some places. The entire Baltimore Association defected to the antimission forces. Large sections of the country found that mission support had dropped drastically. Baptists had become divided over the one thing that had united them.

All of the discord, however, was secondary to the overpowering sectionalism that began to divide the country over the issue of slavery. The story has been told repeatedly, and to cover it in any detail here would be beyond the scope of this work.[28] With regard to Baptist preaching, however, it is important to know that although there were harsh words spoken from pulpits both North and South, there was also much ambivalence. Even some of the most ardent abolitionists knew and loved many of their counterparts in the South. The same is true of many of the Southern preachers, who had hosts of Northern friends. The issue of slavery wrenched the finest preachers among the Baptists to the depths, and the resulting schism of the denomination was the cause of great grief. When William B. Johnson proposed the formation of the Southern Baptist Convention in May 1845, he hoped that "our separation will be attended with no sharpness of contention, with no bitterness of spirit."[29] His hopes may not have been fully met, but there were some great preachers on both sides of the issue who carried forward the best tradition of Baptist preaching. The gracious spirits of Francis Wayland and Richard Fuller provide supreme examples of such preaching.

Francis Wayland

The only person who did not know that Francis Wayland was a great preacher was Francis Wayland. Most of his life had been spent as president of Brown University, where he was internationally recognized as a leader in progressive education. He thought of himself primarily as an educator, a scholar, and an administrator and bemoaned the supposed fact that he was not a great preacher. To his sister he wrote, "God will honor the preaching of the Cross. O that I knew how to preach it, so that he would bless it!"[30] Yet at the end of his life, those who had known him kept remarking on his preaching and the influence he had exerted on them through his sermons.

As the president of Brown University from 1827 until 1855, he was far more than an administrator and fundraiser. He was more like a pastor

---

[28]See Robert A. Baker, *Relations Between Northern and Southern Baptists* (Fort Worth: Marvin D. Evans Printing Company, 1954). For more concise treatments of sectionalism, see Robert A. Baker, *The Southern Baptist Convention and Its People, 1607-1972* (Nashville: Broadman Press, 1974) 153-59, and Robert G. Torbet, *A History of the Baptists* (Valley Forge: The Judson Press, 1963) 282-97.

[29]See Baker, *The Southern Baptist Convention,* 165.

[30]Francis Wayland and H. L. Wayland, *A Memoir of the Life and Labors of Francis Wayland, D.D., LL.D., Late President of Brown University* (New York: Sheldon and Company, 1867) 2:211.

to his students and faculty than anything else. His weekly chapel sermons became events in the life of the university. In those moments he shed all his academic and philosophical language and spoke from the heart. Twenty-one of those university sermons were published in 1849, and they comprise some of the most practical and moving discourses of the nineteenth century.[31] A prominent New England attorney looked back over his years as one of Wayland's students and commented that if he were to recount the most remarkable events in his former teacher's life, he would not dwell upon any of the great philosophical works by which he was known all over the world. Rather, it was Wayland's preaching that exerted the most influence on the remarkable number of students who came under his care during twenty-eight years at Brown.[32]

Perhaps his poor opinion of his own preaching came from his first pastorate. At the age of twenty-five he was called to become pastor of the First Baptist Church of Boston with a vote of fifteen to ten from the membership. In those days "society" (nonmembers who attended the church) also voted. The result was even less encouraging: the society favored him with a seventeen to fifteen vote. From these numbers it is easy to see how the venerable church had declined since the death of Samuel Stillman. It is not as easy to see how young Wayland had the courage to enter a church so divided over his coming. But enter it he did, and for five years he nearly worked himself to death.

His preaching during those years was not, in his opinion, very good. When anyone criticized his preaching, he was the first to agree. He did not like his own sermons—why should others? For the few who were dissatisfied, he proposed that the church should provide carriages to take them to hear some other preacher. No one took him up on his offer.

He was single in those days, and he lived in the home of Thomas Baldwin, pastor of the Second Baptist Church, then at his full power and influence. Wayland did not fail to learn from his elder colleague, just as Baldwin had learned from Stillman a generation earlier. Wayland labored over his sermons, and each Sunday his tall, lean, angular, ungraceful body trembled into the pulpit to deliver what he believed to be the word of God

---

[31] Francis Wayland, *University Sermons* (Boston: Gould, Kendall, and Lincoln, 1849).

[32] James O. Murray, *Francis Wayland* (Boston: Houghton, Mifflin and Company, 1891) 239.

for that day. He was so nervous that he had to keep his hands in his pockets to keep them from visibly shaking. After he had been in Boston for less than a year he wrote to his sister with a note of surprise: "They pay good attention to preaching—very rarely get asleep. I do not know that I have seen one asleep for some months."[33]

No one seemed to have the courtesy to let Wayland in on the secret: he was developing into a great preacher. The first clue he himself recognized came in 1823. The twenty-seven-year-old pastor was invited to preach the annual sermon before the Boston Foreign Mission Society. He chose as his subject "The Moral Dignity of the Missionary Enterprise." The evening came, rainy and chill. Only a few of the faithful came out to hear him. The sanctuary was so cold that he had to wear his overcoat during the whole service. Wayland preached his sermon and went home depressed. The next morning he went to the home of a friend, threw himself onto a sofa in depression and said, "It was a complete failure. It fell perfectly dead." He had no idea that the sermon he had called a failure would mark an era in the history of the missionary enterprise in America.

To Wayland's chagrin, the Foreign Mission Society requested that the sermon be published. He reluctantly agreed, sure that he would be embarrassed by the public consumption of his "failure." To his shock, the first edition, which came out in December, was almost immediately exhausted. Soon another cheaper edition came from the press, and it was followed by other editions. A year later it was printed in England and passed through several editions. Later it was translated into German. The result was immediate acclaim for Francis Wayland as one of the great young preachers among the Baptists. When Robert Hall read it in England he commented that "the author of that sermon will be heard of again."[34] In the South, J. B. Jeter of Richmond had to get up and walk the floor while the sermon was being read, declaring that he could not sit still while listening to it.

Some of the passages from that sermon still leap from the page and cause one to pace the floor. Try to imagine what his voice must have sounded like on that rainy night in 1823.

---

[33]Wayland and Wayland, *Memoir,* 1:136.

[34]Ibid., 1:167.

Our object will not have been accomplished till the tomahawk shall be buried forever, and the tree of peace spread its broad branches from the Atlantick to the Pacifick; until a thousand smiling villages shall be reflected from the waves of the Missouri, and the distant valleys of the West echo with the song of the reaper; till the wilderness and the solitary place shall have been glad for us, and the desert has rejoiced and blossomed as the rose.

Our labours are not to cease, until the last slave-ship shall have visited the coast of Africa, and, the nations of Europe and America having long since redressed her aggravated wrongs, Ethiopia, from the Mediterranean to the Cape, shall have stretched forth her hand unto God.[35]

All the fame produced a change in Wayland. He suddenly discovered that he had the ear of the public. Perhaps even more important, he gained confidence in his own preaching, and he threw himself even more devotedly into the work of the pastorate.

The local church, however, was not to be the sphere of his life work. At the age of thirty-one he became the president of Brown University, then declining in students, money, and morale. Wayland's virtual reconstruction of Brown and his inspiration toward more progressive education in all of America is a story best told elsewhere. His preaching, however, pervaded all of his educational work. Never once did he forsake his calling as a preacher of the gospel. Since his influence on young preachers was multiplied by his new position, it is not outside the boundary of reality to say that no Baptist in the North influenced preaching in his denomination more than Francis Wayland.

The most distinctive element of Wayland's preaching was his total dependence upon the Scriptures to provide the structure of his sermons. He allowed his text to guide his preaching. If he found certain truths in the Bible that were in apparent conflict, he never tried to reconcile them. Rather, he preached them both with equal conviction and left it to the hearer to reconcile them.

Simplicity marked his sermons whether they were preached before the university or the local reform school. He was convinced that academic language in the pulpit was utterly opposed to the gospel. "The minister of the gospel," he said in one of his sermons, 'is not to preach that the ten shall applaud him, while the ninety shall wonder at what they

---

[35]Francis Wayland, "The Moral Dignity of the Missionary Enterprise," 3d edition (Boston: James Loring, 1824) 11.

do not understand."³⁶ He not only maintained a beautiful simplicity in his own sermons, but also insisted upon simplicity from his students. "Say what you mean in language that the commonest mind will not fail to understand it," he urged.

Whenever he listened to the preaching of someone else, he longed for life, fire, zeal, for the truths of the Bible to be enforced in plain and simple language. As he grew older, he was less hesitant to offer charitable criticism to other preachers, many of whom had been his students. The only time he approached harshness in his criticism was when he concluded that a sermon was cold and lifeless, void of warmth and earnestness. The testimony of one such preacher was enough to warn others who might have Wayland as a visitor on a Sunday morning. On one occasion, he took the hand of the preacher and, drawing him aside after the service, said very quietly,

> My son, I have been pained and grieved with your preaching here today. It has been evident to my mind that you have been pleased and proud over your finely-wrought and finished discourse. Those sermons were, as sermons, very creditable to your ability as a preacher, but very discreditable to you as an ambassador of Christ. There was too much learning and too little of Christ in them. Go home, my son, and burn them up, and on your knees weep over your delinquency.³⁷

Yet he offered such criticisms with such a tenderness and concern that he did not make enemies of the preachers.

Along with his emphasis upon the Scriptures and his simplicity, humility undergirded all his preaching. Maintaining such an attitude was a difficult task in a period when the question of slavery was fast spiraling toward civil war. During this time, Baptists looked to Wayland not only for content, but also for tone. That is to say, he exerted a great influence upon the moral attitude of Northern Baptists toward their Southern counterparts. Wayland never visited the South, but he knew Southern Baptist preachers, and loved them. He grieved over the division of the Baptists in 1845, and as tensions escalated toward war, Francis Wayland's voice called for compassion and understanding. His moderate stand was based purely on his own recognition that the people of the North were

---

³⁶Francis Wayland, "Christian Worship," in *Sermons to the Churches* (New York: Sheldon, Blakeman, and Company, 1858), 138.

³⁷Wayland and Wayland, *Memoir,* 2:323.

far from guiltless. To his sister he wrote, "There has been, I think, too much confessing other people's sins, and not enough confessing our own."[38]

Slavery, he believed, was madness; but a greater madness was the slaughter of brothers. "[G]reater madness never existed," he sadly wrote to his son.[39] Thus, in the midst of the emotional extravagance of his era, Wayland dared to speak for moderation. To a newspaper friend he urged that "hard names" not be used to refer to fellow citizens in the South. "Seek to be a peace-maker," he said. "The country is very much agitated. . . . Let us strive to allay party violence and to calm the passions of men."[40] His words, of course, were not heeded. But his spirit lives on among those gracious souls who have the humility to see that they are not all right, just as others are not all wrong.

Perhaps the greatest monument to his humble spirit lies in a published series of letters between Wayland and Richard Fuller. The letters were published in 1856 and demonstrate the degree to which two Christian ministers of differing views can disagree strongly, yet possess a graciousness and genuine affection that must have startled the public. "[S]hould I utter a word that would tend needlessly to wound the feelings of my Southern brethren, there is not one of them that will be as deeply pained as myself," wrote Wayland in the first letter.[41] He followed with a series of eight letters in which he brilliantly answered every instance in which Southerners appealed to the Scriptures in defense of slavery.

Wayland's death came in 1865, just as the slaughter of his fellow citizens came to an end. To his dying day he was never convinced that he could preach well, but the generations who were inspired by his preaching and who learned from his sermons how to preach disagreed with his opinion of his own ability.

Richard Fuller

Richard Fuller was eight years younger than Francis Wayland, but their ministries spanned the same turbulent years. No two people could

---

[38]Ibid., 2:266.

[39]Ibid., 2:263.

[40]Ibid., 1:402.

[41]Richard Fuller and Francis Wayland, *Domestic Slavery Considered as a Scriptural Institution* (New York: Sheldon, Lamport and Blakeman, 1856) 15.

offer a more interesting contrast. Whereas Wayland was shy and studious, trembling into the pulpit in his early days, Fuller virtually wore the task of preaching like a well-tailored suit. Whereas Wayland was born in New York and spent most of his life in Rhode Island, Fuller was a son of Beaufort, South Carolina, one of the most Southern of all Southern towns. Whereas Wayland abhorred slavery from a distance, Fuller inherited several hundred slaves and had to deal with the moral implications from firsthand experience. Whereas Wayland was a polite and courteous child from birth, Fuller was rambunctious and boisterous, taming his temper at times with the greatest of effort.

When Fuller was a teenager, he stepped out onto the back porch of his family's plantation home in Beaufort and saw a vulture perched on the chimney of a neighboring house. The temptation was irresistible. Although it was a long shot over two intervening lots, Fuller took aim and fired. The wounded buzzard disappeared down the chimney. An aged lady, who was ill in her room below, was horrified at the grizzly, fluttering specter coming down her chimney in a cloud of soot and dust. She thought some evil spirit was about to pounce upon her! Fuller was not allowed to forget his famous buzzard shot.[42]

Such was the rambunctious teenager who, at the age of sixteen, left his Southern magnolias and entered Harvard College as a freshman. By the age of twenty-one he had received his Harvard degree and was settled in Beaufort as a promising young attorney. Gifted, handsome, wealthy, he had a great future as a trial lawyer. He was busily climbing the ladder of success when, in the winter of 1831-1832, the Reverend Daniel Baker passed through Beaufort to lead one of the most remarkable revivals anyone could remember. The meetings were held alternately in the Episcopal and the Baptist church, and among the converts were Richard Fuller and his friend Stephen Elliott. Fuller became one of the greatest leaders among the Baptists, and Elliott became the Episcopal bishop of Georgia. "My heart and soul were running over with joy and praise,"[43] said Fuller, and he knew he had to preach.

In 1832 he was ordained and became pastor of the Baptist church in Beaufort. For fifteen years he served that church, composed of both

---

[42]J. H. Cuthbert, *Life of Richard Fuller* (New York: Sheldon and Company, 1879) 32.
[43]Ibid., 69.

slaves and whites. It was there that he developed a style of preaching that one hearer characterized as "logic on fire."[44] His legal training combined with his emotions and filled the church each Sunday. He had a natural eloquence that appealed to the least educated slave as well as to the cultured planter. He developed a power of imagination that could couch an age-old truth in such unexpected language that people never forgot it. Said one who had gone to hear Fuller for the sole purpose of criticizing his sermon, ". . . the man had not been preaching five minutes before I was completely in his power, and he did with me what he pleased."[45]

Such preaching could not go unnoticed. After fifteen years as pastor of the Beaufort church, Fuller turned his face towards Baltimore. He spent the rest of his life—including the war years—as an esteemed Baptist pastor and preacher in Baltimore. At the First Baptist Church, and later at the Eutaw Place Baptist Church, Fuller became a nationally renowned preacher. Even in the North, where abolitionist sentiments were running high before the war, Fuller was invited to preach at Madison University. Some in the village, who had not heard him, protested against a Southern preacher. Word reached Fuller, who shrugged it off by saying that they too needed the gospel. He preached, and after the sermon, the crowd actually tried to carry him to his guest house on their shoulders. The president of the university commented, "Since then the name of Dr. Fuller has been a household word in Hamilton and Madison University."[46]

At the heart of his preaching was Jesus Christ.

> We know that where Christ crucified is not preached, nothing is done for eternity. Much there may be of sublimity and beauty in the orations of the pulpit, but if Christ crucified be not there—while the imagination may be entertained—all will be to the soul only the beauty of frost, and the sublimity of the desert.[47]

That quotation came from the sermon Fuller preached at the Triennial Convention in 1844, a year before the Southern Baptist Convention was

---

[44]Ibid., 133.

[45]Ibid., 136.

[46]Ibid., 134.

[47]Richard Fuller, "The Cross," in *Sermons* (New York: Sheldon and Company, 1860) 345.

formed. The divisiveness in the Convention over the issue of slavery could be felt by all. Richard Fuller's sermon on "The Cross" was never forgotten. Although it did not stop the split, it did remind leaders both North and South that their ultimate unity was in Christ. After the sermon, one of the most prominent abolitionists went up to Fuller, threw his arms around him, and said, "Brother Fuller, I love you."[48] As they stood there, weeping and embracing each other, it was as if for one last moment the Baptists in America were united.

The issue of the day was slavery, and Fuller did his best to turn minds and hearts away from the thought of war. He was one of the forces behind the movement to colonize Liberia with slaves in hopes that something could be worked out to free fellow humans and avert war. He did not believe that slavery was right or good. He had inherited his own slaves, and the testimony of one of them was that Fuller "had united in him the largest proportion of greatness and goodness of any man I ever knew."[49] After the war, when he visited his devastated hometown of Beaufort, two or three hundred former slaves crowded around him and begged him to preach. A soldier who saw the event commented that he would give all he was worth to be loved by as many people as loved Fuller.

Before the outbreak of open conflict Fuller lamented that extremists in the South could not regard an abolitionist as an honest person, while extremists in the North looked upon every slaveholder as nothing less than a pirate. His letters to Francis Wayland were just as gracious and kind as were Wayland's to him, and they showed how great and good men could differ, and differ in love. When the war broke out, Fuller was in a very difficult position. He was a leader in the Southern Baptist Convention, a son of South Carolina, and a slaveholder by inheritance. Yet he was a resident of Maryland, a border state which did not secede. In the spring of 1861, at the meeting of the Southern Baptist Convention in Savannah, Fuller was one of a committee that introduced resolutions of sympathy for the Confederacy. Yet Fuller himself continued his allegiance to the United States throughout the war. Thus, he maintained his influence in both sections of the country even after the war. In 1868, he

---

[48]Cuthbert, *Life of Richard Fuller*, 181.
[49]Ibid., 106.

wrote a letter to Northern Baptist ministers inviting them to attend the meeting of the Southern Baptist Convention in Baltimore.

> Let us, then, seek to bring to the distractions of the country and the church those influences which alone can produce true union by infusing the principles of the gospel—its spirit of peace, forgiveness, love, harmony—into the heart of the nation.[50]

His relationship with Northern Baptists was affirmed in 1872 when he was invited to speak at a convention in Washington, D.C., in behalf of the Southern Baptist Theological Seminary, then located in Greenville, South Carolina. Fuller spoke of his pleasant memories of the old Triennial Convention and pleaded for the good fellowship of the past. He then candidly told them of the crippled condition of the seminary in Greenville and asked for their financial support. Pledge followed pledge, until a large sum of money was collected, testifying not only to Northern Baptist liberality, but also to the confidence they placed in Richard Fuller.

Richard Fuller died in Baltimore in 1876. His last words, murmured in broken accents, were an expression of a deathless faith: "Who'll preach Jesus?" He did, and he did it with a power and eloquence that was not surpassed among nineteenth century Baptists. Even Francis Wayland once said that he would give all his learning and philosophy to be able to preach as Richard Fuller did.[51] Fuller was the best of men in the worst of times. A child of his age, he yet transcended his age through preaching a gospel that judges every age.

CONCLUSION

The unity of the Baptists, of course, was never reclaimed after the Civil War. But there were those days from 1814 to 1845 when Baptists in America spoke with one voice and carried out their mission imperative with one accord. This era is one of the most fascinating to study because it shows clearly how Baptist preaching was part of the age. It was indeed a mixture of gold and clay, a leaky vessel that could still carry enough potent wine to make the head spin. The names of Furman, Staughton, Baldwin, Wayland, and Fuller are only representative of the best of Baptist preaching during the period. There were many more.

---

[50]Ibid., 269.
[51]Ibid., 159.

Perhaps the best paradigm of Baptist preaching during the first half of the nineteenth century comes from Francis Wayland. He told of the life in New York City during the closing days of the War of 1812. The nation was suffering from the effects of the war. Harbors were blockaded, communication between ports was cut off, unemployment was high, American products were moldering in warehouses, and the economy was in shambles. One Saturday afternoon in February, he remembered, a ship entered New York harbor, a ship that carried the American negotiators for peace. No one knew the outcome of their negotiations, and everyone was waiting intensely for news to come to shore.

The hours of darkness grew on, and finally a small boat reached the wharf, announcing the fact that a treaty of peace had been signed and was waiting for nothing but the action of the American government to become law. Upon hearing the news, people rushed everywhere shouting breathlessly to their friends as they ran through the streets, "Peace! Peace! Peace!" Everyone who heard the sound repeated it. The whole city was soon in commotion. When the rapture finally subsided, only one idea occupied every mind.[52]

This era of great Baptist preaching resembled such exciting news. Peace! The word was to be spread to the whole world. Baptist preaching, even during the great internal American slaughter, kept proclaiming that message and urging its hearers to ratify the treaty with God.

---

[52]Wayland, *Sermons to the Churches,* 16-17.

Chapter 10

THE PREPARATION AND DELIVERY OF JOHN A. BROADUS

He has done more than any other man to bind North and South together, for the whole country loved him. He was one of God's greatest gifts to our denomination, and to our generation.

Augustus H. Strong
in reference to John A. Broadus

Baptist history came staggering out of the smoke of the Civil War, and, like the mythical general, rode off in many directions at the same time. Not so with Baptist preaching. Whatever else the war did to Baptist preaching, it exploded any possible tendency toward what William H. Whitsitt called "over-cultivated, weak-thoughted, intellectual exquisites"[1] in the pulpit. Baptist preaching walked calmly from the battlefields of the war to the pulpits of churches both North and South and delivered a message of hope and a challenge to live the gospel in a war-weary land.

Although the latter half of the nineteenth century produced many fine preachers in American Baptist ranks, the greatest attention was focused on one man: John A. Broadus. The fact that he was a Southerner was incidental. The Mason-Dixon line was not a barrier to his words, printed or spoken. He was a Baptist of international influence, to be compared with Maclaren and Spurgeon in quality if not quantity of sermons, and to be held above all in his influence on preaching during his day and well into the twentieth century. To make such a claim for Broadus is not to exaggerate in the least; rather, it is to admit a paucity of words, for it can be said with equal truth that no one in the world of Protestant preaching exerted greater long-term influence than Broadus. To support what must seem such an extravagant statement, especially when other great preachers such as Henry Ward Beecher and Phillips Brooks shared the

---

[1]William H. Whitsitt, "Position of the Baptists in the History of American Culture" (Greenville SC: n.p., 1872) 29. This was Whitsitt's inaugural address as Professor of Biblical Introduction and Polemics at the Southern Baptist Theological Seminary.

era, one can only point to *A Treatise on the Preparation and Delivery of Sermons,* first published by Broadus in 1870.

No sooner was the book published than it became and remained the standard textbook for preaching among non-Catholic seminaries and theological schools in the English-speaking world. Words of praise for the book from every denomination could be piled up to the point of weariness. The simple fact is that for seventy-five years or more every work on preaching was merely a supplement to that of Broadus. Even today, over a century after he first published it, the work of Broadus stands ghostlike behind many a modern approach to preaching.

THE PREPARATION BEHIND THE *PREPARATION*

What, or better who, lies behind *The Preparation and Delivery of Sermons?* John A. Broadus, like many a Virginia farm boy in the 1830s, wanted nothing more in life than to become an Indian chief and live and die in paint and feathers. But reality intruded and the boy from Culpepper County found himself at the age of twenty-three the leading master's graduate at the University of Virginia and a popular young preacher. Not that he particularly wanted to be a preacher. Four years earlier he had written to a friend,

> I was not "cut out" for a public speaker; I have not that grace of manner and appearance, that pleasant voice, that easy flow of words, which are indispensably necessary in him who would make impressions on his fellows by public speaking.[2]

Yet only six months later, with the full intention of studying medicine, he found himself listening to a sermon preached by A. M. Poindexter, a well-known Virginia Baptist. The sermon was based on the parable of talents, and what struck young Broadus was the appeal of the preacher for Christians to consecrate their mental gifts to God. Broadus was well aware of his mental gifts, and he had thought sincerely about the ministry, but it was the sermon by Poindexter that providentially cleared away all his doubts. He must be a preacher.[3]

---

[2]Quoted in A. T. Robertson, *Life and Letters of John Albert Broadus* (Philadelphia: American Baptist Publication Society, 1901) 48-49.

[3]John A. Broadus, "Memorial of A. M. Poindexter," in *Sermons and Addresses* (Richmond: B. F. Johnson and Company, 1887) 397-99.

With Georgetown College calling him to Kentucky to teach ancient languages, Broadus turned instead to a pastorate: the Charlottesville Baptist Church in Virginia, where he could minister to both the town and the university. His congregation was remarkable in its variety. The profound and the ignorant shared many a pew, and it was this challenge that did much to prepare Broadus for his great life work. No Baptist preacher could be studied as a greater model for the perfect blending of depth and clearness. The university, however, could not give him up, and after three years as pastor in Charlottesville he accepted the position of Chaplain to the University of Virginia in 1855.

The accounts of his life during his early ministry never say it, but it is evident that Broadus was struggling to determine the exact nature of his vocation. He never seemed to be entirely happy when his life focused entirely on one of his two loves. When in the pastorate he longed for the classroom; in the classroom he yearned for the pulpit. For a short time he tried to teach a university class in Greek while he was pastor in Charlottesville, but the strain was too great. Both the pulpit and the classroom suffered, so he finally gave up his Greek class.

He struggled on until the light began to break in on him at the meeting of the Southern Baptist Convention in 1857. It was there that he was asked to be a member of a committee of five to plan the organization of an institution to be known as the Southern Baptist Theological Seminary. Joining Broadus were eminent fellow Baptists in the South: James P. Boyce, Basil Manly, Jr., E. T. Winkler, and William Williams. When they met in August of 1857, Boyce proposed an outline of legal arrangements, Manly had drawn up an "Abstract of Principles" for the professors to sign, and Broadus contributed a plan of instruction modeled on the elective system of the University of Virginia. Less than two years later he accepted the invitation to be one of the original faculty members of the new institution. From that day on his life was bound to the seminary. A multitude of offers both from churches and schools in the North and the South would come his way in the long years ahead, but he would remain with the institution in whose foundation he played such a prominent role.

The early years of the seminary constitute an heroic story in itself, for just as the institution showed every promise of success, the Civil War dashed all immediate hopes. Located in Greenville, South Carolina, the seminary was in a volatile state—the first, in fact, to secede. Broadus and Boyce were opposed to secession, and Boyce even ran unsuccessfully for the state legislature in 1861 on an antisecession platform.[4] Nothing seemed capable of staying the bloody hand of war. Even those fervently opposed to secession finally had little choice but to give in. "South Carolina is going to the devil," said one Union leader, "and I'm going with her."

When the war finally broke out, the seminary lost virtually all of its students and had to close in hopes of better days. Broadus preached where he could, and he served as chaplain in Lee's army for a time. But his mind was on the seminary, and on his vision of a textbook for young preachers. As hard as the war years were, the period of Reconstruction was even harder for many in the South. Southern Seminary reopened its doors with almost no money and barely a handful of students.

In later years it became a well-known story that the lectures forming the basis for *The Preparation and Delivery of Sermons* were prepared when Broadus had only one student in his preaching class, and that student was blind. A. T. Robertson later commented that "it was like Doctor Broadus to give this one blind student the best he had."[5] True, but to keep from assigning too prominent a halo over the head of Broadus, it would be helpful to remember his comment in a letter to his wife:

> Really it is right dull to deliver my most elaborate lectures in homiletics to one man, and that a blind man. Of course I whittle it all down to simple talk.[6]

Broadus was obviously human, and nothing was a more blunt reminder of that fact than the failure of his health in 1870, just when his book on preaching was published. The trustees of the seminary sent him on an extended trip to Europe. He had worn himself out teaching and trying to raise funds for the struggling seminary. Not only was his health restored on the journey, but he also made many new friends among European Christian scholars. He was particularly taken with B. F. Westcott and his colleague F. J. A. Hort, who were completing their monumental edition of the Greek text of the New Testament.

---

[4]See John A. Broadus, *Memoir of James Petigru Boyce* (New York: A. C. Armstrong and Son, 1893) 177.

[5]Robertson, *John Albert Broadus*, 214.

[6]Ibid., 216.

The mind of Broadus was expanded and stimulated. Upon his return to the seminary he was recharged with enthusiasm for the fields of New Testament and homiletics. His mind became an insatiable sponge. By the 1880s he had added to his competency in Latin, Greek, and Hebrew a working knowledge of German, French, Spanish, Italian, Gothic, Coptic, and modern Greek. He was a scholar of international stature in the classroom. Editor Philip Schaff even asked him to revise the standard translation of John Chrysostom's sermons on Philippians, Colossians, and Thessalonians for the *Select Library of the Nicene and Post-Nicene Fathers of the Christian Church*. Broadus not only complied with that request, but also wrote an essay on "St. Chrysostom as a Homilist" for inclusion in the famous series.[7]

As a biblical critic he was fully versed in all the leading theories and was capable of forming his own judgments. His *Commentary on the Gospel of Matthew* (1886) was a brilliant demonstration of his ability to use critical methodology effectively. Any suggestion that the heritage of Southern Baptists excludes the use of reason and critical tools in the study of Scriptures dissolves in the work of John A. Broadus. In him, as J. H. Farmer of McMaster University said, "the preacher and teacher met together, the intellectual and spiritual kissed each other."[8]

Broadus also stood as a living witness against the false assumption that a precise scholar must be aloof, somehow separate from the common people. On the contrary, Broadus took great delight in the common folk of his denomination. Once when confronted with the criticism that his denomination had in it a great mass of ignorant people, he checked the temptation to respond, "Well, why haven't you a similar mass?" It was a rare Sunday when he was not preaching in some church, and during the summers he was sought after as a supply preacher from all parts of the country—North and South. Once Broadus tried to distill what to him was the first thing in effective preaching: "sympathy," he said. "And what is the second thing, I should say, sympathy; and what is the third thing, sympathy."[9] He did not define sympathy as being patronizing. He

---

[7]See Philip Schaff, ed., *Saint Chrysostom*, vol. 13 of *A Select Library of the Nicene and Post-Nicene Fathers* (Grand Rapids MI: Wm. B. Eerdmans Publishing Company, 1976) v-vii, 173ff.

[8]Quoted in Robertson, *John Albert Broadus*, 338-39.

[9]Broadus, *Sermons and Addresses*, 39.

called for a genuine camaraderie with the congregation, uniting breadth of view, charity of feeling, and fidelity to truth.

The death of Broadus in 1895 was a jolt to the Baptists. Words of praise for his life rushed in from all over the world. But perhaps the most telling comment was made by Rabbi Moses of Louisville.

> Before I became familiar with Doctor Broadus, I knew Christianity only as a creed which seemed absolutely incomprehensible to me. I judged it mainly from the untold, unmerited misery, the agony of ages which Christian rulers and nations had entailed upon poor Israel under the impulse given by Christian priests and teachers. But when I learned to know and revere in Broadus a Christian, my conception of Christianity and my attitude toward it underwent a complete change. Broadus was the precious fruit by which I learned to judge the tree of Christianity.[10]

Such testimony from a Jewish leader speaks eloquently of what a genuine Christian life can do. It was not primarily the learning or the arguments of Broadus that moved the rabbi to change his opinion of Christianity. Rather, it was the testimony of Broadus's life—his gracious spirit, his love for truth, his breadth of learning—all those merged into one life. That is what moved the rabbi, and that is precisely what made John A. Broadus one of the greatest Baptist leaders of all time.

THE FOUNDATION OF MODERN BAPTIST PREACHING

It was the life behind the book that added luster to *The Preparation and Delivery of Sermons,* but the book could have stood alone without a knowledge of its author. For the last century the work of Broadus has deservedly stood as the foundation of Baptist preaching. The great preachers of the denomination in the late nineteenth and early twentieth centuries were all influenced by Broadus. By the end of the nineteenth century the book had passed through twenty-two editions. Theological schools of every Protestant denomination were using it either as a required text or a highly commended supplement. Two separate editions were published in England. It was translated into Chinese for the mission schools. In 1897 it was revised by E. C. Dargan, a student of Broadus and his successor as Professor of Homiletics at Southern Seminary. Half a century later, in 1943, it was again revised by J. B. Weatherspoon to serve still another generation. Three full generations of Baptist students

---

[10]Robertson, *John Albert Broadus,* 438.

studied either the original or newly revised editions of *The Preparation and Delivery of Sermons.*

Can the Broadus influence on Baptist preaching be described? If there is such a thing as a Broadus stamp on preaching, what does it look like? In my judgment the Broadus influence can be described in three statements.

He based preaching firmly on the informed interpretation of Scripture. To say that Broadus emphasized Scripture as the source of truth in preaching is nothing new. Baptist leaders had been teaching the same concept since the seventeenth century. The great difference came in the fact that Broadus lived in a new era. Biblical criticism had spread from Germany to America, terrifying many Baptists into a fearful biblicism. Afraid that the foundations of their religious experience were crumbling beneath them, some Baptist preachers began to make a subtle move away from the Bible as the *source of truth* and toward setting up the Bible as the *object of faith.* The mood was shifting from the free proclamation of truth to the fearful defense of truth. Some began to substitute preaching *about* the Bible for preaching *from* the Bible. The inevitable result was a reorientation of faith: what one said about the Bible was becoming more important than what one experienced of Christ.

Baptists needed someone to lead them into a new day. He would have to earn the confidence of the very people who were most afraid of biblical criticism. At the same time, he would have to rise to a position of respect among the leading biblical critics of the theological world. Broadus stood between both worlds and spoke eloquently to each.

With mind and heart aglow, he showed his students through his living example that intellectual rigor and evangelistic warmth could be woven into the same cloth. He was less concerned about eloquence than about piety and knowledge: "The preacher can be really eloquent only when he speaks of those vital gospel truths which have necessarily become familiar."[11] Those vital gospel truths, he taught, are found in the Scriptures. Yet Scripture must be interpreted not blindly, but with the use of reason. Spurious passages must not be used as texts. He was no more concerned about the errors common to any translation of the Bible than

---

[11]John A. Broadus, *A Treatise on the Preparation and Delivery of Sermons* (Philadelphia: Smith, English, and Company, 1874) 22.

he was about the grammatical mistakes found in his students' sermons. They both needed to be corrected, but neither altered or modified the basic message.

Thus sermons had to be drawn from the deep truths of the Scriptures. He liked to paraphrase a saying of Bacon: "Truth from any other source is like water from a cistern; but truth drawn out of the Bible is like drinking water from a fountain, immediately where it springeth."[12] Broadus knew the futility of trying to defend the Bible by eulogizing it or attacking its critics. The Scriptures, he believed, would continue to speak religious truth regardless of criticism or praise from without. "The Scriptures in general, and the four gospels in particular, carry credentials of their own on every page."[13]

Broadus was less concerned that preachers teach a system of doctrines than that they proclaim the experience of Christ. Experience was to precede doctrine; only then could doctrine make sense and be held with conviction. In a sermon entitled "One Jesus" he said it clearly.

> The gospel is not a creed simply, is not a society of priests, the gospel comes to us embodied in a person. Jesus is himself the gospel; receiving him we receive the power of God unto salvation.[14]

His understanding of the centrality of Christ underlined the necessity of interpreting the Scriptures with intelligence and precision. He was an avowed enemy of rampant spiritualizing and irresponsible allegory. At a time when it was common for preachers to break away from the laborious study of text and context and, with imagination taking flight, to find symbols of Christ in every dusty corner of the Old Testament, Broadus drew preaching back down to the common earth and virtually forced preachers to say what a passage actually meant. To do otherwise, he claimed, was inexcusable.

Thus from the teaching of John A. Broadus, undergirded by the example of his own preaching, Baptists were guided ever so carefully to an

---

[12]Broadus, *Sermons and Addresses*, 39.

[13]John A. Broadus, *Jesus of Nazareth* (New York: A. C. Armstrong and Son, 1890) 94.

[14]Broadus, "One Jesus," in Vernon L. Stanfield, ed., *Favorite Sermons of John A. Broadus* (New York: Harper and Brothers, 1959) 54.

informed interpretation of Scripture. The Bible was not always taken literally by Broadus, but it was always taken seriously and reverently.

He gave the Baptist sermon a distinctive shape. Broadus once described a sermon that seemed to have as little congruity as "the human head, a horse's neck, a body composed of parts brought from all directions and covered with many kinds of feathers, and the whole ending in a fish's tail."[15] Such disorganization was unfortunately all too common among preachers in his day. Too many preachers were simply not trained to use logic and order in sermons. Preaching was sometimes splattered over a congregation with no sense of unity, resulting in a messy, ill-defined understanding of the gospel.

The teaching of Broadus helped give shape to Baptist preaching—not necessarily "three points and a poem"—but at least a logical progression with a definite beginning and ending. "The movement," he said, "must not be wild and irregular, like undisciplined cavalry."[16] Rather, it should vividly portray the meaning of the text in logical steps. His aim was not to make it *possible* for a person to understand the text, but to make it impossible for one *not* to understand it.

Broadus taught that the divisions of a sermon should be stated in plain Anglo-Saxon language, not in words of Latin origin often used in theological textbooks. *Felicity* was not to be used when *happiness* could just as easily be employed. The conclusion should be carefully prepared, for it was, he believed, a very solemn moment: "Do not be thinking of your reputation, good brother, but of your responsibility, and of your hearers' salvation."[17]

He invested Baptist preaching with a distinctive style Baptist preachers were, for the most part, not familiar with the Broadus style and delivery of a sermon. They tended toward one of two extremes. Either they gave no preparation to a discourse and depended upon the inspiration of the moment, or they prepared a manuscript and read it Broadus taught a middle course. He rarely wrote out an entire manuscript sermon. Rather, he meticulously prepared a skeleton of his sermon, including a fully written introduction and conclusion, and then *left it in his study* when

---

[15]Broadus, *Preparation and Delivery,* 270.
[16]Ibid., 262.
[17]Ibid., 288.

he went to preach. The result was extemporaneous preaching based on careful preparation. He did not memorize, but the wealth of preparation fed his mind as he preached. He refused to take notes into the pulpit with him because he wanted eye contact with the people, but even more important, he wanted to remain open to spiritual leadership as he preached. "How can a man pray that God will guide him through a forest, when he has already blazed the entire path, and committed himself to follow it?" he asked.[18] Such was his method of preaching, and sometimes even lecturing. Baptist preaching largely followed his lead, thus creating a certain style one elderly woman once said she could always recognize.

But there was more to the Broadus style than the method of delivery. There was a certain elegance, a decorum, a manner of respect, which came from his influence. Broadus was vehemently opposed to anything that seemed ostentatious or showy or arrogant in the pulpit. For Broadus, there was a sacredness to the preaching task that excluded exhibitionism of any kind. Alliterative outlines, ostentatious clothing, kneeling before the pulpit, the use of the "royal *we*," affectations of voice or tears—all these, in his view, were merely signs of egoism and therefore hurtful to the gospel. Such matters of style, Broadus taught, were not just trifles. They reflected the character of the preacher. A trifling preacher would preach a trivial gospel, and in the days of Broadus—indeed in any day—a trivial gospel was the last thing needed. From the influence of Broadus came generations of preachers who knew that what a preacher *is* goes far to determine the effect of what he *says*. That knowledge, along with Broadus's training in the preparation and delivery of sermons, produced a distinctive style of Baptist preaching.

CONCLUSION

During the last century, and even early in this one, there was a true story about Broadus that was generally circulated and known among Baptists all over the country. The first person to be converted under the influence of Broadus was a slightly retarded man named Sandy, who lived near the Broadus farm. Broadus, at the age of sixteen and only a few months after his own conversion, ventured to speak to Sandy about his salvation, and eventually Sandy professed his faith in Christ. Soon Broadus left for college and the brilliant calling that lay before him. But whenever

---

[18]Ibid., 429.

he returned to his home community in the years ahead, Broadus could always count on hearing the voice of Sandy running to meet him. Always Sandy had the same greeting: "Howdy, John? thankee, John. Howdy, John? thankee, John." Broadus would sometimes tell that story and would add, "And if I ever reach the heavenly home and walk the golden streets, I know the first person to meet me will be Sandy, coming and saying again, 'Howdy, John? thankee, John.' "[19]

It would not be hackneyed or trite to add that Sandy would not be the only one to rush toward Broadus in gratitude for what his life and work had meant. Baptists, indeed the universal church, are largely in his debt. Like the ripe fruit that gathers all the dew and sunshine of the summer, Broadus distilled the best traditions of preaching from his own denomination, added to that a knowledge and understanding of the Scriptures drawn from nineteen centuries of Christian thought, mixed with that a contemporary awareness of critical study, combined with that a genuine affection for common folk, and produced a work that nourished the pulpit ministry of many a church in this country and abroad. All those who have a stake in effective preaching, and that is all of us some of the time and some of us all the time, have reason to rise up and call him blessed.

> *Thus, though oft depressed and lonely,*
> *All my fears are laid aside:*
> *If I but remember only,*
> *Such as these have lived and died.*[20]

---

[19]Robertson, *John Albert Broadus*, 35.
[20]Ibid., 436.

Part III

LIVING THE HERITAGE

Chapter 11

GIVING SHAPE TO THE HERITAGE

Have you ever read the sermons written by a famous preacher of another era and found yourself yawning? I have, but it was not because they were poor sermons. These sermons were great in their day; however, they may not be great today if they are preached in the same way. The gospel they proclaim is timeless, the words they use are appealing and sometimes beautiful, but the form is a horse and buggy loping down an expressway.

How do we give modern shape to the Baptist heritage of great preaching? How can we best proclaim the age-old gospel in the language of today, while still honoring the tradition of preaching? Many a modern preacher stands in the pulpit week by week and represents the best of the Baptist heritage. They are doing it, whether they know it or not, by standing on the shoulders of those who preceded them. In Robert Burns's words, "We clamb the hill thegither."[1] We give modern shape to our heritage in a joint effort with the communion of saints.

PREACHING THAT FITS

The greatest preaching always creates a form fit for the age in which it lives. To repeat the lesson of parts one and two, Baptist preaching, like Christian preaching in general, has gone through repeated cycles of decline and revival. In periods of decline sermons become locked into the form and style of a past era of preaching. Revival occurs when through the newness of God's Spirit sermons take the shape of the age in which they are preached.

Are we in a revival or a decline of preaching today? How long it might last remains to be seen, but there is a fresh new breeze blowing in the world of preaching. In spite of the host of books published in the field during the last decade, the interest is not just academic. The renewed in-

---

[1] Robert Burns, "John Anderson My Jo," in Raymond Bentman, ed., *The Poetical Works of Burns* (Boston: Houghton Mifflin Company, 1974) 223.

terest in preaching was found in the local pulpit long before it spilled over into academia. There has been an almost spontaneous renewal of preaching led not so much by the princes of the pulpit as by the many nameless pastors who have made it their business to put the Word into words. These preachers are both men and women who labor in churches of all sizes. They share the joys and frustrations of their times and of their people, whom they know and love. The really great preachers of today, and there are many, have at least one thing in common: they all somehow manage to shape the age-old gospel into sermons that will speak precisely for today. They "rightly handle the word of truth" (2 Timothy 2:15). Not many of these sermons gain wide popularity, precisely because they are just right for a limited congregation.

WHAT ARE THE CLUES?

What are the clues for discovering such preaching among Baptists? How can one identify preaching that builds on the heritage described, yet speaks in terms of the present age?

Biblical

The Baptist denomination was born, suffered, and has lived trying to interpret the Bible from the pulpit. It is this interpretation that often led to pain and prison, but they insisted upon no other written authority. Interpretations have varied, leading to General and Particular Baptists in England, as well as Regular and Separate Baptists in America, to mention only a few of the divisions. But whatever the interpretation, it has been the Scriptures to which reference has been made.

Likewise, in the pulpit the best of Baptist preaching has steadfastly refused to use a text as merely a tag to be attached to the sermon. Rather, great Baptist preaching has always been expository. To use the Bible seriously in the pulpit is a mark of the finest Baptist heritage.

Broadly Liberal in Outlook

One of the precious jewels whose meaning has been mangled and twisted by well-meaning people is the word *liberal*. "No one in hell," wrote a recent president of the Southern Baptist Convention, "is glad he went to a liberal church."[2] It is strange that the leader of a denomination once

---

[2]Bailey Smith, "Southern Baptists' Most Serious Question" (1982 SBC News Kit, Dargan Carver Library, Nashville) 1.

persecuted for its ecclesiastical liberalism would describe liberalism as an avenue to hell.

Let it be said clearly: *a preacher can be theologically conservative yet broadly liberal in outlook.* The best heritage of Baptists is indeed theologically conservative, but until this century the greatest Baptist leaders were eulogized as "liberal in spirit." When William Rogers conducted the funeral for Oliver Hart, for example, he praised Hart for his "liberal mindedness."[3]

Liberalism is indeed one of the grandest words in the English language. When Patrick Henry stood and made history with his "give me liberty or give me death" speech, he was a political liberal. When the Apostle Paul opposed Peter over the question of circumcision (Galatians 2:11ff.), he stood as a theological liberal. When Thomas Helwys informed the king of England that he "hath no power over ye immortall soules of his subjects,"[4] he was an ecclesiastical liberal. Baptists were born in liberalism, sustained and nurtured by liberal minded people, supported by liberal contributions, and strengthened by liberal thinking. If liberalism does indeed send people to hell, then hell must be filled with the giants of religious history, including Jesus, who was so liberal that he challenged the stuffy, worn-out religious institutions of his own day.

The word *liberal* comes from the Latin *liber,* which means "free." Its derivatives run the entire gamut from liberty to libertine, the one praised and the other scorned by conservatives and progressives alike. *Liberal* was originally used to describe a person of free birth who, unlike the slaves, was allowed to study languages, art, science, philosophy, and literature, thus the term "liberal arts."

So what is a "broadly liberal" Christian? Some would shudder at the thought of those two words standing side by side, but liberal and Christian stand together in the New Testament just as liberty and justice are bound together in our national consciousness. *A liberal Christian is one who is free under the Lord Jesus Christ to seek the truth.* Jesus spoke of Christian liberalism when he said, "You will know the truth, and the truth shall set you free" (John 8:32). The Apostle Paul spoke of Christian lib-

---

[3]William Rogers, "A Sermon Occasioned by the Death of the Rev. Oliver Hart" (Philadelphia: Lang and Ustick, 1796) 23.

[4]Thomas Helwys, *The Mistery of Iniquity* (London: The Kingsgate Press, 1935) frontispiece.

eralism when he said to the conservative Galatians, "For freedom [or liberalism] Christ has set us free; stand fast therefore, and do not submit again the yoke of slavery" (Galatians 5:1).

Take a closer look at the definition of a liberal Christian. "One who is free . . . to seek the truth" is eternally restive in the presence of God. Regardless of the degree to which the liberal Christian has come to experience and understand the Christian faith, there is always more depth of experience and understanding to be found. Thus there is a genuine humility in a true liberal that was characteristic of all the great Baptist preachers. The Baptist heritage points toward an eternal discontent with superficiality in religion, either from the right wing or the left. The broadly liberal Christian lives by faith, but always whispers the prayer of confession: "I believe; help my unbelief!" (Mark 9:24).

Yet there is guidance in the search for truth, for the liberal Christian is not just free, but free *"under the Lord Christ."* Some mistakenly characterize a liberal as one who mocks Christ and laughs at the faith "once for all delivered to the saints" (Jude 3). Such intellectual snobbery has no rightful place in the Baptist heritage. Baptist leaders have always searched for deeper truth because they have experienced Truth. "I am . . . the truth," said Jesus (John 14:6).

Baptist preaching that lives the heritage seeks the truth wherever it may be found. There is an openness, a graciousness, a friendliness, that comes from the Lord Christ who saw the best in those who were condemned by the conservative Pharisees. At the same time there is an unwavering commitment to Christ that is not threatened by cultural movements or intellectual novelties. As John A. Broadus once said, "You must know how to unite breadth of view, and charity of feeling, with fidelity to truth."[5]

Adventurous

There is no mistake in using a word that comes from the Latin *adventus,* "to come." Whenever the great Baptist preachers stood in the pulpit, people knew something was coming; something was about to be born. Living the heritage means moist palms and a lump in the throat

---

[5]John A. Broadus, *Lectures on the History of Preaching* (New York: Sheldon and Company, 1876) 233.

whenever one is about to preach. Wherever there is advent, there is adventure.

Like any adventure, things move, happen, you go somewhere. Great preaching has a destination, and it leads the congregation through every exciting turn until it arrives at its destination. It invites the people to join the adventure; poor preaching merely tells them about the adventure.

When John Clifford packed the Westbourne Park Baptist Church in London with eager hearers, it wasn't because they could predict exactly what he was going to say. There was adventure in his preaching. They knew he would preach the gospel, but they never knew exactly where Clifford would take them with the gospel.

Suppose one were to preach a sermon based on Galatians 5:22: "But the fruit of the Spirit is love, joy, peace, patience, kindness, goodness, faithfulness, gentleness, self-control." Poor preaching would immediately see a nine-point sermon in that verse and proceed to expound on each point with suitable arguments, illustrations, and examples. An impeccable outline of the sermon could be recorded by the twelve-year-old sitting beside his mother on the fifth pew next to the window, if it were not for the more interesting designs he preferred to draw in the hymn book. The poor congregation is courageous and determines to listen attentively to all nine points because, after all, Holy Scripture is being discussed. After the first ten minutes of the sermon the old deacon sitting on the front pew looks at his watch and says to himself, "Good heavens! Ten minutes gone and he's only on 'joy'!" It doesn't take a genius to figure out that at that rate "self-control" is thirty-five minutes down the way, so he quietly lets his mind wander off to the golf course, has a jolly good time racking up his best imaginary score of the year, and comes back only to hear the preacher say, "And in conclusion . . ." for the third time! The very fact that they keep coming back to that kind of preaching is a testimony either to God's amazing Spirit or to the congregation's collective faithfulness.

A nine-point sermon on that text may appeal to those who love memorizing lists, but it is not adventurous. Each point is entirely predictable and academic. Yet hidden behind that list is an adventure: when Paul discovered the love of Christ that would transform even Saul of Tarsus, he found each of those nine qualities to be simply love in another form. How can a preacher make that boring?

Imaginative

Baptist preachers who have used intellectual rigor as well as evangelistic warmth have not been dry academics in the pulpit. On the contrary, those who studied the text most minutely were in the best position to use their imagination to the fullest. Alexander Maclaren, one of the most marvelously imaginative preachers of all time, compared the study of the preacher to that of an astronomer. One studies the lights of God's Word, and the other studies the lights of God's universe. An outside observer would imagine that the astronomer spends most of his time delighting in the majesty and beauty of the universe, but in reality, the competent astronomer spends long hours working out dry mathematical problems, which are nonetheless abstract and difficult because the planets have given the data. Only then is an astronomer in a position to use his imagination to the fullest in comprehending the universe. The preacher's work, claimed Maclaren, is analogous to the astronomer's: "Dry toils with lexicon and grammar and concordance, laborious discrimination of finely-shaded meanings, and the slow elaboration of results into a coherent system, are not in themselves favourable to devout emotion."[6] It is that kind of intellectual labor that taps the worthiest Christian imagination.

Such preaching does not mean that every Sunday the congregation enters the sanctuary with fear and trembling, never sure exactly what the preacher will spring on them that day. Dramatic monologues, story sermons, dialogue sermons, and the like are often imaginative, but they can rarely be served as a consistent weekly diet. Ordinary folks in the pews are longing for the preacher to take the Scripture seriously, to proclaim its truth, and to do it imaginatively! Pulling out all the gimmicks one knows in one sermon cannot compete with that kind of biblical preaching.

Rigorous thinking during the day often leads to the best imagination at night. One should use all the critical tools at his disposal in studying the Scripture; then when the mind is at rest later in the day, there is often a receptivity that allows the imagination to function at its best. Ideas and possibilities come to mind that were never considered in the more analytical study of the text. While driving to the hospital or making pastoral

---

[6]Alexander Maclaren, "Counsels for the Study and Life," *Review and Expositor* 22 (April 1925):173-74.

calls, many a busy preacher experiences flashes of truth and insights that he can attribute only to the strange working of the Spirit of God.

Imagination in preaching can be learned. It is aided by the senses, so that after (and during) an intense analytical study of Scripture the preacher imagines he is walking into the setting of the passage he is studying. Like an invisible guest, he wanders around in the setting, never as an intruder and always being polite. After all, the biblical characters just might not appreciate his presence! So he wanders into the home of the prodigal son and carries on a conversation with the father and the older brother. The aroma of the fatted calf floats through his mind as the homecoming party is prepared. He sits down in the shade of a tree to discuss the situation with the older brother. How can a sermon lack imagination after such a journey?

Brief

Baptists emerged during a century when sermons were long, long, long. Reading them is sometimes hard enough, but the idea that anyone with normal physical resources could sit on a hard bench and listen to them attentively is extraordinary. One description of seventeenth-century public fast days in England says that the preacher commonly began at nine in the morning with a prayer for about a quarter of an hour, followed by the reading of Scripture and expounding for about forty-five minutes, followed by a long prayer lasting an hour, and then another prayer of only half an hour. After that, the preacher rested and ate lunch for a period of fifteen minutes while the people sang hymns. Then he came again into the pulpit, prayed for another hour, and gave them another sermon of about an hour's length. After a closing prayer, the service was ended.[7]

Sermons did become shorter among the Baptists as the centuries wore on, but even as late as the time of Broadus a twenty-minute sermon was considered extremely brief, and a forty-five minute sermon was far more common. Were they that much better at preaching than we are today? Or perhaps the congregation failed to maintain attention for that long? The fact is that customs were different. People expected the sermon to be a certain length, and if it was too short many felt cheated

---

[7]Described in John A. Broadus, *Lectures on the History of Preaching* (New York: Sheldon and Company, 1876) 211-12.

somehow, especially if they had ridden a considerable distance to hear the preacher.

Our age has grown accustomed to little snippets of information shot machine-gun-like through the media. Sustained logic and arguments drawn out to their logical conclusions are rare. Should the modern preacher succumb to those facts of life? Or should the pulpit be the last holdout for sustained explanation and appeal? There are some preachers who have such a gift of imagination and genuine eloquence that they can hold a congregation spellbound for long periods of time. But most preachers must face facts realistically and hold sermons to within twenty minutes.

Such a time limitation is a great challenge and could in the long run improve preaching. Short sermons require more preparation. The preacher who is long-winded in the pulpit is often short-winded in the study. Short sermons mean that every word must work. Perhaps Jesus had preachers in mind when he said something about being held accountable for every careless word uttered (Matthew 12:36).

Appropriate

The pulpit has often been a favorite haunt of verbal exhibitionists. Not so with the best heritage of Baptist preaching. Francis Wayland, among the most erudite of all the preachers in the Baptist heritage, was almost childlike in his use of language in the pulpit. "The minister of the gospel," he claimed, "is not to preach that the ten shall applaud him, while the ninety shall wonder at what they do not understand."[8]

The best heritage of the Baptists forbids the use of cheap slang in the name of good communication. Even more abhorrent is the telling of a joke to "warm them up." How sad to see and hear such insecurity! Yet through the history of the Christian church, congregations have occasionally been subjected to just such preaching. During the fifteenth century the use of off-color stories in the pulpit became so common that the Italians said of any spicy and not too delicate joke that "it was good enough for a ser-

---

[8]Francis Wayland, "Christian Worship," in *Sermons to the Churches* (New York: Sheldon, Blakeman, and Company, 1858) 138.

mon."⁹ Finally the Lateran Council of 1512, and later the Council of Trent, passed rules against the practice.

The best heritage of Baptist preaching avoids the public display of Greek or Hebrew words. All that is homework, and great preaching does not preach its homework. Those who work well in the original biblical languages need not display their knowledge. In the sixteenth century, Erasmus, among the most brilliant of all Christian leaders in the history of the Church, chided preachers in his *The Praise of Folly*. The personified Folly says,

> It has seemed well, you note, to imitate the rhetoricians of our time, who believe themselves absolutely to be gods if they can . . . weave a few Greekish words, like inlay work . . . into their Latin orations, even if at the moment there is not place for them . . . with the idea . . . that those who understand will be vastly pleased with themselves, and those who do not understand will admire the more.¹⁰

Use language that fits, language that ordinary people understand, always remembering the sage advice of a wise preacher: "Remember that the Lord said, 'Feed my sheep,' not my giraffes."

Contemporary

The best Baptist preaching has never dodged the burning questions of the day. Rather, it has led the way in asking them. Yet the best sermons do not offer simplistic answers, perhaps not even very religious sounding answers. The best preaching grapples with the searing questions in the light of the gospel. Even if the preacher and the congregation cannot make their way to full light, at least they find strength and patience enough to wait for more light, and they do it together.

Reverent

From the very beginning, the best of Baptist preaching has had an aura of reverence about it. When the preacher stood in the pulpit, the people knew that he was conducting serious business. "I have no time to

---

[9]Quoted in E. C. Dargan, *A History of Preaching* (London: Hodder and Stoughton, 1905) 302.

[10]Desiderius Erasmus, *The Praise of Folly*, trans. Hoyt Hopewell Hudson (Princeton: Princeton University Press, 1941) 10-11.

trifle with men's souls," wrote Samuel Stillman of Boston.[11] In reference to Richard Furman, William B. Johnson wrote, "When *he* arose to speak . . . all eyes were turned upon him, with profound attention, and reverential awe."[12] Such preaching was not without its light moments, but the humor was always natural, not forced.

Worship, in the best tradition of the Baptists, leads naturally into the sermon. It is never mere entertainment, something done *for* the congregation rather than something done *by* the congregation. Some well-meaning Baptists have come close to shifting the nature of worship to that of performance by those on the stage. There's nothing particularly new about that temptation. A century ago Søren Kierkegaard sadly compared Danish church worship to a theater performance.[13] Worshipers become an audience that meets not in a sanctuary but an auditorium. They are not given orders of worship but programs, outlining the numbers to be sung and the people to perform. Leaders stand on a stage, which, in some buildings, is equipped with lighting and amplification systems that compete favorably with those in Broadway theaters. The main performance is that of the preacher, who is sometimes spotlighted while the rest of the auditorium lights are dimmed. Why should anyone wonder over applause in the church? Of course it is appropriate *if what takes place is entertainment.*

The best Baptist tradition flatly refuses to be a part of ecclesiastical entertainment. If the "foundations of the thresholds shake," it should not be from the thunderous applause of an audience, but from the voice of the seraphim who call.

> *Holy, holy, holy is the Lord of hosts;*
> *the whole earth is full of his glory.* (Isaiah 6:3)

The Baptist tradition traced in this book insists on active worship. The prayers, spoken by the pastor, are the "prayers of the people." Thus the pastor always uses the plural "we" in public prayer. Why? It is not the

---

[11]Samuel Stillman, *Select Sermons on Doctrinal and Practical Subjects* (Boston: Manning and Loring, 1808) xvi.

[12]In William B. Sprague, ed., *Annals of the American Pulpit* (New York: Robert Carter and Brother, 1860) 6:164.

[13]Søren Kierkegaard, *Purity of Heart Is to Will One Thing,* trans. Douglas V. Steere (New York: Harper and Brothers, 1938) 162-65.

pastor's private prayer. It is one person trying to express in words the united prayers of the people. Albert Schweitzer once said to his congregation that when he led in public prayer, "it seems to me that your thoughts, rising around the words of my prayers, form wonderful harmonies around a simple melody."[14] The sermon points to God made known in Jesus Christ, not to the preacher made known by stage lights. Anthems and hymns are no longer performances, but the inevitable voice of praise and thanksgiving from a faithful people.

Such reverence in the act of worship does not impede evangelism; rather, it enhances genuine evangelism. If the sermon resorts to some kind of mental coercion in order to force public decisions, then the Baptist preacher is betraying the best heritage of his denomination. With William Carey, the pioneer of modern missions, the faithful Baptist preacher lives with the conviction that "we have no faith in makings."[15] We cannot make anyone into a Christian by mental coercion. The preacher must preach Christ in the faith that "the wind blows where it wills" (John 3:8), and the results are best left with God.

CONCLUSION

So there are the major contours of the Baptist heritage in preaching. It has a shape; it can be recognized; it is distinguishable from other kinds of preaching. There are, of course, other traditions among the people called Baptists. Doubtless a book of similar length to this one could be written tracing other Baptist traditions in preaching. But no other heritage has led and sustained the denomination over the entire course of its history. No other heritage has provided such depth to match its evangelistic appeal. No other heritage has so consistently sustained a people with hope and courage to face whatever a day may bring. In short, no other heritage of preaching has sent so many ordinary yet extraordinary people out into the world with the words of Isaiah on their lips: "Here am I! Send me!"

---

[14]Albert Schweitzer, *Reverence for Life,* trans. Reginald H. Fuller (New York: Irvington Publishers, Inc., 1980) 42.

[15]S. Pearce Carey, *William Carey* (New York: George H. Doran Co., 1923) 264.

Chapter 12

MAKING CLEAR THE GOSPEL

The preacher is one of the few speakers whose object must be the same on every occasion. The subjects will change, but the object is always constant: making clear the gospel. Nothing outside that objective can be considered preaching. Many an honest and hard-working preacher has discovered that a lifetime of preaching has not exhausted the possibilities of subjects to reach that one object. Great preaching bears witness to an event, an event that took place in history, an event by which all other events are judged, an event that, when reproduced in a person's life, makes that life absolutely different. This event is the intervention of God in human history, it is Jesus Christ.

That gospel literally captured the early Baptist preachers and refused to let them go. When debate and controversy over doctrinal matters threatened to overshadow that gospel, they absolutely refused to be diverted from their one object. "Rage and Fury," said John Gale in the eighteenth century, "are inconsistent with Christianity; and where these govern, that [the gospel] can find no place."[1] A century earlier John Bunyan claimed never "to meddle" with theological controversy. Instead, he asserted, "it pleased me much to contend with . . . the Remission of Sins by the Death and Sufferings of Jesus."[2] They were convinced that the gospel needed no defense, only proclamation. So they preached the gospel.

WHAT THE GOSPEL IS NOT

The gospel may seem so obvious, so blatant, that we need not consider what the gospel is *not*. Yet many have heard enough sermons to be fully aware that there is often some confusion over the gospel.

---

[1] John Gale, *Reflections on Mr. Wall's History of Infant Baptism* (London: Printed by J. Darby, 1711) 3.

[2] John Bunyan, *Grace Abounding*, 284.

The gospel is not a defense of the Bible. There has probably never been a greater expository preacher among the Baptists than Alexander Maclaren. He lived during an age when biblical criticism was producing a rage of controversy over the Bible. In all his hundreds of published sermons, I do not remember a single time when he felt it was necessary to defend the Bible. Whatever his subject, he eventually led the sermon to the great subject—Jesus Christ. "Take it as a piece of the simplest prose . . . that Christ is *everything,*" he said.[3]

The Bible can stand on its own. To rant and rave over one's pet theory of inspiration is an ingenious way to fail to preach the gospel. To attempt to prove that the Bible is inerrant and infallible in every aspect—historically, philosophically, scientifically, as well as religiously—is not only to attempt to prove what is intrinsically unprovable, but to divert one's ultimate faith away from God made known in Jesus Christ to a tangible object. In biblical terms, that is the sin of idolatry. It is not unlike what Moses found when he came down from Mount Sinai. Tired of an invisible god, the people had insisted upon a tangible god. So Aaron fashioned a golden calf out of their most valuable possessions (Exodus 32). Some extreme inerrantists have taken what is most valuable and beautiful—their religious faith—and fashioned a god that can be handled. The Bible to them is no longer the Word of God, it is God's very self. To try to preach such a god is not only a mistake, it is heresy.

The gospel is not a book, it is a Person. The early disciples traveled through the Empire, not with a book in their hands, but with a presence in their heart. The blood of martyrs was willingly spilled not as a witness to a book, but as witness to a Person. When Christ was departing, he trusted his gospel in the world to the keeping of the Holy Spirit, who "will guide you into all the truth" (John 16:13). William Newton Clarke, one of the greatest Baptist leaders of the early twentieth century, said flatly that Christ "never promised an infallible church, or an infallible book, or any infallible visible guide, but committed his kingdom to the Spirit and the divine life."[4]

---

[3]Alexander Maclaren, *Psalms for Sighs* (Grand Rapids MI: Wm. B. Eerdmans, 1945) 83.

[4]William Newton Clarke, *An Outline of Christian Theology* (Edinburgh: T. and T. Clark, 1900) 46.

Baptist preaching has been devoted to the Bible. It has taken the Bible seriously at every turn, but it has not worshiped the Bible. Rather, it has opened the Bible and studied it, proclaimed its truth, and lived it. Some assume that the Bible must be defended; great Baptist preaching has allowed the Bible to defend itself. Some hesitate to ask embarrassing questions of the Bible for fear faith may crumble; great Baptist preaching has carried on a constant dialogue with the Bible and found faith strengthened. Some measure final authority by the Bible; great Baptist preaching has found ultimate authority in the God of the Bible. It has lived in the faith that through an honest and searching study of the Bible, God can be encountered. Such preaching explores the Scriptures fearlessly and comes face to face with many a person whose words are, like Jeremiah's, "a burning fire shut up in my bones" (Jeremiah 20:9). When that happens, Baptist preaching frequently discovers that both the preacher and the congregation have been addressed by God.

To appeal to the supposed inerrancy of the "autographs" of the Bible is, as John Clifford said, "as mischievous as it is unwarranted."[5] Why appeal to something that does not exist? Not even one page! It is to stake one's faith on a theory. The victories have been won through the centuries with the *present* Bible, with all its problems of translation and explanation.

The authority of the Bible needs no defense. There will always be varied theories of inspiration just as there will always be critics of the truth of the Bible. But the Bible's authority is not ultimate. Ultimate authority for the Christian is God made known in Christ. Scripture will never be in danger of losing its appropriate authority, for to discard the Bible would be to discard the only means of understanding the historic Christ. H. Wheeler Robinson put it succinctly: a Christian "holds the Bible to be authoritative because of the truth of its teaching; he does not hold the teaching to be true simply because he finds it in the Bible."[6]

The gospel is not the mere presentation of Bible stories. Even apart from its religious significance, the Bible contains some of the most interesting and exciting stories in world literature. Old Testament stories, however,

---

[5]John Clifford, *The Inspiration and Authority of the Bible* (London: James Clarke and Company, 1895) 64.

[6]H. Wheeler Robinson, "The Bible and Protestantism," *The Congregational Quarterly* 16, no. 1 (1938):48.

told from the pulpit merely to draw moral lessons from some patriarch's life may be both interesting and helpful, but they are not gospel preaching. Even New Testament stories may be told with the same attention to the facts and still not be gospel preaching.

It is easy to be lured by the idea that teaching the content of the Bible is the same as preaching the gospel. Many a preacher is understandably concerned about the widespread ignorance of the bare facts of Scripture. So there is a great temptation to use the allotted time in the pulpit simply to teach the basic stories of the Bible. Great Baptist preaching, however, has always insisted on going beyond the stories to the truth that underlies them. Take for example, the story of Jesus calling two fishermen to follow him. The *facts* are these: their names were Simon and Andrew; they were casting their nets in the Sea of Galilee; they left their nets to follow Jesus. But the *truth* is something much deeper than the facts. The truth has something to do with a call we still hear, and it has everything to do with the lives behind the faces peering up at the preacher at that very moment.

The Old Testament prophets based their message on a formula that is mistranslated in the King James Version. What we know as "Thus saith the Lord" is a perfect tense in the Hebrew and is better translated "Thus Yahweh has said." That is, preaching proclaims what God *has said* through Scripture in a certain historical setting—that is fact. But the best preaching also proclaims what God *is saying*—that is truth. The former without the latter is just telling stories. The latter without the former has no mooring. But taken together—fact and truth—the gospel is discovered, and once again the eternal Word finds its way through the stories and into hearts of faith.

Narrative preaching, which has produced some of the finest contemporary sermons, is far more than just telling factual Bible stories. At its best, narrative preaching tells The Story in such a way that it transcends time. It always moves the hearer to the level of saying, "That is also *my* story!"

The gospel is not a political philosophy. Jesus came preaching the Kingdom of God, not a political philosophy. To identify Christ with right-wing or left-wing politics is to betray the one crucified by political pressure from right and left. Jesus steadfastly refused to be a part of the three groups wielding power in his day. Neither the chief priests (religious power), the elders (aristocratic power), nor the scribes (legal power) could claim his support. They all soon became his enemies.

To state it bluntly: Christ is the judge of all politics, and to try to identify him with any political philosophy is to confuse the judged and the judge. Baptist preaching was born in a political world and has never left it. Politics opened the door of many a prison cell to early Baptists, and politics slammed the doors of the great universities in the face of dissenters of all kinds. It established Congregationalism in Massachusetts and Anglicanism in Virginia, and it laid the lash on the bleeding back of Obediah Holmes. Baptist preaching has never been divorced from politics; it has never been wedded to politics.

What has been the relationship? Ultimately, the best Baptist preaching has never winked at taking sides on political issues. John Clifford was a familiar face in the halls of the English Parliament. Samuel Stillman, and later Thomas Baldwin, were asked to preach the annual election sermon in Massachusetts. Isaac Backus campaigned for the separation of church and state all the way to Independence Hall in Philadelphia. The line of Baptists involved in politics is unbroken. The greatest Baptist preaching has been consistent with regard to politics; it has always held up Christ as the judge of all politics.

The gospel gives no detailed political instructions, but it does bear testimony to something no political philosophy would dare say: there is no disgrace in giving up power and privilege in the name of the Crucified. Thus, the gospel stands above politics as its judge, and at the same time moves many a thoughtful Christian into the thick of political battles.

The gospel is not advice to be good. Who could have been more good, more moral, according to the standards of the age, than the Pharisees? Yet Jesus' life judged their impeccable morals just as he still judges even the best of our morals.

The temptation to reduce the gospel to legalism is always present, not only in the preacher but also in the people. Legalism always provides one with a tangible record of success or failure. The report card has the advantage of showing whether one passes or fails.

Great preaching has no business peddling pious moralisms. The problem with most "children's sermons," as well as many adult sermons, is that they often consist of telling a story in order to teach a moral—be kind to grandma, always say "please" and "thank you." A moralism reflects a culture; the gospel reflects a Person who judges all cultures. A moralism tells people what to do or not to do; the gospel frees people to be or not to be.

The gospel is not the promotion of faith and goodwill. Who could deny that genuine faith and goodwill exist among all religions? Jews, Muslims, Hindus, and Buddhists, to say nothing of post-Christian humanists and even outspoken atheists, are sometimes so full of faith and goodwill that they put many a Christian to shame. There is nothing inherent in the gospel that gives Christians a corner on genuine faith and goodwill.

The question is this, faith in whom? Or what? Goodwill in the name of whom? Of what? The gospel answers those questions not in any abstract principle or theory, but in a historical person, Jesus of Nazareth.

FOCUS ON THE GOSPEL

Now we have reached a turn along this rather familiar road. We must now think in more positive terms of what the gospel *is*. At the outset it should be recognized that great Baptist preachers have always confessed a certain humility about the gospel. It has not so much been something they possessed as something that possessed them. They have not enclosed the gospel within the Baptist fold as though other denominations have no part of it. Rather, great Baptist preaching has always echoed the sentiments of Ernest Payne: "Christians clearly need help from one another if they are to find the right way."[7]

The gospel we preach is not our own. The words should be ours, and the manner of presentation should be ours, but not the substance of our preaching. The substance belongs to all Christians and to history itself. The substance of our preaching centers around the event of Jesus Christ. This is borne out by the Apostle Paul's definition of preaching the gospel: it is the passing on of the news "that Christ died for our sins, in accordance with the scriptures; that he was buried; that he was raised to life on the third day . . . and that he appeared to Cephas . . . and afterward to all the apostles" (1 Corinthians 15:3-7). In spite of all the diverse and sometimes incompatible *kerygmata* of the New Testament,[8] there is a unity in the gospel message. The essence of the gospel is Jesus Christ.

---

[7]Quoted in W. M. S. West, *To Be a Pilgrim, A Memoir of Ernest A. Payne* (Guildford, Surrey: Lutterworth Press, 1983) 201.

[8]See James D. G. Dunn, *Unity and Diversity in the New Testament* (Philadelphia: The Westminster Press, 1977) 11-32.

But as P. T. Forsyth stressed, we are only partially right in saying that Christ is the gospel: "the gospel is a certain interpretation of Christ which is given in the New Testament."[9]

For that reason great Baptist preaching from the outset has been dedicated to the study of the Bible. Living the heritage calls for Baptist preachers to summon all their training in the use of the tools of biblical study, all their training in theology and ethics, all their knowledge of church history and current events, and all their imagination and linguistic skill to focus on the critical study of the Bible. This does not slam the door on the voice of the Holy Spirit. Many an honest preacher has discovered that the more critical knowledge he or she has of a passage, the more frequently is heard that "still small voice."

To preach the gospel obviously does not mean reciting C. H. Dodd's understanding of the bare kerygma each Sunday.[10] The Old Testament, for example, can spring to life with insights current to our century, but it must always be preached as it relates to the event of Jesus Christ. The story of the tower of Babel preached to increase a congregation's understanding of early worship along the Tigris and Euphrates rivers is not gospel preaching. But that same story set over against Luke's account of Pentecost in Acts 2 throws open the windows and lets the light stream in. Likewise, the New Testament epistles must be preached as they were written, in the shadow of the Christ event.

JESUS AS THE GOSPEL

Now let us take a closer look at this Christ event. It is obvious that the early Church did not proclaim merely the *message* of Jesus or a certain *philosophy* that Jesus proclaimed. The early Church *preached Jesus*. That is, they proclaimed not Jesus' gospel, but Jesus himself as the gospel. Whereas the heart of Jesus' message was the coming of the Kingdom of God (Mark 1:15, Matthew 10:7, Luke 21:31) the heart of the Christian message is that Jesus himself is the personification of the Kingdom of God. A radical Marxist can preach the message of Karl Marx without reference to Marx himself; a faithful Jew can preach the law of

---

[9]P. T. Forsyth, *The Person and Place of Jesus Christ* (London Independent Press, Ltd., 1961) 1.

[10]C. H. Dodd, *The Apostolic Preaching and Its Developments* (New York: Harper and Brothers, 1935) 17.

Moses without reference to Moses himself; but the Christian message is forever united to the living Christ. "We preach Christ crucified," said Paul, "a stumbling block to Jews and folly to the Gentiles" (1 Corinthians 1:23). Great preaching always bears witness to his life—his *whole* life—for it is in the entire event of his life that the "Word became flesh and dwelt among us" (John 1:14).

He shared our humanness. Perhaps the most dangerous heresy among conservative Christian theologies in any age is the old docetic notion that claims that because Jesus was "spiritual" he somehow did not share our humanness. A spiritual Christ can feel no pain, either his own or ours. A spiritual Christ does not really agonize over what direction his ministry should take (Matthew 4:1-11), much less share in the struggle of our vocational decisions. A spiritual Christ need not weep real tears at the death of a friend (John 11:35), much less weep with a mother whose son has died of a drug overdose. A spiritual Christ need not feel the pain of Jerusalem (Matthew 23:37), much less the pain of the ghetto. That is to say, a spiritual Christ is a domesticated Christ who attends only to the spiritual concerns of people. Such a conception invites the compartmentalization of life into the sacred and secular and opens wide the door for those who want to save the soul but forget the body.

To deny Christ's humanity is a recrucifixion on a religious cross. Jesus was recognized as Jesus of Nazareth long before he was proclaimed the Christ of God. His friends knew him as the son of Mary and Joseph, from the northern part of a remote, politically powerless country on the periphery of the Roman Empire. He limited his short ministry largely to the Jews; his family at one time thought he had lost his mind (Matthew 12:48); he had a country accent (Matthew 26:73); he was executed like the lowest slave. Not only the Cross, but also his genuine humanity, have proved to be a scandal to every generation.

The greatest battles of the early centuries of the Church centered around the true humanity of Jesus. Even the Council of Nicea in A.D. 325, which proclaimed the "consubstantiality" of Jesus with God, never denied the humanness of Christ. Later, the Council of Chalcedon in A.D. 451, underlined the full humanity of Jesus.

Even the Apostle's Creed, recited by countless Christians every Sunday, places great emphasis on his humanity: *"born* of the Virgin Mary . . . " (what is more earthy than a birth?), *"suffered* under Pontius Pilate

. . . " (what is more human than suffering?), "was *crucified, dead,* and *buried*" (what is more inevitably physical than death?).

Great Baptist preaching has never failed to bear witness to the fact that Jesus shared and bore our humanness. Even those who most fervently preached the deity of Christ never failed to confess and proclaim his humanity. Hear Richard Fuller of Baltimore:

> A knowledge of our ignorance is a very important department of human wisdom. . . . Let us open the pages of inspiration in the spirit of docility, and we will confess that, however baffling to our thoughts, there is not truth more clearly revealed than the incarnation of the divine Being in the man Christ Jesus.[11]

"The *man* Christ Jesus," he said. His emphasis on the incarnation was couched in the fact that Jesus was truly human.

The story does not end with his humanity. As Donald Baillie stressed, "God was in Christ."[12] In a way beyond the scope of human words, Jesus is so closely identified with God that the same people who knew his humanness from firsthand experience proclaimed him as the long-awaited Messiah, the Son of God, the one now exalted to the right hand of God. Jesus as human friend became Jesus the Lord whose very presence judges our sinfulness. Somehow, the Word that called forth the light and scattered the stars across the heavens was in him to the extent that Paul described him as "the image of the invisible God" (Colossians 1:15) and declared that "In him all the fulness of God was pleased to dwell" (Colossians 1:19).

This is the point where Christian preaching reaches down and slips off its shoes, for it is entering holy ground. Who can describe in human words that which overflows the cup of reason? Baptist preachers have proclaimed Christ as the risen Lord, not because they could explain it, but because they have experienced it. They have pointed to the Crucified One and said, "The love of God is something like that!" They knew that if the one event that split history down the middle could be explained in human terms it would not be of God's action at all.

The Cross has been central to great Baptist preaching, not because the preachers have been preoccupied with a gruesome death, but be-

---

[11]Richard Fuller, *Sermons* (New York: Sheldon and Company, 1860) 15.

[12]See Donald Baillie, *God Was in Christ* (New York: Charles Scribner's Sons, 1948) 4.

cause they have been possessed by one who overcame death. Who can look at the Cross without seeing the depth of human sin? Any attempt to do away with sin and guilt because of the naive theory that people have enough guilt laid on their shoulders outside the church results in an immature theology. Great Baptist preaching has never joined the peace-of-mind cult. The Cross forbids it! Christ does not offer peace of mind but the peace of God, something far better. Jesus did not have peace of mind as he agonized in the Garden of Gethsemane, but he had the peace of God, which enabled him to face even the Cross.

The Cross is a reminder of our age-old attempts to be our own god, which is ME written in capital letters, or the expansion of ME into FAMILY or COUNTRY or RACE. Great Baptist preaching has dealt with not only private sin, but corporate sin, national sin, world sin. All of this sin is caught in a spiral of history and converges at the Cross. In a society "whose official creed is optimism, and which is knee-deep in blood,"[13] this kind of preaching faces evil realistically.

If the Cross represents the depth of human sin, why is every dime store filled with cheap crosses? Why does it adorn every Christian church? In short, why has this ancient implement of torture and death become the logo of the Christian faith?

It would have been extremely easy for the early followers of Jesus to proclaim him as one of the martyred prophets whose tombs were venerated throughout the land. Not only easy, but safe. Anyone can venerate a dead man. Can you imagine a Pharisee venerating the prophet Amos to his face? A dead prophet is a safe prophet. But how strange that no cult arose at the grave of Jesus. We are not even certain of the location of the tomb.

Something else happened. The unanimous claim of the disciples was that not even death could stop him! The Resurrection is not an event to be argued rationally; it is suprarational. Neither is it to be proven scientifically; it is beyond science.

Great Baptist preaching states flatly that the Resurrection was an act of God; therefore, belief is an act of faith. The Resurrection is not preached as evidence to authenticate faith but as the object of faith. The passion story would hardly have been written if it were not for the Res-

---

[13]Jurgen Moltmann, *The Crucified God* (New York: Harper and Row, 1974) 4.

urrection. The dejected and defeated disciples somehow *experienced* the risen Christ. It was not their faith that created the Resurrection; it was the Resurrection that created their faith. Thus Christian faith begins at Easter.

Baptist preaching at its best does not try just to defend or even to describe the Resurrection. Rather, it attempts the humanly impossible: namely, to allow the Resurrection to happen again and again in the hearts of believers. Great preaching does not attempt to reconcile the various descriptions of the Resurrection any more than the gospel writers did. There is something far greater at stake, and it has everything to do with the living Christ in the midst of believers—what the Church has traditionally called the presence of the Holy Spirit.

The story continues with the Holy Spirit. Belief in the present spirit of Christ may be the most neglected and abused element of the gospel. With nearly every appearance of the risen Christ described in the New Testament there was some kind of calling. Vocation followed appearance; mission followed encounter. Finally, the early disciples, called and supported by a power they could not explain, much less understand, began their audacious spread of the gospel. They were not mere faith healers. Healing was only a sign of something far greater: a coming Kingdom where there would be no more pain or suffering. Neither were they cheerleaders for glossolalia, placing speaking in tongues on the center stage of history. Even Paul, who gave it place, refused to give it centrality. Given the immaturity of the Corinthian church, one wonders if Paul was simply enduring their glossolalia in order to bring "a still more excellent way" (1 Corinthians 12:31) to the forefront.

The preaching of and dependence on the Holy Spirit has nothing to do with a ghostlike spirit of Jesus that would be more at home on Halloween than any other day of the year. Still less is it the idea of some psychological presence living on after the death of Jesus. It is the *Holy* Spirit, the spirit of God, the spirit (Hebrew, *ruah;* Greek, *pneuma*) that according to Genesis was "moving over the face of the waters" (Genesis 1:2) and was the agent of creation. The Holy Spirit is the power of God, the same spirit who empowered the Old Testament prophets, gave new life to defeated and dejected disciples, and who has given hope and courage to every believer from the Decopolis to the megalopolis. To reduce that power to something magical for a selected few is to squeeze God into a magician's hat.

Great preaching not only preaches on the Holy Spirit but depends on the Holy Spirit. For preaching is merely stale bread if it has no power that again and again transforms human words into the divine Word.

CONCLUSION

Alexander Maclaren, in looking back over a lifetime of preaching, spoke of the necessity of building one's preaching on a solid foundation. In a striking illustration he said that if a person wished to build a house in Rome or Jerusalem, he must go fifty or sixty feet down, through potsherds and broken tiles, and the dust of ancient palaces and temples. "We have to drive a shaft," he concluded, "clear down through all the superficial strata, and to lay the first stones on the Rock of Ages."[14]

This chapter has attempted to describe the Rock of Ages on which all great preaching is built. The next three chapters will make some proposals for the future of Baptist preaching, but none of that is as important as *what* is preached. Baptist preaching may not always be eloquent, but it must always make clear the gospel.

---

[14]David Williamson, *The Life of Alexander Maclaren* (London: James Clarke and Company, n. d.) 130.

Chapter 13

BACK TO THE OLD GRIND

You may remember the story of Robert Robinson, the eighteenth-century Baptist preacher who served the church at Cambridge. Throughout his mature ministry he urged preachers to work hard in preparation for sermons, but as a young man he sometimes entered the pulpit without prior study, apparently believing that God would always supply him with a sermon. On one occasion it was almost time for him to preach and he had absolutely no idea what to say. During the last verse of the hymn preceding the sermon, a verse came to him from the Song of Solomon: "Comfort me with apples, for I am sick of love." He preached on the text, but never again did he enter the pulpit without intense preparation.[1]

HARD LABOR

There is no way to make sermon preparation easy. Fun? Sometimes. Exciting? Frequently. Easy? Never. Even on those rare occasions when the sermon flows from your pen as quickly as you can write it, you can be assured that next week's sermon will flow at the rate of cold molasses. God has more than one way to keep a preacher humble, and many would state that sermon preparation is one of the best. To say it bluntly, sermon preparation can be a grind, and the great heritage of Baptist preaching offers no exceptions.

No wonder preachers sometimes immerse themselves in other pressing duties of the pastorate and allow sermon preparation to slide. As pressing as other duties are, they may not be as terrifying as sitting alone behind a desk facing an open Bible and a sheet of paper as blank as your mind feels. It does not take long for a preacher to discover that sermon preparation takes work, hard work. But it must be added that study and preparation for sermons is not *just* a grind. It "is obviously a matter

---

[1] See George Dyer, *Memoirs of the Life and Writings of Robert Robinson* (London: G. G. and J. Robinson, 1796) 26.

of books, and family love and concerts and fishing and community campaigns and hospital calls and books again."[2]

There is an alternative, however. In the Middle Ages preachers regularly read other people's sermons in the pulpit, and the quality of preaching suffered accordingly. In the twelfth century, Werner of Ellerback published a collection of sermons entitled *Deforationes Patrum,* or "Flowers Plucked from the Fathers." In his introduction he stated that his purpose was to offer a new collection of sermons for the use of preachers, since the old ones had become somewhat stale and the people needed a fresh supply. So also was the purpose of another book of sermons entitled *Sermones Dormi Secure* ("Sleep Well Sermons"), which went through twenty-five editions.[3]

So there is always that option: you can preach other people's sermons. Enough have been published to keep you well supplied. Some companies even specialize in keeping pastors supplied with sermons for each Sunday of the year. One company advertises, "Pastors, let us take the burden out of your sermon preparation." They can take all the heavy burden out of sermon preparation, except the heavier burden of guilt for preaching the work of others. However, it is an option, and if you decide to take it, you need not read further, just enjoy a good night's sleep.

From the religious ferment of Cambridge University in the early seventeenth century came evangelical preachers who were committed to laboring over their sermons. To use their quaint phrase, they would sometimes exhaust their "animal spirits" in sermon preparation. In a time of great religious controversy, when to preach at all in a Baptist church carried its attendant dangers, Baptist preachers had to know not only *what* they would say but also *why* they were saying it. John Gill, whose voluminous published works almost all originated in sermons, accused anyone who failed to labor over sermon preparation of being "nothing less than idle and lazy."[4] Robert Hall worked so hard on his preaching that he had a complete physical breakdown in 1804 and had to stop preaching for

---

[2]Theodore A. Gill, in *To God Be the Glory,* ed. Theodore A. Gill (Nashville: Abingdon Press, 1973) 13.

[3]E. C. Dargan, *A History of Preaching* (London: Hodder and Stoughton, 1905) 201, 207ff.

[4]John Gill, "The Duty of a Pastor to His People," in *A Collection of Sermons and Tracts* (London: Printed for George Keith, 1773) 2:5.

months before he returned to the pulpit. In America the names of Furman, Staughton, Hart, Stillman, Baldwin, Manning, Backus, and many more all testify to the reality of hard labor in preaching. The truth is that great Baptist preaching was no accident.

HOW TO BE PREPARED

The minutes of triumph in the pulpit most frequently follow on the heels of hours in the study. Even those periodic flashes of inspiration, when just the right words come to mind, occur most often when the mind is keen from constant study. The problem with Sunday is that it comes around once a week. But many a busy pastor would think it was vacation time if only one sermon a week had to be prepared. Usually there are two or three sermons, plus talks for church organizations, civic clubs and book review clubs, and the many other groups that invite pastors to speak. Of course you don't accept every invitation, but it is likely that you will accept some, and even if you use something you have prepared before, it takes time to review. Unlike many politicians, the preacher has no professional sermon/speech writer to help with the task. So the question is constant: how to be prepared?

A basic principle underlying all sermon preparation is the *ability to think theologically*. Great preaching does not form sermons out of books; it forms sermons out of life. And that, of course, includes books. Thinking theologically is not looking for a catchy sermon illustration in every daily event. It is the ability to draw theological significance from the common, ordinary happenings every person experiences. Perhaps you are driving downtown, frustrated over the traffic and heat and interminable traffic lights that turn red just as you reach them. You turn your car radio dial in search of some soothing music and accidentally tune in the new Christian radio station in town. Before you can twist the dial, out comes a syrupy soprano voice oozing with sweet religiosity,

> *No more sorrow, no more strife,*
> *Since Jesus came into my life.*

She sings the lyrics with a smile you can almost see through the radio dial. You begin to think theologically. Are the lyrics to that song, heard by an unknown number of people in your own congregation, faithful to the gospel? Do they even make sense? That experience may or may not appear in a sermon, but you tuck the event neatly into some corner of your brain so it can be ready for use when and if the time comes. Examples of thinking theologically are infinite, for they relate to everyone you meet, everything you see or hear or smell or taste, everything you do.

One word about general reading. Most preaching manuals, and many preachers, are afflicted with the "Haven't-you-read-so-and-so?" disease. It is an extremely easy illness to catch, and it is very difficult to cure. The aspiring preacher, with his college diploma still close to his breast, reads his first preaching manual in preparation for a seminary class in homiletics. There, in black and white, from someone who ought to know, is the advice to read everything under the sun, including the great novels, biographies, several significant newspapers on a regular basis, and, of course, the Bible. All of this should be done while keeping up with his Greek and Hebrew, serious biblical studies, weighty theology books, ethics, and a few forays into church history. Then in all the time left over, he is supposed to do all the work of a pastor.

The only cure for the "Haven't-you-read-so-and-so?" disease is to recognize the fact that writers of preaching manuals normally speak from the perspective of a lifetime in the ministry. They are the beneficiaries of a great wealth of wisdom that has enriched their own ministries through a lifetime of reading and reflecting. Their advice is meant to provide an exciting guide for future reading, not a burden of guilt to lug into the ministry. So plot a course, read the great books, and don't fritter away time reading junk books.

How to Find a Text

Now to the specific task of preparing the sermon for next Sunday morning: how to find a text? Fortunately, there is an easy answer to that problem. There is absolutely no reason for a preacher to lose half the week running around trying to find a text. Baptist preachers have enjoyed complete freedom in choosing a text for each sermon. That freedom has been both a blessing and a burden. It is a blessing because passages of scripture can be chosen to suit the occasion. It is a burden for the same reason: choosing the appropriate passage is not always easy. Many have found that a plan is a necessity.

There is no reason for a Baptist preacher to be afraid of using a lectionary. It has the advantage of providing the preacher with a plan of preaching, or at least the general direction, for the whole year. While always free to change the plan, you have the advantage of knowing well in advance the texts to be used Sunday by Sunday. Frequently sermon material will fall into your lap two months before it is needed. Each Monday morning you will already be equipped with a text, and frequently some idea or illustrations that have been gathered over the weeks. A lectionary has other advantages: it rescues you from your own pet interests. It persuades you to travel the full orbit of the gospel in a year's time and forces you into areas of the Christian faith that may have escaped your attention before.

Baptist preachers have another option that many find most rewarding. You can make your own lectionary. The first requirement for the task is to have a sufficient amount of time each year during which you are freed from church responsibilities and can concentrate on planning for the coming year. This is not vacation time; it is planning time and should be so understood by the church.

Once you have established a time and place for planning, here are a few essential tools: a calender marked with all the special days and seasons you intend to observe, one or more lectionaries that can serve as general guides and offer good suggestions, a good set of commentaries, and a Bible. The first day or two can be spent mapping out the general contours of the year's preaching. An obvious method is to break the year into seasons: Advent to Christmas, Christmas to Easter, Easter to the end of the summer, and September to Advent. Gradually get more and more specific until you can return to your church with a good grasp of what you will be preaching over a year's time. This method has the same advantage as a lectionary as long as you are careful not to dwell on your pet subjects or favorite passages of scripture.

Now that you have mapped out the entire year, you are free to concentrate on next Sunday's sermon. The view from the mountaintop has been invigorating, but now you are in the valley with a million things to do, people to see, programs to conduct; and Sunday, that inevitable Sunday, looms ahead.

Exploring the Text

Before jotting down a single note regarding the text, remember that Baptist preaching must be based on an a priori decision to be honest. That may not be as easy as it sounds. A preacher as great as Origen commonly engaged in wild and irresponsible allegory, and there was hardly any improvement until the time of the Scholastics. Origen, however, can be more easily excused than today's preachers, for allegory was the accepted method of interpretation in his day, especially in third-century Alexandria where he was trained and spent much of his ministry. Baptist preachers have inherited the accumulated knowledge of centuries of biblical study. To be honest with that heritage is the first requirement. Sermons must not be prepared to prove already held convictions. The task is to hear God's Word through the Scripture, not for God to hear your word through the sermon.

Now that you have determined to be honest, there is one more step—a vital step—to take before turning to the commentaries. Trust yourself enough to believe that you too might have something significant to say about that text, something as significant to your setting as the wisdom of any commentator, no matter how brilliant he or she may be. If early Baptists had depended wholly on available commentaries for their interpretation of Scripture, there never would have been a Baptist denomination. They spoke with a humble confidence that they too could read and understand the Word and interpret it correctly.

Try to block out all your prior understanding of the text and read it as if you were seeing it for the first time. There are two advantages to this: (1) you have a knowledge of your own congregation and circumstances that no commentator, no matter how brilliant, can have. That first impression you jot down may provide the most important link between the text and the people because it pulsates with life for them. (2) Your first impression is often a clue for your introduction. Take, for example, a certain preacher who wanted to preach from the story of Noah. The first thing that popped into his mind as he was preparing the sermon was how in the world an ancient story like that could pertain to people today. The next Sunday the first sentence in his sermon was this: "How can an ancient story like this, handed down from generation to generation by word of mouth and finally put in written form centuries later, have anything to say to us?" Instantly the people thought, "Yes! I've wondered that myself!" And they knew that the fellow in the pulpit was sure to be honest. So trust yourself. Your impressions may be few but are likely to be extremely important.

The next step is to turn to the commentaries and other tools of biblical study you have been taught to use and feel comfortable using. If you despise translating Greek or Hebrew, don't spend the entire week translating. Just pick out a few key words and do some word studies. To paraphrase Jesus, biblical languages are for the preacher, not the preacher for biblical languages. Read the best commentaries you can afford or can borrow. In short, familiarize yourself so thoroughly with the setting and content of the passage that you can enter the text and look around. You suddenly find yourself standing in the middle of a crowd of sick and groaning people beside the pool of Bethesda (John 5:1-9). Use your senses. What do you see? Smell? Hear? Can you bring yourself to touch anything? Take notes on all of this. By midweek, using this method, you will have enough notes to give you some idea about how the sermon might be structured.

Before we turn to the outline, it is well worth noting the two different ways of thinking we have used. Jerome Bruner has called them "right-handed thinking" and "left-handed thinking."[5] Right-handed thinking uses all the resources at hand and records what is logical and obvious about a text. Right-handed thinking is objective. Left-handed thinking, on the other hand, is far different. It is that receptive state of mind that is always ready to record that flash of truth, that light from beyond the horizon, which gives us a glimpse of the mind of God. Right-handed thinking gives the sermon a body; left-handed thinking gives the sermon a soul. Great preaching uses both ways of thinking.

Writing the Sermon

Not every preacher writes the introduction first; some wait until last. Whenever you prepare your introduction, be aware of this: it is crucial. It is the beginning of the trail, and although you cannot see all that is ahead just from the entrance, many a traveler will judge your entire journey by its beginning.

One preacher I know would judge the success or failure of his introduction by whether or not a certain deacon who always sat on the front side pew would leave his hearing aid turned up! Nothing will make a congregation turn off their ears quicker than some canned joke that supposedly "warms them up" but really only cheapens the gospel. Yet, humor—natural humor—has its place in a sermon, but only if the humor is not superimposed. Genuine humor can come only from those who are seri-

---

[5]Jerome Bruner, *On Knowing* (Cambridge: The Belknap Press of Harvard University Press, 1962) 2-8.

ous enough to see their own foolishness. It comes in flashes as natural as sunlight. Natural humor is not buffoonery.

Let your introduction belong to that sermon and that moment in history, and belong nowhere else. Introductions are not mix-and-match commodities to be chosen from the sermon shelf and matched with any sermon as an attractive accessory. The first few words of a sermon should have an organic relation to the rest of the sermon, so that what you say in the introduction naturally leads to what you say in the body.

One pastor, whose church was filled with avid basketball fans, was faced one Sunday morning with hundreds of red, sleepy eyes staring at him. No, they had not all been on a binge; they had all stayed up the night before watching the finals of a college basketball tournament in which two local teams had played. The congregation was roughly divided in their loyalties to each team. Here are the first two sentences of his sermon that day: "By your faces I have no problem telling whose team won last night. Let's talk about someone whom everyone thought was a loser." He then proceeded to preach a sermon on the death of Jesus, and everybody was with him. That introduction was perfect for that sermon at that time.

Some introductions fail not because they are not interesting enough but because they are too interesting. To begin the sermon on the mountain peak is to have no place else to climb. Where would you go, for example, if you began a sermon with Elie Wiesel's moving account of the little boy who refused to die while hanging from the gallows in a Nazi concentration camp?[6] Everything else would be anticlimactic. A good introduction is short, to the point, and causes people to think, "That preacher has something to say that I want to hear."

Now we come to the main body of the sermon, where the tradition of Baptist preaching has been to divide the discourse into sections, or points. Each point is divided and subdivided by explanation, argument, illustration, and an infinite number of further subdivisions. It is here that I want to propose a basic shift in our understanding of points. The problem with points is that they are static. They fail to lead to a destination, and frequently the preacher believes he or she is successful if people can

---

[6]Elie Wiesel, "Night," in *Night, Dawn, the Accident* (New York: Hill and Wang, 1972) 70-72.

remember the points. Many a preacher falls for gimmicks such as printing the points in the weekly bulletin, so that people can remember them. Space is even allowed in the bulletin outline for people to take notes, as though the prize will go to the hearer who can remember not only points but also subpoints and arguments and illustrations. As Jesus once said in a different context, "they have received their reward" (Matthew 6:2): a church composed of people who remember points.

Read the powerful description of black preaching written by Henry Mitchell.[7] Black preaching demonstrates that sermons must move more than the brain. Paul Tillich warned that in the course of time an intellectual gospel would appeal only to intellectuals.[8] Preaching must move both the head and the heart. When that happens, the attempt to remember points will be irrelevant, because somehow through God's Spirit the congregation has been lifted through the medium of that sermon to a higher plane of life. They leave the sanctuary at a different level. This is *not* structureless preaching. It is preaching in which the structure is somewhat concealed in order to reach a greater goal than the retention of points. The new preaching moves; it leads the congregation on an exciting journey.

Imagine that you have studied a text until the meaning has placed you on a mountaintop. The text has become God's Word for you, and you want the sermon to lift the people to the same mountaintop. So you walk back down the mountain to where the people are. Because you know them and love them as a pastor, your introduction begins down in the valley just where they are. Now you want to lead them up the mountain until they, too, can experience the exhilarating view from the top. So you begin walking just ahead of them, quietly and patiently showing the way. As trails lead off in different directions, you call them back to the main trail that leads to the top. From time to time you stop to rest. Few can make it to the top without a few rest stops. With that kind of leadership you finally bring them into a clearing at the summit where they can see so far that they seem to be able to see even beyond the horizon. As they leave that place, they may have to go back down into the valley, but they will

---

[7]Henry Mitchell, *The Recovery of Preaching* (San Francisco: Harper and Row, 1977).

[8]Paul Tillich, *The Protestant Era,* trans. James Luther Adams (Chicago: The University of Chicago Press, 1948) 227-28.

never be the same again, for their eyes have seen a vision of something more, something that lives on in the valley even when the way is difficult.

Thus great preaching takes people to the mountaintop. The number of rest stops along the way will depend on the preacher's intimate knowledge of the congregation, how strong they are, and how far their legs can carry them. Martin Luther King, Jr., in his "I Have a Dream" sermon, led an entire nation to the mountaintop. The momentum was more than merely powerful—it was suprapowerful. Even in listening to it again through a recording one can sense his patient leadership up the path, until the millions who hung on his words could see his vision of "all of God's children, black men and white men, Jews and Gentiles, Protestants and Catholics," who will "join hands and sing with the Negroes in the spiritual of old, 'Free at last, free at last, Great God A-mighty, We are free at last!'"[9] That sermon must be among the most powerful ever preached. Now a sharp question: who can remember its points? Of course, the points are not the point! What counts is that a whole nation saw the dream. The nation was led upward, step by step, over a well-planned path until we reached the mountaintop. Because of that vision, the nation has never been quite the same.

This model for sermon construction leaves a great deal of freedom for each preacher to lead his people along the path he or she finds most appropriate. There is more than one way to climb a mountain. A path may go straight up, or it may circle the mountain in a gradual incline, or it may zigzag up the mountain. But they all reach the top, and the view is worth the effort.

Concluding the sermon is one of the most difficult parts of sermon construction. Baptist preaching has enough faith, however, to allow God the privilege of creating the view from the mountaintop. The preacher may lead the people up, but he or she cannot make them look. There is not a preacher in the world who can *force* anyone to see the horizon.

The most important thing to remember about conclusions is a negative: do not exploit people's emotions. You must care enough for the people to honor their freedom. The conclusion, therefore, should be short. It should never be just a summary of points, but should complete

---

[9]See Stephen B. Oates, *Let the Trumpet Sound, the Life of Martin Luther King, Jr.* (London: Search Press, 1982) 259-62.

the journey you have traveled together. In writing the conclusion, a good question to ask yourself is this: "What do I want to happen?"

Speaking of writing, should a sermon be written? Is that even possible for the overworked pastor who must preach three or more different sermons a week? Probably not, at least not for all three. But the main sermon of the week should be written. Only by the discipline of writing can just the right word be found. Only by writing can the correct rhythm be achieved. Without the discipline of writing, sermons will be filled with hackneyed phrases. It is enough here to be reminded that Jesus said that on the day of judgment people will render account for every careless word they utter (Matthew 12:36). That day of judgment comes every time you stand up to preach.

CONCLUSION

A little over a century ago Phillips Brooks gave his famous series of lectures on preaching at Yale Divinity School. In one sentence he summed up the task of the preacher as he prepares: "There is nothing a sermon ought to be except a fit medium of truth."[10] Every principle of sermon preparation I have mentioned has been for the sole purpose of making the sermon a "fit medium of truth"—*the* Truth—for ordinary people.

Let Baptists prepare each sermon as a Jewish prophet prepared for sacrifice: it must be a sermon without blemish, suitable to offer as a sacrifice to God before all the people. And as it goes up in smoke before the altar, the people will look up and see the Lord "high and lifted up." Then the song of the seraphim will be our song: "Holy, holy, holy, is the Lord of hosts: the whole earth is full of his glory" (Isaiah 6:1-3).

---

[10]Phillips Brooks, *Lectures on Preaching* (London: H. R. Allenson, Ltd., 1877) 114.

Chapter 14

A WAY WITH WORDS

Great Baptist preaching has had a love affair with words. Words are the preacher's most important tools. Just the right word used at the perfect time can make the difference between success or failure once he reaches the pulpit. Thus, Baptist preaching lives under double orders: to have something to say and to know how to say it. That is not as easy as it sounds. Plenty of well-prepared sermons have something vitally important to say, but the message never gets across. The task of delivery is to have a perfect balance, to utter words that are at the same time an urgent message from God and a clear message to ordinary people.

The task of a good delivery is like that of a good interpreter. An interpreter hears a message for people in a language they do not understand and translates it into their own language. A good interpreter must have a thorough knowledge of at least two languages: that in which the message comes and that in which it is to be delivered. The preacher spends a lifetime trying to master both the language of theology *and* the language of ordinary people. The two are rarely the same, as every new theology student soon discovers. Often failure in the delivery of a sermon is a result of a preacher saying good things but using theological lingo nobody in the congregation understands.

A friend preached for a whole year before one person in the congregation had the courage to approach him after the service and ask what he meant by the word *pericope*. Every week he had used that word in reference to the scripture reading, and evidently the people had been so confused by it that they did not hear what he said *about* the pericope. Soon after my friend told me of that experience I happened to tune in a radio preacher who was informing his listening audience that a certain Greek verb being discussed was a second aorist imperative. I wondered how many in his radio audience knew or cared about the verb tense.

Yet just as often the preacher fails in sermon delivery because he does not understand the language of theology. What he says is plain and understandable, but because the preacher never bothered to learn the language of theology the sermon's message is shallow.

So the preacher is a faithful interpreter of the Word. This is exactly what Paul advised Timothy: "Do your best to present God as one approved, a workman who has no need to be ashamed, rightly handling the word of truth" (2 Timothy 2:15).

THE LANGUAGE OF WORDS

One of the recurring temptations for any preacher is to look out over a crowded sanctuary and daydream that all those people came to hear him or her preach. Once you succumb to that subtle temptation it is easy to become a clerical exhibitionist. The clerical exhibitionist, through the words used and attitudes expressed, focuses attention toward the person preaching instead of the living Christ. Exhibitionism comes on very subtly and sometimes unconsciously for the preacher. But comments by the congregation will offer clues for the exhibitionist.

CLUE #1: "Dr. Booklove is a mighty smart preacher because he uses such big words. Last Sunday he preached a great sermon; I wish I had been smart enough to understand it."

CLUE #2: "One thing I love about Brother Jolly's sermons is that he keeps us laughing. He could be another Bob Hope."

CLUE #3: "Isn't it wonderful that Reverend Travelogue has visited so much of the world! He has a personal experience to illustrate everything. And he always makes the scripture come alive by telling us about his trips to the Holy Land."

CLUE #4: "I wish I could be as humble as Dr. Sensitivity. His confessional sermons always bring tears to my eyes."

CLUE #5: "Don't you love Brother Lovesong's voice? I could listen to it all day, especially when it quivers with emotion."

All of these comments focus on the kind of preacher who consciously or unconsciously builds up a loyal following. To succeed as a clerical exhibitionist in a church is to risk clerical crucifixion, and many a preacher has left a church dazed and covered with scars because the congregation could not give up their loyalty to the previous pastor.

Great Baptist preaching avoids any form of exhibitionism. There are some positive principles on the use of language which, when followed, permit the preacher to retain his own special way of expressing himself while at the same time focusing the attention of the people on the living Christ.

Anglo-Saxon Words

The English language is a fascinating combination of two basic strands of language: Anglo-Saxon and Latin. Words derived from Latin are the ones you hear in a university classroom, but they are *not* the ones you hear around the breakfast table. In everyday speech, ordinary people use Anglo-Saxon words, many of which consist of one syllable. That is one reason for the overwhelming popularity of the King James Version of the Bible. It used mostly one syllable Anglo-Saxon words: "O taste and see that the Lord is good" (Psalm 34:8). Compare that to the ordinary book of theology.

Most people in a normal congregation use simple language in everyday conversation, not that they do not know bigger words or more complex sentence structure. Far from it. Many in an average congregation can easily correct the preacher's grammatical mistakes. Just as the gospel is centered around a divine Incarnation, sermon delivery must be centered around a type of language incarnation. That is to say, language must take on the flesh and sounds of that particular congregation. That does not mean adopting every slang word or ill-constructed sentence. It simply means the constant use of the simple Anglo-Saxon words used in the everyday speech of the congregation: no scientific jargon (like biofeedback), no psychological talk (like neurosis), no administrative slang (like counterproductive), and above all, no theological jargon.

The problem is not in theological language. Christian people would be enriched by a knowledge of specialized theological and biblical terms like "myth," "exegesis," "etiological," and many other terms that speak clearly to the theologian but are not in common usage. Theological terms can be taught in small classes where discussion takes place, but not splattered on an innocent congregation that has no chance to talk back.

One reason Paul's letters are sometimes difficult to understand is that he was the apostle to the Gentiles—the intellectuals. They used Greek and Latin words so Paul often had to use the same words in writing to them. There is just no way to translate "justification" into a common one-syllable Anglo-Saxon word. So, if you are preaching from one of Paul's letters, remember that behind every tongue-twisting word is an experience. Always ask, "What experience in Paul's life lies behind these words?"

Words that Appeal to the Senses

Someone once asked Jesus about neighborliness, and he responded by telling the story of the good Samaritan. Someone asked him about the forgiveness of God, and he responded with the story of the prodigal son. Someone asked him about faith, and he talked about a mustard seed. This language appeals to the senses, and the people never forgot it.

George Buttrick used to say that "truth travels best on the wings of a metaphor" (incidentally, that was a metaphor). He was a master at the perfectly timed use of metaphors; his sermons and everyday language were filled with them. The language of Jesus was full of metaphors: "You are the salt of the earth," "You are the light of the world," "This is my body," "This is my blood."

The new preaching clothes its sermons in words the people can see, taste, touch, not just words they can hear. In a flash of clarity Paul wrote, "We are the aroma of Christ" (2 Corinthians 2:15), and not a soul missed his point.

The Active Voice

The Old Testament rarely employs the passive voice. God revealed himself in active participles, continuous action. The Hebrew phrase for "God created" means that God created and *keeps on* creating. To use the passive voice in a sermon is to slam on the brakes.

Compare some of the well-known biblical statements that have great force and vitality in the active voice to what they might sound like in the passive voice.

ACTIVE	PASSIVE
Render therefore unto Caesar the things that are Caesar's.	Let therefore the things that are Caesar's be rendered unto Caesar.
Drink of it, all of you.	All of you, let it be drunk.
Go therefore and make disciples of all nations.	Go therefore and let all nations be made disciples.

Feed my sheep.	Let my sheep be fed.
Go, wash in the pool of Siloam.	Be gone, let your face be washed in the pool of Siloam.

One of the most striking examples of the use of the active voice in the long history of Baptist preaching is found in a sermon by Richard Furman, preached on the occasion of the death of George Washington. In lamenting on the death of a great national hero, Furman frequently used the passive voice, because he was referring to what had ended, "Washington, the great, the virtuous, the magnanimous, the brave, the father of his country, is numbered among the dead!" But then Furman turned his attention to the future and addressed the American people.

> Citizens of America! his political children, dry up your tears! Turn away your eyes from the desolate mansion, where his presence is no longer seen; turn them from the dreary vault on Potomack's bank, where his mortal part lies mouldering in dust; view him in the realms of light, united in blest society with saints and patriots, who have finished, like him, the toils of virtue, and now share the vast rewards of grace: See him holding high converse with the Angels of Light; and, with them, approaching the Divine Presence in humble adoration, perfecting, in high, immortal strains, those grateful acknowledgements of the divine interposition, goodness, and mercy, which he began on earth.[1]

What a contrast to the dreary passive voice of the verbs earlier in the sermon. Here he changed gears; here he looked to the future; here he regained vitality and hope, and challenged the people of America to look to the future. It is no accident that he employed a litany of active verbs: turn away, turn them, view him, see him—all active verbs. To continue the use of the passive voice at that point would have been to maintain the funeral cadence of the sermon. Movement, hope, progression, and challenge in sermons must come in the active voice.

Too Many Adjectives and Adverbs

Beauty and clarity are not dependent on decoration. Meaning can be obscured by too many modifiers. The great poets have known this. How many adjectives do you count in these familiar lines from Robert Frost?

> *Whose woods these are I think I know.*
> *His house is in the village though;*

---

[1] Richard Furman, "Humble Submission to Divine Sovereignty the Duty of a Bereaved Nation" (Charleston SC: Printed by W. P. Young, 1800) 27.

> *He will not see me stopping here*
> *To watch his woods fill up with snow.*

Not a single adjective, yet who can fail to see those woods blanketed with snow?

Great Baptist preaching, even the most eloquent, has not favored the accumulation of modifiers. These preachers knew that sentences decorated with too many adjectives and adverbs would tend to draw too much attention to the modifiers and obscure the thrust of thought. So the most eloquent preachers were sometimes the most simple. This is especially true for the conclusion of a sermon, when all thought needs to be compressed into one idea, the one thing that the preacher wants the congregation to grasp or to grasp them. Listen to this conclusion written by Richard Fuller in the nineteenth century:

> Think how soon we must go hence and be no more. Land of the *living?* No, this earth is not the land of the living; yonder, yonder is that land all burning in the sun. This is the land of the *dying.* We may repel the image of death, but we cannot repel death.[2]

How bare of modifiers it is, yet how powerful.

THE LANGUAGE OF ATTITUDE

Words are crucial, but there is something else that communicates from the pulpit just as much as words. That something is attitude. I recently heard a sermon on God's love in which the preacher acted as though he hated his hearers. "God loves you!" he growled, and not a soul missed the double message: the message of his words and the message of his attitude.

The most important attitude for the new preaching is humility. For the preacher truly to believe that he or she is the bearer of the Word of God is enough to make one humble. Preachers more than anyone else know their own inadequacies and failures. They realize that no one is worthy to preach. Yet a prevalent caricature of the preacher is the pompous, slightly overweight, balding, moralistic dolt with a pious twang and a pretentious air. That may be a caricature, but even caricatures are based on some degree of truth. Many sincere people, including preachers, have a hard time believing that preachers are human, and no clerical collar or ordination or string of academic degrees or published works can change that basic fact.

---

[2]Richard Fuller, *Sermons* (New York: Sheldon and Company, 1860) 183.

Run as fast as you can from theatrical temptation: there is no room for a holy tone, a tremolo, or a purposeful sob caught in the throat. A smart-aleck voice affects the congregation just like scratching a chalkboard. The best preaching speaks naturally, and adequate sound systems in most places allow the voice to rise or fall naturally with the feeling level of the sermon. One voice in the pulpit and another voice for the front door will make people wonder which one is real.

Speaking of humility is a good time to mention clothes. If you do not preach in a pulpit gown, there are some important things to remember about the clothes you wear. The key is to select clothes that do not draw attention away from the sermon. Anything that stands in the way of the message is taboo. The pulpit is no place for a style show, but neither is it a place to sport your commitment to volunteer poverty. Both extremes draw attention to themselves. Congregations still echo the words of the Greeks: "We would see Jesus" (John 12:21).

The best preaching also emanates from a respect for the people in the congregation. Christianity is not a mystery religion in which only the initiated have knowledge of the mysteries. The faithful Sunday school teacher may know nothing of the twelve-tribe amphictyony, but he may know more about the message of the Bible from years of reading and meditation than does his pastor. Many a preacher has learned far more about everyday Christian living from lay people than he ever learned from books. Many a pastor is amazed at the depth of faith and commitment to Christ that can be found in the most quiet and unassuming people of a local church. When one becomes a part of a community and shares the lives of a congregation, only a clerical robot could fail to have a profound respect for the capacity of people to hear and respond to the gospel.

A farmer in a little country church once said that he never liked a certain preacher's sermons because "he always spoke down" to the people. There is a great difference between preaching a simple gospel and preaching a simplistic one. Many a time the tone of a pastor's delivery reminded Phillips Brooks of the sermon by a medieval preacher on the subject of cooperation between clergy and laity, whose text was taken from Job 1:14: "The oxen were plowing, and the asses feeding beside them."[3]

---

[3]Phillips Brooks, *Lectures on Preaching* (London: H. R. Allenson, Ltd., 1877) 53.

Another important attitude for the new preaching is realism—a realism that knows that the entire burden of bearing the gospel is not on your shoulders alone. You may wear the "whole armor of God" (Ephesians 6:13), but you are not the whole army of God. You recognize that you also wear the whole armor of humanity, and because of that double armor you know exactly what Paul meant when he spoke of "the foolishness of God" (1 Corinthians 1:25). Thus, great preaching has enough faith in God's providence to be serious with a twinkle in the eye. You do not shun humor precisely because you are sincere enough to see the ludicrous side of yourself and life around you.

All these attitudes speak clearly to the congregation, but there is one more attitude present in great preaching that is essential: courage. The preacher who is afraid of the congregation will preach sermons to please them. He or she will be like the court prophet saying, " 'Peace, peace'; when there is no peace" (Jeremiah 6:14). If you are a slave to the opinions of your congregation, go do something else. Fit them in the finest clothes. Fill their cars with gasoline. Invest their money. But do not spend your life preaching sermons to please them. I am reminded of the statement of a courageous Baptist pastor who was fired during the 1960s for his stand on the church's receiving black members: "A church may fire me," he said, "but it can never hire me." The preacher is not for hire. The call is from God, and the answer must ultimately be from God. Real courage is not blind; it comes when the faithful pastor, shaking with fear, does what he or she believes is right under God.

CONCLUSION

Where does the preacher's power really come from? There must be something in addition to excellent preparation and delivery of a sermon. There must be something more than precise words and proper attitudes. The constant wonder of preaching is the power of God. Somehow, in spite of all his blunders, a preacher can make, "tongues like flames of fire" (Acts 2:3) come down and rest on his words. The miracle of Pentecost takes place once again, and the preacher's frail words become the Word, which somehow breaks down the walls that separate Jew and Gentile, black and white, rich and poor. That is precisely the reason you never really learn to preach. You just do your best and pray for the miracle. The joy of preaching is that the miracle so often happens—and in the most unexpected ways.

EPILOGUE: THE CHALLENGE OF WORLD PREACHING

In Thornton Wilder's play *Our Town,* two children are discussing a letter written by the local minister to their friend Jane Crofut. The dialogue is revealing:

> Rebecca: "I never told you about that letter Jane Crofut got from her minister when she was sick. He wrote Jane a letter and on the envelope the address was like this: It said: Jane Crofut; The Crofut Farm; Grover's Corners; Sutton County; New Hampshire; United States of America."
>
> George: "What's funny about that?"
>
> Rebecca: "But listen, it's not finished: the United States of America; Continent of North America; Western Hemisphere; the Earth; the Solar System; the Universe; the Mind of God—that's what it said on the envelope."
>
> George: "What do you know!"[1]

This exchange between Rebecca and George could very well serve as a paradigm of Baptist preaching. Great Baptist sermons are indeed addressed to individuals, as the letter was addressed to Jane Crofut, but in an ever-expanding context. Individuals are a part of a nation, a hemisphere, a world, a universe—ultimately the mind of God. The preacher who misses the larger context ultimately misses the gospel altogether, for the Christian faith has always been individual and social.

To answer the challenge of world preaching has been the task of the kind of preaching described in this book. It has always attempted to ad-

---

[1]Thornton Wilder, *Three Plays by Thornton Wilder* (New York: Bantam Books, 1957) 28.

dress the needs of the individual, but it has also attempted to proclaim a message that transcends local time and place. Only a transcendent message has any pertinence in our world.

WHAT BAPTIST PREACHING CAN OFFER

The other day an acquaintance in New England whom I see from time to time asked me what I do for a living. When I told him that I teach preaching in a Baptist seminary he was astonished. More correctly, I should say that he was aghast. His idea of Baptist preachers was the caricature of the panting screamer with arms flailing. After his initial astonishment subsided, we continued with a stimulating conversation about the church and Christian preaching. This man was not unlike many people in our society. Far from being an opponent of the church, he was very pleased to discover that he knew someone who was deeply involved with the church in general and with preaching in particular. Soon I discovered that he had great respect for preaching and wanted to know more about the Christian faith. The conversation could not have been more natural or more fulfilling.

It is that kind of person for whom I believe Baptist preaching has a particular appeal. He was searching for a kind of preaching that would challenge him both emotionally and intellectually. He represents countless thousands in our society who hunger for the kind of preaching that has undergirded the Baptist heritage. He and many like him constitute a challenge that I believe the Baptist heritage uniquely meets with three characteristics: piety, community, and praxis.

Piety

Piety is not one of those subjects that make modern society quiver with excitement. Most folk find appealing the lines written above the fireplace in the Alcott house in Concord, Massachusetts: "The pious ones of Plymouth, who, reaching the Rock, first fell upon their own knees and then upon the aborigines." To be called pious is not always a compliment. Piety conjures up an image of such hypocrisy and sticky sweetness that some would rather run for the woods than be called pious.

Yet there is another side to piety, a side that draws with such gentle persistence that it cannot be ignored. It has nothing to do with what Shakespeare called "pious action [in which] we do sugar o'er / the devil himself."[2] The history of Baptist preaching is filled with people of warmth and steady conviction who never paraded their piety, but for whom devotion to God was the source of a rather rugged commitment.

As a result of this kind of piety, Baptist preaching never lost touch with the Bible. Although the tradition I have described in this book used critical biblical study to advantage, it never viewed historical-critical methodology as the sine qua non of effective preaching. Such preaching, in fact, rejected the implied position among some scholars that only highly trained specialists are capable of understanding the Bible correctly. Baptist preaching has carried on a constant and respectful dialogue with lay people who are encouraged to read the Bible for themselves. Naturally, Baptist preaching has had to live with some eccentrics who insist on numerological or quasimagical readings of every passage in the Scriptures, but it has continued the dialogue and attempted to guide biblical interpretation along sound lines.

The result of such an approach is a denominational legacy in which genuine piety is alive and well. Our so-called secular society—religious to the core—is yearning for genuine piety. Piety regards God as burning holiness, yet of such love that even the worst among us can find wholeness. Genuine piety is real, one of the few things in a consumer society that lives up to its billing. It does not glibly say, "I'm O.K." Piety gratefully says, "I'm not always O.K., but it's O.K., because God has forgiven me." Piety, in other words, is grown in humility.

In a world full of lonely people, Christian piety offers challenge and hope because it knows perfection has not been fully attained. Piety has friends because it looks on others with a sense of gratitude and friendliness. In the end, piety has God, for its very sense of humility comes from a vision of holiness.

Not only does our society need that heritage of genuine piety, but mainline Christianity needs it. Baptists who live out the tradition described in this book may be among the brightest hopes for some who have lost touch with the transcendent. On the other hand, the tradition described in this book may be the best hope for fundamentalism. Some fundamentalists find distasteful the rigidity of their tradition. They would gladly embrace a heritage of openness and intellectual rigor coupled with

---

[2]*Hamlet,* act 3, sc. 1, line 47.

evangelistic warmth. To meet the challenge of world preaching, Baptists would do well to maintain their tradition of genuine piety.

Community

The Baptist preaching heritage has encouraged community. Democratic church polity was a key factor in the spread of Baptist churches after the Revolutionary War in America. Baptist preaching resisted the authoritarian role that placed the preacher on a commanding platform in the church. Called and supported by the local church, the Baptist preacher was subject to the congregation. Church decisions were made by the church, not the preacher. Deference, not obedience, was given to the pastor.

As a result, Baptist preaching has lived and prospered in community. Sermons have been shaped as much by the needs of the congregation as by the academic rigor of the preacher. Baptist preaching has made the discovery that great sermons are created as much by the congregation as by the preacher; therefore, it is no surprise that great congregations have spawned great preaching.

Extreme specialization in the preaching ministry will ultimately be harmful to the preaching task. The pastor who insists on devoting his full time to the preparation of sermons during the week with little or no contact with lay people is ironically diminishing the quality of preaching for that church. Churches with very large memberships, numbering in the many thousands, have often discarded genuine democracy in the name of efficiency and adopted a business model in which the deacons become in effect the board of directors and the pastor becomes the president. Decisions are made in the hierarchical structure, a practice that is indeed much more efficient. But what does it do to the preaching? Often those who administer the church in an authoritarian mode also begin to preach in an authoritarian mode. The pastor is no longer the trusted friend who speaks with moral authority that has been earned; rather, the pastor becomes the almost untouchable legal authority who dispenses the correct answers with little opportunity to be challenged. Such an arrangement hurts not only the church, but also the preacher and the preaching.

Baptist preaching has thrived in community. It is that sense of community preaching that offers one of the bright hopes for preaching in our lonely world.

Praxis

I am borrowing a word that Harvey Cox used to describe liberation theology, which he said was first and foremost a "theology of praxis."[3] What Cox meant was that liberation theology has grown out of the practical tasks of living among the poor of the third world. It has not trickled down from the universities to the people; rather it has been hammered out in the ongoing interaction between reflection and engagement with real problems.

No better word could be used for one of the great strengths of Baptist preaching. One of the persistent problems in preaching in the Western countries has been the separation of the theological school and the everyday world of the ordinary church member. Like every other discipline, theology has developed its own language which, when used in the pulpit, has been utterly foreign to those in the pews. In many cases, theology students were not allowed to preach until they completed their theological education and were ordained. Some have even left theological school with a haughty contempt for those uninitiated in the churches who were not privy to the mysteries of theology.

Baptist preaching has been largely able to overcome that separation between the pulpit and the pew. Preachers among the Baptists, whether educated or not, have been called by the local church. That, of course, has inevitably produced some extremely unprepared preachers, but at the same time it has produced preaching that has grown out of action. Baptists have always assumed that theory and practice must be inseparable, and what God has joined, Baptists must not put asunder.

When Baptists began educating their preachers, theory and practice remained intact. "Field education" as a separate course was unnecessary because nearly every student already had a field of service. Many had been in the pastorate for a number of years, and others had held church positions during their years of theological training both for the experience and for the financial help. Theological professors also remained in close contact with the churches through frequent preaching and Bible studies. Thus theological education for the Baptists has always been characterized by praxis.

---

[3]Harvey Cox, *Religion in the Secular City. Toward a Postmodern Theology* (New York: Simon & Schuster, 1984) 136-37.

Baptists must always maintain a "preaching of praxis." This great strength of the Baptist heritage is needed more than ever in a world increasingly alienated from those who are known as specialists in their fields. Maintaining a preaching based on practice will protect Baptists from three dangers.

The first is the danger of arrogance. Preaching that constantly interacts with real problems among church members and in our society will never become arrogant. The pastor will be reminded constantly that many church members know more about some things than he does. Thus, the pulpit will learn from the pew, reflect on that knowledge through biblical study and prayer, and deliver a message that is not just relevant but also pertinent.

Preaching based on praxis will likewise protect us from the danger of misunderstanding. Lay people will force the preacher to translate theological lingo into ordinary language that everyone understands. The temptation to impress the congregation with theological knowledge will dissolve in the mingling of people and action and ideas. When the preacher is unclear in a statement, actions during the week and interactions with the people will make it clear.

The third danger such preaching guards against is the danger of imitation. Sermons that grow from the soil of praxis do not come out of a sermon book. They come out of life in interaction with the Word of God. The greatest problem in preaching someone else's sermons in such a context is not its dishonesty, but its irrelevance. In a context of praxis, no one else can preach with more burning pertinence than the pastor.

PREACHING BEYOND TIME

The story of the Baptist preachers that I have recounted in much of this book has been two-dimensional. They were born, they lived, they died. That is as far as I was able to take the story. But their preaching, like all great preaching, was three-dimensional. Through faith they looked beyond the horizon and preached beyond time.

Baptist preaching must remain three-dimensional. The present life must not be disparaged, but must be loved as both precious and full of promise. But there is another world that can be known only by faith. We know it intuitively, not just because we are part of the church. The whole world has a dim awareness of it. We say, "Time is swift," precisely because we have a vantage point above time as well as within time. Baptist preaching will continue to say that God is God—a Being not confined within time, but the Lord of time. We cannot speak of God without thinking of eternity.

At the same time, we cannot preach three-dimensionally without thinking of humanity. Baptist preaching has been nurtured by the whole Church. Richard Fuller of Baltimore was fond of telling a story about William Jay. Jay walked out one day in a dense English fog. Presently he saw a huge and monstrous object approaching him that made him start. As he drew nearer, the shape turned out to be a gigantic man. When they met, he saw that it was his own brother John.

Baptist preaching in the future would benefit from recognizing other approaches to preaching the gospel as part of the same family. Baptist preaching is a small chapter in a much larger book. Effective sermons are being preached by Christians of every denomination and every branch of the Church. Baptist preaching has much to offer and much to learn.

INDEX

Adams, John, 146, 171
Adams, Samuel, 146
Adler, Hermann, 74
Augustine, 43

Backus, Isaac, 114, 152-56, 217, 227
Bacon, Francis, 194
Baillie, Donald, 221
Baker, Daniel, 182
Baker, Robert A., 161, 162
Baldwin, Thomas, 146, 148, 150, 158, 171-75, 177, 185, 217, 227
Bedgegood, Nicholas, 143
Beecher, Henry Ward, 187
Beecher, Lyman, 84
Beza, Theodore, 139
Boone, Daniel, 156
Botsford, Edmund, 142, 143
Boyce, James P., 189
Brainard, David, 43
Brantly, Sr., William T., 144, 157, 160, 165
Brine, John, 42, 58
Broadus, John A., xii, 187-97, 204, 207
Brooks, Phillips, 187, 235, 243
Brown, John, 72, 87, 88
Bruner, Jerome, 231
Bunyan, John, xii, 12-15, 17, 43, 98, 213
Burns, Robert, 201
Buttrick, George, 240

Callender, Elisha, 117-23
Callender, Ellis, 118, 119
Callender, John, 107
Callender, Jr., John, 120-23
Calvin, John, 3, 42, 43, 139
Campbell, Alexander, 175
Carey, William, 21, 40, 41, 46-48, 52-59, 61-63, 66, 92, 158, 167, 170, 211
Chanler, Isaac, 140
Charles II, King, 11, 108, 109

Chauncy, Charles, 123
Chesterton, G. K., 74
Chrysostom, John, 191
Churchill, Winston, 74
Clarke, Elizabeth, 108
Clarke, John, 105, 108-11, 114, 115, 121, 123
Clarke, William Newton, 214
Claude, John, 38, 39
Clay, Henry, 137
Clifford, John, 67-78, 205, 215, 217
Columbus, Christopher, 54
Comer, John, 119, 122, 123
Condy, Jeremiah, 121-23
Cooke, Captain James, 36, 53
Cornwallis, Lord Charles, 158, 159
Cotton, John, 107
Cox, Harvey, 249
Crandall, John, 110, 111, 114, 115
Crofut, Jane, 245
Cromwell, Oliver, 109
Crosby, Thomas, 3, 8, 9, 18, 27

Dale, Robert W., 25
Dargan, E. C., 192
Davenport, James, 127, 128
Denne, Henry, 10, 11
Dodd, C. H., 219
Doyle, Arthur Conan, 74
Drowne, Shem, 119
Dungan, Thomas, 129
Dunster, Henry, 111-15, 119, 123

Eaton, Isaac, 125, 130-33, 136, 137, 141, 150, 151
Eaton, Joseph, 130
Edwards, Jonathan, 43, 126
Edwards, Morgan, 132-34
Edwards, Thomas, 10
Eliot, John, 43

Elizabeth I, Queen, 5
Ellerback, Werner of, 226
Elliott, Stephen, 182
Emerson, Ralph Waldo, 68
Evans, Caleb, 32-36, 44, 59, 62
Evans, Hugh, 31-36, 44, 62

Fairbairn, A. M., 92
Farmer, J. H., 191
Forsyth, P. T , 219
Foskett, Bernard, 30-33, 44
Foster, John, 63
Franklin, Benjamin, 127
Frelinghuysen, Theodore, 126
Frost, Robert, 241
Fuller, Andrew, 41, 43-53, 56, 58, 60-63, 66, 158, 167, 170
Fuller, Richard, 176, 181-85, 221, 242, 251
Furman, Richard, 27, 115, 137, 140, 144, 158-67, 172, 174, 175, 185, 210, 227, 241
Furman, Wood, 160

Gale, John, 21-25, 28, 213
Gano, John, 132, 135-37, 156, 162
George, Lloyd, 67
Gerneaux, Francis, 135
Gibbon, Edward, 36
Gill, John, 27-29, 42, 226
Goen, C. C., 128
Goold, Thomas, 115
Gould, G. P., 74
Gregory, Olinthus, 62
Guild, Reuben A., 152

Hall, Robert, xii, 37, 41, 47, 59-66, 178, 226
Hardin, Elizabeth, 120
Hart, John, 130
Hart, Oliver, 125, 140-44, 147, 149, 162, 163, 165, 203, 227
Helwys, Gervase, 5
Helwys, Thomas, xii, 4-6, 203
Henry, Patrick, 203
Holmes, Obediah, 110, 111, 114, 115, 217
Hood, Robin, 55
Hort, F. J. A., 190
How, Thomas, 30
Howard, Joseph, 161
Hume, David, 36
Hutchinson, Ann, 108

James I, King, 251

Jay, John, 251
Jay, William, 251
Jefferson, Thomas, 110, 156, 171
Jessey, Henry, 6-9, 11
Jeter, J. B., 178
Johnson, William B., 164, 165, 176, 210
Jones, Samuel, 134, 137-39
Jones, Jr., Samuel, 138
Jones, Thomas, 138
Judson, Adoniram, 158, 166

Keach, Benjamin, 16-18, 26, 27, 129
Keach, Elias, 18, 129
Kierkegaard, Søren, 210
King, Jr., Martin Luther, 234
Knollys, Hanserd, 8, 9, 11
Knox, John, 3

Lathrop, John, 7
Latimer, Hugh, 3
Lawrence, Joshua, 175
Lee, Robert E., 190
Liddon, Canon H. P., 77
Luther, Martin, 3

Maclaren, Alexander, xii, 25, 79-89, 187, 206, 214, 224
Maclaren, David, 79
Maclaren, Marion, 80
McLoughlin, William G., xiv, 113, 123
Magus, Simon, 116
Manly, Sr., Basil, 144, 189
Manning, James, 132, 151, 152, 154, 227
Maring, Norman, 134
Marshall, Daniel, 133
Marx, Karl, 219
Maston, T. B., 152
Mather, Cotton, 115, 116, 118
Mercer, Jesse, 163
Mercer, Silas, 163
Miller, Benjamin, 133
Milton, John, 19, 112, 113, 160
Mitchell, Henry, 233
Monroe, James, 158, 159
Morgan, Abel, 133-35
Myles, John, 117

Napoleon, 65
"Notewell, Nicholas," 95

Oakes, Urian, 105, 116
Origen, 229

Index

Paine, Thomas, 36
Parker, Daniel, 175
Parker, Joseph, 77
Payne, Ernest, 218
Pearce, Samuel, 167
Peck, John Mason, 166, 174
Penn, William, 129
Peter Pan, 52
Pitt, William, 65
Poindexter, A. M., 188
Pollard, F. W., 92
Pope, Alexander, 160
Pugh, Evan, 161

Ransom, Elisha, 173
Reese, Joseph, 161, 162
Revere, Paul, 146
Rice, Luther, 158, 166
Rippon, John, 33
Roberts, J. E., 83
Robertson, A. T., 190
Robertson, Frederick W., 25
Robinson, H. Wheeler, 91-101, 215
Robinson, John, 77
Robinson, Robert, 37-40, 225
Rogers, William, 203
Rushbrooke, J. H., 74
Russel, John, 105, 117
Ryland, John, 18, 41, 46-48, 52, 57-63, 65, 66
Ryland, John Collett, 47, 57, 58, 62, 167

"Sandy," 196, 197
Schaff, Philip, 191
Schweitzer, Albert, 211
Screven, William, 115, 142
Shakespeare, William, 246
Shaw, George Bernard, 74
Smith, Hezekiah, 150, 151
Smyth, John, 4-6, 8, 11
Spurgeon, Charles H., xi, xiii, 77, 84, 187
Stanley, Arthur, 15
Staughton, William, 36, 157, 158, 167-72, 174, 175, 185, 227

Stearns, Shubel, 133
Stillman, Samuel, xii, 125, 143, 146-50, 173, 177, 210, 217, 227
Stinton, Benjamin, 26, 27
Stone, Barton W., 175
Strong, Augustus H., 187
Sutcliff, John, 41, 46
Swift, Jonathan, 160

Taylor, Dan, 42
Taylor, John, 175
Tennent, Gilbert, 126, 135
Terrill, Edward, 30
Tertullian, 110
Thielicke, Helmut, xii
Thompson, Wilson, 175
Tillich, Paul, 233

Ugly Duckling, 52
Upham, Edward, 122, 123

Vedder, Henry C., 123

Wall, William, 23
Wallis, Beebe, 48, 59
Washington, George, 136, 157, 241
Wayland, Francis, 174, 176-83, 185, 186, 208
Weatherspoon, J. B., 192
Welch, James F., 174
Wescott, B. F., 190
Wesley, John, 21, 43
Whitefield, George, 21, 38, 43, 61, 126, 127, 136, 151, 153, 155
Whitley, W. T., 22, 24
Whitsitt, William H., 187
Wiesel, Elie, 232
Wilder, Thornton, 245
Williams, Roger, 105, 107, 109, 121
Williams, William, 189
Winkler, E. T., 189
Witter, William, 110
Worcester, Noah, 145, 146

Young, Doyle L., 47

Zwingli, Ulrich, 3